Economic Development
of Tropical Agriculture

Economic Development
of Tropical Agriculture

Theory, Policy, Strategy, and Organization

Edited by

W. W. McPherson

University of Florida Press ● Gainesville ● 1968

A University of Florida Press Book

Library of Congress Catalog Card Number: 68-24368

PRINTED BY THE STORTER PRINTING CO., INC.
GAINESVILLE, FLORIDA

BOUND BY DOBBS BROTHERS LIBRARY BINDING CO., INC.
HIALEAH, FLORIDA

Foreword

The publication of this book, *Economic Development of Tropical Agriculture*, inaugurates a series of publications to be sponsored by the Center for Tropical Agriculture (CTA) of the University of Florida. Supporting the publication of scholarly work is considered an integral function of the CTA. The curriculum is thereby enriched and results in research are disseminated in a wide and timely manner. This strong academic concern for the tropics renders technical assistance programs more effective. The series will reflect the Center's scope of interest in tropical agriculture. It is hoped that this book and future works will contribute to a better knowledge of the potentials and limitations of the production of food and other farm products in the tropics.

This first book represents the breadth and depth of thinking of a group of internationally recognized experts who have had substantial experience in tropical development. The papers which comprise the book were presented in a series of seminars given on the University of Florida campus between January and November, 1966. Dr. W. W. McPherson, Graduate Research Professor of Agricultural Economics at the University of Florida, was chairman of the seminar committee, contributed the lead paper, and served as editor of the resulting book.

This volume should be useful to many persons, not only to the large number of individuals who have an interest in the economic development of tropical agriculture, but to those who have an interest in agriculture and economic development in general.

E. T. YORK, JR., *Provost*
Institute of Food and
Agricultural Sciences

HUGH L. POPENOE, *Director*
International Programs and
Center for Tropical Agriculture

v

Acknowledgments

T he assistance of the seminar program committee, Doctors H. B. Clark, C. C. Moxley, and Leo Polopolus, and Mr. Antonio Gayoso, is gratefully acknowledged. The full support of Dr. E. T. York, Jr., Provost, Institute of Food and Agricultural Sciences (IFAS); Dr. Hugh L. Popenoe, Director of International Programs and the Center for Tropical Agriculture, IFAS; and Dr. K. R. Tefertiller, Chairman of the Department of Agricultural Economics of the University of Florida, is greatly appreciated. To the authors, who were kind enough to divert their time from very busy schedules in order to participate in this program, we are deeply grateful. Also, we express thanks to the Editor of *Lloyds Bank Review* for kind permission to reprint Professor Harry G. Johnson's paper (Chapter 7). In addition to the authors whose papers appear in this book, we offer thanks to Mr. Oscar Collado, Ingeniero Agrónomo, Head, Rural Credit Department, National Bank of Costa Rica, and to Dr. Gustav F. Papanek, Director, Development Advisory Service, Harvard University, for participating in the special seminar program.

Financial support, which made this venture possible, was provided by the Center for Tropical Agriculture, which is financed in part by funds received from the Ford Foundation.

Editorial revisions of the papers were kept to a minimum, mainly to matters of format. Each author worked independently of the others. As might be expected, there are occasional duplications of ideas as well as differences in ideas among authors. However, no attempt to reconcile these differences and duplications was made as they were judged to be "healthy" ones and may well lead to further fruitful inquiry and discussion.

W. W. McPherson, *Editor*
University of Florida
April, 1967

Authors

Chiang, Alpha C., Visiting Professor of Economics,
Cornell University

Dr. Chiang received the B.A. degree from St. John's University, China, the M.A. from the University of Colorado, and the Ph.D. from Columbia University. He has taught at Denison University, the Chinese University of Hong Kong, and Cornell University. He is currently Visiting Professor of Economics, Cornell University, on leave from the University of Connecticut. In 1963-64, he was at Yale University as a National Science Foundation Fellow.

Coutu, Arthur J., Director,
North Carolina State University Mission to Peru

Dr. Coutu was born in Connecticut. He received the B.S. and M.S. degrees from the University of Connecticut and the Ph.D. from North Carolina State University. He has been a member of the North Carolina State faculty since 1952. He was a member of the North Carolina State University Mission to Peru from January, 1963, to August, 1965, Chief of Party of that Mission from 1964 to mid-1965, and Director since January, 1966.

Fei, John C. H., Professor of Economics,
Cornell University

Dr. Fei was educated at Yenching University, China (B.A., 1945), the University of Washington (M.A., 1948), and the Massachusetts Institute of Technology (Ph.D., 1952). He has taught at M.I.T., Antioch College, the University of Washington, and Yale University. He is currently Professor of Economics at Cornell University. During 1960-61, he served as research adviser to the Institute of Development Economics in Karachi, Pakistan. He is a senior economic adviser to the National Planning Association, working on development problems of the Philippines and Thailand.

ix

Gaitskell, Arthur, Member of the Board,
    Commonwealth Development Corporation

Mr. Gaitskell was born in England and received his education at Winchester College and Oxford University. He served with the Sudan Plantation Syndicate, Gezira Scheme, 1923-52, was Manager of the Syndicate, 1945-50, Chairman and Managing Director, Sudan Gezira Board, 1950-52, and Consultant, 1952-53. He served as a member of the Executive Council of the Sudan and as Chairman of the Council of Khartoum University. He also served as a member of the Royal Commission on East Africa and the Committee of Experts on the Development of Africa of the Council of Europe. More recently, he was with the World Bank and the Food and Agriculture Commission in Pakistan. He has also been a consultant to Mitchell Cotts in Ethiopia, to Kenya African National Union in Kenya, to the Ford Foundation in Nigeria, to the Euphrates Project Authority, to Sir Alexander Gibb & Partners for the Indus Basin Comprehensive Survey, and with the Food and Agriculture Organization in Mexico. He has served as Lecturer at the Economic Development Institute, World Bank, Washington, D.C.

Gittinger, J. Price, Lecturer, Economic Development Institute,
    International Bank for Reconstruction and Development
    (World Bank), Washington, D.C.

Dr. Gittinger was born in California and received the B.S. degree from the University of California and the M.S. and Ph.D. degrees from Iowa State University. He served as Agricultural Economist with the United States Overseas Mission to Vietnam, 1955-59; Agricultural Economist with the Harvard University Advisory Group, Plan Organization of Iran, 1960-61; and from 1963 to 1965 he was Visiting Professor, Institute of Agriculture, Bogor, Indonesia, under the auspices of the Agricultural Development Council. He was Associate Director of the Center for Development Planning, NPA, just before moving to his present position where his responsibility includes supervision of the Institute's Annual Agricultural Projects Course for senior agricultural administrators from the Bank's member countries.

Green, James W., Chief, Community Development and Local Government Advisor to the Government of Peru and to the United States AID Mission to Peru

Dr. Green is a native of Virginia. He received the Ph.D. degree in sociology from the University of North Carolina, and has pursued additional study of economic and social development at the

School of Advanced International Studies, Johns Hopkins University. He served on the faculties of North Carolina State University and Cornell University, and as Specialist in Land Use Planning for the North Carolina Agricultural Extension Service. From 1954 to 1959 he was initially Associate Chief and later Chief Community Development (Village Agricultural & Industrial Development) Adviser to the Government of Pakistan; from 1960 to 1964 he served as Community Development and Local Government Adviser to the Government of Southern Rhodesia and Senior AID Community Development Staff Adviser for the Central African Federation. From 1964 to 1967, in addition to the position held in Peru as listed above, he served during part of 1965 as Consultant to the United States AID Mission to the Dominican Republic on local government, community development, cooperatives, and agricultural extension. Early in 1967 he moved to Panama for work in community development.

Heady, Earl O., Charles F. Curtiss Distinguished Professor of Agriculture, and Executive Director of the Center for Agricultural and Economic Development, Iowa State University

Dr. Heady was born in Nebraska. He received the B.S. and M.S. degrees at the University of Nebraska and the Ph.D. at Iowa State University. He holds honorary degrees from the University of Nebraska, the University of Uppsala, and the Agricultural College of Sweden. He is a Fellow of the American Farm Economics Association, Econometrics Society, and American Statistical Association. Dr. Heady has served as Visiting Professor at Harvard University, North Carolina State University, and the University of Illinois. He has served extensively as consultant in Greece, India, and European countries, and is participating in the development of Agricultural Economics at the University of Nuevo Leon, Monterrey, Mexico.

Johnson, Glenn L., Professor of Agricultural Economics, Michigan State University, and Chairman of the Consortium for the Study of Nigerian Rural Development

Dr. Johnson is a native of Minnesota. He holds the B.S. degree from the University of Illinois, the M.A. from Michigan State University, and the Ph.D. from the University of Chicago where he was a Social Science Research Council Fellow. He also studied at American and George Washington Universities and Cambridge University. He was on the staff of the Bureau of Agricultural Economics and the faculty of the University of Kentucky before joining the faculty of Michigan State University. He has been a Visiting Professor at the University of California and the University of Manchester, England. He has served with the Norwegian Agricultural Economics Institute, as a member of the joint economic military evaluation on the United States Overseas Mission in Thailand, as Director of the Economic Development Institute, University of Nigeria (1962-64), and as consultant to the Rockefeller Foundation (University del Valle, Cali, Colombia) with emphasis on agricultural economics and attention to agricultural development associated with the Foundation's "Conquest of Hunger" program. He has been Director of the Nigerian Consortium since 1965.

Johnson, Harry G., Professor,
    London School of Economics

Born in Toronto, Canada, Dr. Johnson received the B.A. degree from the University of Toronto and Cambridge University, the M.A. degree from the Universities of Toronto, Harvard, Cambridge, and Manchester, and the Ph.D. from Harvard. He has served as a member of the faculty of St. Francis Xavier University, University of Toronto, Cambridge University, King's College of Cambridge, Stanford University, University of Indiana, Instituto Torcuato di Tella in Argentina, the University of Western Ontario, Manchester University, the University of Chicago, and the London School of Economics. Other professional posts held by Professor Johnson include: Lecturer, International Economic Association, refresher courses for Asian economists: Karachi (1956), Singapore (1956), Murree (1958), and Poona (1966); External Examiner, the University of Malaya in Singapore, 1959-61; Honorary Member, Japan Economic Research Center, since 1966; Member, Foreign Advisory Board, Pakistan Institute of Development Economics, since 1966. Editorial positions have been held with the *Journal of Political Economy, Review of Economic Studies*, and *The Manchester School*. He has served as President of the Canadian Political Science Association, Consultant to the Board of Governors of the Federal Reserve System, and on numerous national and international committees and commissions. He is a Fellow of the American Academy of Arts and Sciences. In 1966 he moved from the faculty of the University of Chicago to his present position with the London School of Economics.

King, Richard A., M. G. Mann Professor of Economics,
    North Carolina State University

Dr. King was born in Massachusetts. He received the B.S. degree at the University of Connecticut; the M.S. at the University of California, Berkeley; and the M.P.A. and Ph.D. at Harvard University. A year of postdoctoral study was spent as a Fellow in Political Economy at the University of Chicago. He has served on the faculties of the University of Connecticut and North Carolina State University. From February, 1964, to July, 1965, he served as an Economic Adviser with the North Carolina State University contract in Peru, and since returning to the campus he has continued active participation in the Peruvian project.

Langham, Max R., Associate Professor of Agricultural
    Economics and Economics, University of Florida

Dr. Langham is a native of Illinois. He attended Southern Illinois University and received the B.S., M.S., and Ph.D. degrees from the University of Illinois. He served on the faculty of Louisiana State University before joining the faculty of Agricultural Economics, University of Florida in 1962. His graduate teaching and research are in the areas of production economics and econometrics. For a period in 1966 he was in Costa Rica. He is currently supervising research on the economic opportunities of livestock production in Costa Rica.

McPherson, W. W., Graduate Research Professor,
    University of Florida

Dr. McPherson, born in North Carolina, holds the B.S. degree from North Carolina State University, the M.S. from Louisiana State University, and the Ph.D. in economics from Harvard University. He has served with the Bureau of Agricultural Economics, United States Department of Agriculture, and has been on the faculty of North Carolina State University (1949-59). From 1955 to 1957 he was adviser to the Planning Board of Pakistan with the Ford Foundation-Harvard University Advisory Team. He was Head of Economics and Statistics Research (1959-61) and Assistant Scientific Director (1961-62) with the Division of Tropical Research, United Fruit Co., and worked in Honduras, Guatemala, Costa Rica, Panama, the Dominican Republic, Colombia, Ecuador, and Nicaragua. In the spring of 1963, he served as consultant to AID in Trinidad and Tobago, and in the summer of 1966 he was with the International Research Institute in Brazil. He joined the University of Florida faculty in 1962.

Ruttan, Vernon W., Professor and Head, Department of
    Agricultural Economics, University of Minnesota

Dr. Ruttan was born in Michigan. He attended Michigan State University in 1942-43 and received the B.S. degree from Yale in

1948. The M.A. and Ph.D. degrees were received from the University of Chicago. From 1963 to 1965 he was with the Rockefeller Foundation as Agricultural Economist at the International Rice Research Institute, Laguna, Philippines. He had previously held positions with the Council of Economic Advisers, Purdue University, the University of California, and the Tennessee Valley Authority.

Contents

1

Status of Tropical Agriculture and Preview of Subsequent Chapters

W. W. McPherson

Countries within the tropical and subtropical zones of the world are predominantly agricultural and, with few exceptions, have per capita incomes below the world average. Although discussions of theory, policy, strategy, and organization for development presented in this book have reference and application to economic and agricultural development beyond the boundaries of the tropics, they are of particular interest with reference to the countries in the tropical and subtropical zones because of the predominance of agricultural activities and prevalence of low incomes.

STATUS OF TROPICAL AGRICULTURE

Income Levels.—Levels of income are presented here, not because income is believed to be identical with ultimate goals or to be a perfect measure of the ultimate welfare of individuals or society, but because we have yet to come up with a more satisfactory concept with respect to economic growth. An increase in output (income) possibilities certainly should indicate an increase in the range of opportunities from which choices may be made. Moreover, level of income is usually associated in a positive direction with other "desirable" conditions such as food supply, health, level-of-living indexes, and life expectancy. As Schumpeter (1947, 2) has stated so succinctly, "I speak of economic growth during any stated period if the *trend values of an index of per capita total output of goods and services* have increased during that period" (my italics); or Lewis (1955, 9), "The subject matter of this book is growth of output per head of population. . . . The definition must, however, relate to goods and services—'economic' output, in the old fashioned meaning of 'economic'—and not to some such concept as welfare, satisfaction or happiness."[1]*

The problems of measuring income or output in agriculture, especially *trend*, are particularly difficult. Among the conditions that give rise to these difficulties are the wide period-to-period variations that occur as a result of uncontrolled factors such as weather, the large but often changing share of output in the subsistence (non-market) sector, and the differences in the share of the farm segment of the total agricultural sector. There is evidence that estimates of farm incomes in comparison with non-farm incomes and incomes in lower-income countries in relation to incomes in higher-income countries are likely to have a downward bias. For example, one estimate raises the 1950 per capita figure in Africa, for comparison with $1,550 in the United States, from $48 to $177— an increase of more than 350 per cent (Millikan, 1956), but the difference is still almost beyond comprehension. Thus, differences in average incomes cannot be interpreted as exact measures of differences in welfare, but they may provide a "very rough approximation" to an index of differences in output of economic goods and services that have been incorporated into the national accounts.

Even when considered only as "a very rough approximation" to an index of real differences, the conclusion that average income levels in tropical countries arc generally quite low in relation to those of much of the rest of the world, appears to be rather obvious (Table 1.1). For convenience, the data on tropical areas are presented on the basis of the subregions developed by the United States Department of Agriculture (USDA) even though these areas do not, in all cases, meet the necessary criterion with respect to location. For example, Chile is included in "Other South America," Saudi Arabia is not included in any one of the

*Notes for this chapter begin on page 20.

TABLE 1.1.—INCOME, POPULATION, AND AGRICULTURAL LAND: UNITED STATES, TROPICAL SUBREGIONS, AND THE WORLD

Subregion[a]	National income per capita 1960-62	Population 1959-61 Midpoint		Projected annual growth rate 1959-61 to 1970
		Total number	World share	
	U.S. dollars	Million	Per Cent	Per Cent
United States	2,342	179.9	6.0	1.5
Tropics				
Central America and Caribbean	227	32.3	1.1	2.7
Mexico	281	34.9	1.2	3.1
Brazil	211	70.6	2.3	3.1
Other South America	263	51.5	1.7	2.8
East Africa	86	48.6	1.6	2.3
West Central Africa	81	108.8	3.6	2.1
North Africa	112	84.8	2.8	2.2
India	69	431.7	14.3	2.2
Other South Asia	69	126.4	4.2	2.5
Other East Asia	82	246.2	8.2	2.5
TOTAL TROPICAL	103	1,235.9	41.0	2.5
World	b	3,011.5	100.0	1.8

Source: USDA (1964).
a. A list of countries included in each subregion is given at the end of this chapter.
b. Data not available.

subregions shown, Afghanistan and Nepal are included in "Other South Asia," and South Korea is included in "Other East Asia." For 1960-62, the estimated average annual national income per capita amounted to only $103 for the tropical areas, or less than 5 per cent of the United States average. For 1958, the latest year for which income estimates for most of the countries are available, countries deemed to be tropical and mostly tropical or subtropical contained about 56 per cent of the population (excluding USSR, Eastern Europe, Mainland China, North Korea, North Vietnam, and Outer Mongolia), but produced only 13 per cent of the income.[2] Moreover, among the tropical countries, only three—Venezuela, Puerto Rico, and Trinidad and Tobago—had per capita incomes above the world average.

Population Growth.—Substantial annual increases in total output are required merely to maintain constant levels of per capita income in the tropics. In the less-developed countries, in general, the crude birth rate around 1960 averaged 40 per thousand in contrast to 21 per thousand in regions regarded as more developed, and 34 per thousand for the world as a whole (UN, 1966a, 1). The combination of high birth rates and the "amazing decline in death rates" (Davis, 1956) is producing population growth rates well above the world average. In Costa Rica, for example, the crude birth rate was 45.3 per thousand in 1948 and 42.7 in 1963, whereas the death rate dropped from 13.2 to 8.5 during this period. In El Salvador, in the same years, birth rate increased from 44.6 to 49.0 and death rate dropped from 16.9 to 10.9 per thousand (UN, 1965, 98-99).

Evidence of an increasing public recognition of, and concern for, the problem of population pressure is shown by the fact that a decade ago only one country, India, had adopted a population policy in the form of public support for the promotion of family planning, whereas today, if we include Mainland China, about five-eighths of the 2.3 billion people in the developing regions live in countries that have expressed policies favoring family planning as a means of reducing birth rates (Kirk and Nortman, 1967).[3] However, the degree of effectiveness of these policies is yet to be determined. Among the tropical regions, Western and Eastern Africa, the Caribbean area, South Asia, Polynesia, and Micronesia reported increases in annual population growth rate during the 1958-64 period (UN, 1966b, 24).

Economic Importance of Agriculture.—An indication of the economic importance of the farm sector in regions that include the tropical areas of the world is given by the report that 70 per cent of the population of Africa, 64 per cent in Asia (excluding Mainland China), 56 per cent in Central America, and 45 per cent in South America, were engaged in agriculture in 1960 (FAO, 1966, 20). A number of countries report levels well above the geographic averages. For example, in Haiti, Liberia, Ivory Coast, Thailand, and Cambodia, the levels are over 80 per cent (FAO, 1966, 21). The much lower figure of 8 per cent in North America in part reflects the fact that in more highly developed countries a larger share of the economic activities of the agricultural industry, including factor and product processing and marketing as a whole, is carried on in the non-farm sector. However, part of this difference also reflects the fact that in the less-developed countries a much larger share of the labor force is engaged in the production of the subsistence items.

The predominance of agriculture in tropical economies is indicated further by the share of the gross domestic product that originates in that sector. Generally, more than 25 per cent of the gross domestic product reported in national accounts is generated in agriculture, and very frequently this figure is 35 per cent or more. Usually the percentage of gross domestic product attributed to agriculture is much less than the percentage of the population reported to be engaged in agriculture (Table 1.2). Although part of this difference may be due to tendencies to underestimate farm income, as a result of the large non-market share of the economic activities in agriculture, a substantial amount of the difference is undoubtedly a result of lower incomes received by labor in agriculture in comparison with returns in other economic activities. It is rather evident, also, that large numbers of agricultural families probably have not shared well in the benefits of growth that have occurred in the total economy. Mexico, for example, reports 18 per cent of the gross domestic product generated in agriculture (1964) with 54 per cent of the population engaged in that field (1960).

Another feature of tropical countries is the very high level of dependence upon agricultural exports for their foreign exchange earnings. In many instances, especially in the case of the smaller countries, production for export accounts for the bulk of the commercial agriculture. Generally, with the exception of countries with important mineral resources (such as Venezuela with its large oil deposits), tropical agricultural commodities—coffee, cocoa, rubber, bananas, tea, sugar, and palm products—account for 75 per cent, and often more than 80 per cent, of the total value of exports.

Food Supplies.—Diets in the tropical areas are characterized by a high level of carbohydrates. From 70 to 80 per cent of the

TABLE 1.2.—Shares of gross domestic product originating and population employed, in agriculture, selected countries[a]

	Agriculture	
Country	Per cent of gross domestic product	Per cent of population
Bolivia	24	63
Brazil	28	54
Colombia	31	54
Costa Rica	32	49
Ecuador	36	56
El Salvador	32	60
Guatemala	28	68
Honduras	45	67
Jamaica	13	39
Mexico	18	54
Nicaragua	36	60
Cambodia	41	81
Taiwan	27	40
India	47	73
Indonesia	56	68
Pakistan	49	75
Philippines	33	57
Thailand	35	82

Source: FAO (1966, 21) for employment and UN (1966c, 457-465) for incomes.

a. Countries for which data are available in a recent year, mostly 1960-1964.

calories usually come from crop products high in carbohydrates (Table 1.3). The particular staple crops vary among the different environments—sorghum and millets in the lower rainfall areas of Africa; rice in Asia, and to a lesser extent in certain areas of Africa and Latin America; maize in Mexico, the Central American countries, Bolivia, and a number of areas in Africa; bananas and plantains throughout the wet areas of the tropics; manioc (cassava) rather generally in Africa to the south of the dry north-

TABLE 1.3.—AVERAGE NUMBER OF DAILY PER CAPITA CALORIE STANDARDS AND LEVELS, AND PERCENTAGE OF CALORIES FROM SELECTED FOOD GROUPS IN UNITED STATES AND TROPICAL SUBREGIONS, AVERAGE 1959-61

Subregion[a]	Calorie standard	Calorie level	High carbohydrate	Wheat	Rice	Other grains	Other starchy crops	Fish, meat, eggs, and milk products
United States	2,650	3,190	40	17.4	0.9	2.5	3.1	30.4
Tropics								
Central America and Caribbean	2,450	2,240	69	8.8	9.4	23.0	12.7	12.4
Mexico	2,450	2,580	70	11.1	1.6	42.2	1.8	11.4
Brazil	2,650	2,710	71	8.6	14.5	11.2	20.9	12.2
Other South America	2,500	2,260	70	16.9	5.9	16.0	15.5	14.5
East Africa	2,450	2,390	83	2.3	8.4	55.9	12.4	6.0
West Central Africa	2,400	2,460	81	1.2	5.7	27.2	45.3	2.6
North Africa	2,350	2,210	73	26.4	3.1	36.2	1.3	9.1
India	2,300	2,060	74	11.3	33.1	19.0	2.6	6.4
Other South Asia	2,300	2,120	79	19.4	47.1	4.9	1.0	7.4
Other East Asia	2,350	2,150	78	1.8	50.1	7.7	12.7	4.8

Source: USDA (1964).
a. A list of countries included in each subregion is given at the end of this chapter.

ern areas, Indonesia, Brazil, and a number of the Central American countries. Sweet potatoes and yams are also important sources of carbohydrates in a number of countries. Over a period of years the native farmers have fitted these crops into economic production systems consistent with the ecological and economic conditions and the population-land relationships under which rural people lived.[4] The general policy, of course, has been to adjust to environmental and economic conditions rather than to change these conditions. The need for developing economical sources of protein is obvious. Where sufficient additional land is available to be brought into production, food supplies of the existing kinds for an increasing population can be produced under existing systems. However, as land becomes a limiting factor, adjustments in farming systems are required merely to maintain constant levels of per capita food supplies. In fact, land is already quite scarce in the tropical countries of Asia, in which almost 27 per cent of the world's population lives on a little more than 7 per cent of the estimated agricultural land; population density is already above 100 persons per 100 acres in India and 154 persons per 100 acres in "Other East Asia" (USDA, 1964). Central America and the Caribbean areas, with 61 persons per 100 acres of agricultural land, are relatively densely populated also. On the other hand, the tropical countries of South America and Africa are much less densely populated. On the basis of the USDA regional groupings, the population per 100 acres varies from 25 in "Other South America" down to ten in East Africa. These data, of course, can provide only a very rough index of the level of population pressure because of differences in the dependence upon types of economic activity other than farming, the physical, technological, and economic factors that affect land productivity, and the inaccuracies of estimates. However, it appears that land, in its broadest sense (including climate), is already a serious limitation to production in the Asian and Caribbean areas. In South America and Africa there is some time left, but in the absence of checks on population growth and/or technological change, population pressure can be expected to reach critical stages by the end of the twentieth century, if not before that time.

Recent Growth Trends.—Estimates of total food production show consistent annual increases in Latin America, Asia, and Africa in recent years (Table 1.4), yet there is no evidence of any sustained

TABLE 1.4.—INDEX OF PRODUCTION OF FOOD, TOTAL AND PER CAPITA, SELECTED AREAS (1952/53-1956/57 = 100)

Period	Total food production			Food production per capita		
	Latin America	Far East[a]	Africa	Latin America	Far East[a]	Africa
Pre-World-War II average	69	82	69	104	106	98
1948/49-1952/53 average	88	87	89	97	93	99
Year ending in						
1954	96	98	98	98	101	101
1955	100	100	101	100	100	101
1956	102	100	100	99	102	98
1957	109	108	106	103	103	101
1958	112	107	103	103	100	96
1959	116	112	107	105	103	97
1960	116	118	110	102	106	97
1961	118	122	116	101	107	99
1962	121	124	114	100	107	95
1963	123	126	119	100	106	97
1964	128	128	121	101	105	96
1965[b]	130	129	124	101	104	96

Source: FAO (1965, 14-15).
a. Includes: Burma, Ceylon, China (Taiwan), India, Indonesia, Japan, Republic of Korea, Malaya, Pakistan, Philippines, and Thailand.
b. Preliminary.

growth in food production per capita. The patterns for total agricultural output are very similar to those for food production (Table 1.5). In view of the difficulties of making accurate estimates of agricultural production and the wide year-to-year variations in output caused by weather and other uncontrolled factors, it appears to be unrealistic to attach any significance to short-term differences of only a few percentage points. However, some significance may very well be attached to the difference in indexes of agricultural production per capita, in the developed countries in comparison with the less-developed countries[5] (Table 1.6), that appeared between 1960 and 1966. These indexes are consistently higher in the developed countries, and the difference appears to have widened despite the fact that output was under restrictive programs in the United States. From the standpoint of general welfare these differences are especially important because agriculture accounts for such large shares of the total economies of the less-developed countries.

One hypothesis is that technology and factor proportions in agriculture of the tropical countries have been relatively constant. Consequently, output has tended to grow in proportion to the increase in labor (or population) as additional land (including water) has been brought into cultivation. In India, according to Brown (1965, 25-26), "Grain yields per harvested acre averaged 296 kilograms per acre during 1901-05; 277 kilograms from 1956 to 1960; and 305 kilograms from 1961 to 1963." On the other hand, Hendrix (1965, 16-21) and the USDA (1965, 19-25) have attributed a substantial share of the growth rate in crop output, 1948 to 1960-63, to higher crop yields per acre in a number of tropical countries. It is quite doubtful that the application of additional labor alone would have produced the higher yields. However, the share of the higher yields that may have resulted from expansion of acreage on higher yielding lands has not been determined. For new inputs other than chemical fertilizers, data are quite scarce; and, whereas the applications of chemical fertilizers have increased in recent years, it is believed that most of these increases were applied to export crops. Although there are exceptions in some areas, it is quite doubtful that the increases have yet been sufficient to have noticeable effects upon aggregate production levels of crops other than those produced for export.

Another interesting point, however, is the fact that each

TABLE 1.5.—INDEX OF AGRICULTURAL OUTPUT, TOTAL AND PER CAPITA, SELECTED AREAS (1952/53-1956/57 = 100)

Period	Total agricultural output			Agricultural output per capita		
	Latin America	Far East[a]	Africa	Latin America	Far East[a]	Africa
Pre-World-War II average	73	84	67	110	109	95
1948/49-1952/53 average	88	87	88	98	93	97
Year ending in						
1954	96	98	98	98	100	100
1955	100	100	101	100	100	101
1956	103	104	101	100	102	99
1957	107	108	106	102	103	101
1958	113	107	105	104	100	97
1959	117	112	109	106	103	99
1960	121	116	112	106	105	99
1961	121	120	118	103	106	101
1962	125	123	115	104	106	96
1963	127	125	122	103	106	99
1964	130	127	125	102	105	99
1965[b]	129	129	128	99	104	99

Source: FAO (1965, 14-15).
a. Includes: Burma, Ceylon, China (Taiwan), India, Indonesia, Japan, Republic of Korea, Malaya, Pakistan, Philippines, and Thailand.
b. Preliminary.

region has shown a decline in the percentage of the population engaged in agriculture. Food and Agricultural Organization (FAO) (1966, 20) data for 1937 and 1960, respectively, show: Central America, 63 and 56 per cent; South America, 62 and 45 per cent; Africa, 76 and 70 per cent; and Asia (excluding Mainland China), 73 and 64 per cent. This decline in the share of the population, of course, does not necessarily mean a reduction in the total number employed in agriculture. Does this reduction in the share of the labor force employed on farms mean that more labor is employed on an increasing share of the agricultural activities carried

TABLE 1.6.—WORLD AGRICULTURAL PRODUCTION, BY SPECIFIED AREAS
(*Index numbers 1957-59 = 100*)

	Total		Per capita	
Year	Developed countries[a]	Less-developed countries[b]	Developed countries[a]	Less-developed countries[b]
1960	106	108	103	103
1961	107	111	103	103
1962	111	112	105	102
1963	113	117	106	103
1964	116	119	108	103
1965	116	120	106	101
1966[c]	121	123	110	101

Source: USDA (1967, 2).
a. United States, Canada, Europe, USSR, Japan, Republic of South Africa, Australia, and New Zealand.
b. Latin America, Other Far East, Western Asia, and Other Africa.
c. Preliminary.

on outside the farm sector—such as the supply of commercial inputs or the transportation, processing, and marketing of farm products? Does it mean that labor can be drawn from the agricultural sector without reducing agricultural output per capita?[6] Or, has there been an increase in the productivity of labor? Although the index of output per capita in Africa has been somewhat above the pre-World-War-II average, it has been below that average in Latin America and the Far East (Table 1.5). Are workers being "pulled" away from farms by increasing opportunities outside agriculture, or are they being "pushed" away to unemployment and the slums of urban centers by declining opportunities in the rural areas? Much more empirical work needs to be done, but answers to these questions are necessary for the formulation of appropriate programs and development strategies.

Despite the importance of agriculture as indicated by its share of total employment, gross domestic product, and export earnings in tropical countries, its direct share in development assistance from external sources (and usually domestic sources, as well) has been relatively small. Agricultural loans of the World Bank (IBRD) and the International Development Association (IDA) (1963-64, 20), from inception to June 30, 1964, in millions of United States dollars were as follows:

Area	Total agricultural	Total all purposes
Africa	65.4	1036.0
Asia and Near East	282.5	3235.2
Latin America	122.2	2077.7
Total	470.1	6348.9

Total agricultural loans amounted to 7.4 per cent of total loans for all purposes. In 1962, of the official foreign aid committed for development projects by the United States, United Kingdom, France, Federal Republic of Germany, and IBRD-IDA, only 10 per cent was allocated to food and agriculture (UN, 1964, 242); manufacturing and mining received 25 per cent, 20 per cent was committed to power, 30 per cent to transportation and communication, 10 per cent to social infrastructure, and 5 per cent to other categories.

Some Other Features of Tropical Agriculture.—The tropical and subtropical areas of the world are by no means homogeneous with respect to environmental conditions. Short distances often mean substantial contrasts in rainfall, topography, and other features. However, it is of particular importance to note that these areas are distinguished from the temperate zones by frost-free temperatures (except at high altitudes), smaller seasonal variations in length of day, and differences in soils.[7] Thus, the "seasons" usually are a matter of rainfall or cloud cover rather than length of day and temperature variations. These differences from conditions in temperate zones are particularly significant because they limit the ability to obtain similar results from similar plants, animals, and production practices; disease, pest, and weed control are especially difficult. Systems of farming vary from those considered to be very primitive, where practices have changed very little over the centuries, to those that employ quite modern technology. These different systems may exist in close proximity, but the latter are usually confined to export production although in some cases they may also be found in the commercial agriculture near the larger cities. By far, the most common systems are those in which very little capital is employed in relation to labor. This, of course, is a result of the character of the production possibilities and the relatively low price of labor in relation to capital. In sparsely populated areas, grazing of livestock or production of crops in a shifting rotation are common systems. In the latter case, only small acreages per family are cultivated in any one year, but the long fallow period means that a large total acreage per family is required. Acreage per worker is quite low in the rice systems of the densely populated areas.[8] The data on farming systems tend to support the hypothesis that output in the aggregate is likely to expand in proportion to labor expansion—fixed proportions of land, labor, and simple capital—when sufficient land is available. In the absence of new and improved inputs, farmers are likely to shift from one crop to another in accordance with production possibilities in response to relative price changes. However, there is little opportunity to change output in the aggregate in response to changes in level of prices unless supplies of commercial inputs are a major part of the system (McPherson, 1965).

In the tropical areas research and development of agriculture have been limited mainly to export products, at least until after World War II. High levels of productivity have been achieved in tropical areas of developed countries, with bananas, cocoa, coffee, palm oil, and other export crops in tropical countries, and with food crops in Mexico in recent years. Thus, the higher levels of productivity in temperate zones may very well be due to differences in research and development efforts rather than to differences in endowed resources (McPherson and Johnston, 1967). The universities of Latin America, established a hundred years or so before the first ones of the United States, only recently began to work in research and education oriented toward the problems of agriculture and rural people.

The lack of *effective* research, education, and development organizations is very characteristic of tropical countries. The term *effective* is emphasized because in many countries there are numerous organizations. In Brazil, for example, there is no dearth of planning activities, but implementation is a different matter (Robock, 1963). The early situation in Pakistan probably is not very different from circumstances in many other countries. "While government policies have a clear and definite bias in favor of development, the administrative system, wedded as it is to the *status quo* in its approach, organization and procedures, tends to pull in a different direction. . . . We are of the view that in the period immediately ahead the inadequacies of Pakistan's administrative machinery will operate as the most serious single impediment to the maximum economical use of the country's financial and material resources" (Govt. of Pakistan, 1957, 91). A balance between stability and flexibility of government is essential. A certain degree of stability is necessary in order to assure foresight and the long-term investments in infrastructure and technological development. On the other hand, the government must be sufficiently flexible to accommodate changing conditions and to promote actions necessary for progress. Traditionally, governments in tropical countries, with a few exceptions, have tended to be categorized by rigidity or a high degree of instability.

Finally, product and input markets are often found to be imperfect even from a static viewpoint. On the other hand, much more than improvements in the static sense is needed. Markets and marketing firms can play a growth-generating role in development (McPherson, 1965). Many of the inconsistencies found in market policies arise from attempts to keep prices low in the interests of urban consumers, while little or nothing is done to increase supply.

PREVIEW OF SUBSEQUENT CHAPTERS

The primary purpose of the preceding sections of this introductory chapter was to summarize some of the main features in the present status of tropical agriculture as related to economic development and agricultural growth. The subsequent chapters deal in depth with a number of these matters and present ideas with respect to what might be done about them. This section presents a very brief preview of the chapters that follow.

There is evidence of extensive existence of persistent population pressure and relatively static production functions. Fei and Chiang

(Chapter 2), with respect to a theory of stagnation, show that two characteristics of any economy, namely, "a persistent population pressure, and the lack of technological progress," constitute a sufficient condition for stagnation. The importance of agriculture in terms of employment, contribution to gross domestic product and to foreign exchange earnings has been emphasized, yet agriculture has often received a small share of the development resources. Gaitskell (Chapter 3) explains the reasons for the "preference for industry" and then discusses "the case for complementary development of agriculture and industry" and the problem of development strategy; conflict between growth rate and the proportion of the population that shares in the gains is also discussed.

Heady (Chapter 4) presents the following recipe for development: "Lower prices and increase availability of resources, add certainty and greater quantity to product prices, blend with knowledge and a firm or tenure structure which relates input productivities appropriately with resource/product price ratios." Heady also argues for higher priorities for agricultural development, suggests appropriate guidelines for establishing priorities within agriculture under different sets of conditions, and emphasizes the need for checks on birth rates in connection with long-run policies. Use of "excess agricultural capacity" of more advanced countries to feed the low-income countries at present population growth rates could provide only temporary relief. The long-run solution is to develop the agricultural economies of the low-income countries.

King (Chapter 5) states that product market development involves planning, implementing, and continuous evaluation and revision. The simple model of price differences over time, space, and form is suggested as a very effective analytical tool for evaluating alternative strategies.

Glenn L. Johnson (Chapter 6) draws heavily from direct experience and observations in Nigeria in his discussion of factor (or input) markets. A distinction is made between efficiency of operations within a given market structure and efficiency to be gained through changes in the market structure. The biggest problem in the operation of existing markets is deemed to be the governments' policies, especially the heavy rates of taxation which kept farm incomes low and distorted investments in agriculture. However, restraints on development appear to fall mainly in the category of structural problems. Needed structural changes involve the credit market, land market, labor market, and development of new technology. With respect to the labor market, "This tendency to overpay governmental and business labor has combined with the governments' heavy taxation on agricultural export crops to create what appears to be a premature, mass exodus of labor from agriculture."

In view of the fact that the export of agricultural commodities plays such a major part in the economy of the tropical countries, an analysis of one of the primary current issues is very much in order. Harry G. Johnson (Chapter 7) discusses the topic of trade preferences and developing countries, with particular reference to the proposal for temporary trade preferences in industrial products to be granted by the advanced countries. The respective contributions that aid and trade can make to the promotion of economic development are examined, and the case for and against trade preferences for developing countries as a means of promoting development, especially industrial exports of the less-developed countries, is discussed. Johnson argues that preferences might have a more powerful influence in promoting development than "conventional wisdom" suggests. The conventional evaluation procedure focuses wrongly on averages of the tariff rates applied to commodities, and fails to consider the really relevant barrier—the effective rates of protection of "value added" implicit in national tariff schedules. However, protection policies pursued by the less-developed countries may be sufficient barriers to their exports to prevent their deriving much benefit from preferences granted by the developed countries, unless major changes are made in their exchange-rate and protective policies.

Langham (Chapter 8) illustrates the use and discusses the potential and limitations of a dynamic linear programming model for development planning and analysis at the farm level. The very low growth potential in the absence of technological progress under present conditions on a Maya Indian reservation in British Honduras is also demonstrated.

Next, we turn to some area-oriented studies. Ruttan (Chapter 9), with regard to rice in Southeast Asia, argues that the yield increases of the last decade and the yield differences among major rice-producing areas within Southeast Asia at the present time reflect primarily differences in the environmental conditions of the areas (especially soil, season, water, and weather) rather than differences in variety or cultural practices. Yet, there have been significant changes in technology over the last decade and a half. Implications are: lack of development of environmental control of water (irrigation and drainage) and of crop diseases and pests have prevented farmers from achieving yield potentials inherent in existing varieties and will present an equally severe limitation on future varieties designed to be even more sensitive to effective environmental control, technical inputs, and management. "Thus, the same public investment and institutional innovations required to narrow the gap between typical and potential yields under present circumstances will represent a necessary condition if introduction of the new varieties is to be reflected in higher aggregate yields." These inferences indicate that a failure to make adequate public investment in irrigation and disease and pest control will severely reduce returns from investment in research and development on varietal and cultural practice improvements. Failure to invest adequately in research and development will limit returns from investment in irrigation and programs for the control of diseases and pests. Thus, the strategy should be to move forward on both fronts in order to reap the rewards of this complementary relationship.

Gaitskell presents two additional area-oriented studies: one covering the Indus Basin of West Pakistan (Chapter 10), and the other dealing with Africa, south of the Sahara (Chapter 11). From the standpoint of the size of these areas and the range of problems and possibilities illustrated by them, these regions are of particular interest to persons interested in the development of tropical agriculture. Gaitskell presents a lucid review of these two important areas in terms of political, social, physical, technical, and economic problems and possibilities with emphasis on development policies, strategy, and organization. He offers both a critical review of the past and positive proposals for the future.

Organizations, particularly in reference to development planning, are discussed by Gittinger (Chapter 12), who covers distinctive features of agriculture in low-income countries as related to problems of development planning and policies. Green (Chapter 13) provides a review of extensive experience with organizations for local development in Asia, Africa, and Latin America.

Particular attention is given to problems of organization at the local level, to specialist support, and to staff training. It is suggested that organizations at the local level should take account of social and cultural units, enlist the active participation of local people, be designed to use most effectively the very scarce technical competence with non-technical work given to those with less-technical competence, and deal with the broad set of problems, including but not limited to agriculture, faced by rural people. Green's conclusions (Chapter 14) concerning advising on development organization are: "The impracticability of merely copying organizational forms and functions from any other country should be obvious. Broad-scale organization analysis in depth is the *sine qua non* of the organizational advisor. Capacity to comprehend multiple aspects of existing 'wholes,' and to construct, if necessary, new organizations which are functionally integrated with the whole, or to reconstruct existing forms is the role of the organizational advisor."

Finally, Coutu (Chapter 15) suggests some reasons for greater United States university involvement abroad. He argues that United States universities should play a more positive role in defining their long-run goals and developing their international dimension, rather than merely servicing programs planned outside the university, and that continuity and sufficient staffing in depth are essential. He concludes that the United States university has a clear responsibility for greater international involvement, but the history of past experience has not been outstanding. "However, there are challenging opportunities for innovation and for service by the United States universities as well as by those in the emerging nations."

COUNTRIES INCLUDED IN SUBREGIONS OF TABLES 1.1 AND 1.2

1. Central America and Caribbean: Cuba, Haiti, Guatemala, Dominican Republic, El Salvador, Honduras, Jamaica, Nicaragua, Costa Rica, Panama, Trinidad and Tobago, British Honduras, Puerto Rico, Windward Islands, Leeward Islands, Bahamas, Bermuda, and Virgin Islands.

2. Other South America: Colombia, Peru, Chile, Venezuela, Ecuador, Bolivia, Paraguay, British Guiana, Surinam, and French Guinea.

3. East Africa: Tanzania, Malami, Zambia, Rhodesia, Kenya, Malagasy Republic, Uganda, Mozambique, Rwanda, Burundi, Somali, Mauritius, Reunion, Seychelles, and French Somaliland.

4. West Central Africa: Nigeria, Congo (Leopoldville), Ghana, Angola, Cameroon, Ivory Coast, Guinea, Sierra Leone, Togo, Liberia, Upper Volta,

Mali, Niger, Senegal, Chad, Dahomey, Central Africa Republic, Congo (Brazzaville), Portuguese West Africa, Mauritania, Gabon, Gambia, and Spanish West Africa.

5. North Africa: UAR (Egypt), Ethiopia, Sudan, Morocco, Algeria, Tunisia, and Libya.

6. Other South Asia: Pakistan, Ceylon, Afghanistan, Nepal, Bhutan, and Sikkim.

7. Other East Asia: Indonesia, Philippines, Thailand, Burma, Taiwan, Malaysia, South Korea, South Vietnam, Cambodia, Hong Kong, Laos, Brunei, Melanesia, Micronesia, Polynesia, and Ryukyu Islands.

NOTES

1. For other views and further discussion of definition and measurement see Frankel (1952), Hicks (1940), Kuznets (1948), Kuznets (1947), Little (1949), Nutter (1957), Kuznets (1956), and Usher (1963).

2. Calculated from data in UN (1964).

3. See Kirk and Nortman (1967) for a summary of policies and actions taken in each of the countries.

4. For further discussion, see McPherson and Johnston (1967). Also, for further discussion of manioc, in particular, see Jones (1957).

5. The "less-developed" countries are heavily weighted by, but not limited to, tropical countries.

6. For a recent discussion of "surplus" agricultural labor and economic development, see Paglin (1965) and references cited in that article.

7. For more detailed discussions, see McPherson and Johnston (1967), also Bennett (1962).

8. Space does not permit detailed discussion of the major farming systems. Selected references for further reading include: McPherson and Johnston (1967), which includes a number of references on technical aspects of tropical agriculture, McPherson (1965), Nye and Greenland (1960), Dumont (1957), Terra (1958, 1959), Jones (1959), Wickizer (1960), Reynders (1961), Allan (1965), Crist (1964), Johnston (1958), Jones (1965), and other recent articles on Africa in *Food Research Institute Studies,* Stanford University.

LITERATURE CITED

ALLAN, W. 1965. The African husbandman. Barnes and Noble, N.Y.

BENNETT, MERRILL K. 1962. An agroclimatic mapping of Africa. Food Research Institute Studies III(3): 195-216.

BROWN, LESTER R. 1965. Increasing world food output. USDA, ERS, Foreign Regional Analysis Div., Foreign Agr. Econ. Rep. 25. Washington, D.C.

CRIST, R. E. 1964. Tropical subsistence agriculture in Latin America: some neglected aspects and implications. Smithsonian Report for 1963 (Smithsonian Institution Publication 4586): 503-519.

DAVIS, KINGSLEY. 1956. The amazing decline of mortality in underdeveloped areas. Am. Econ. Rev. XLVI(2): 305-318.

DUMONT, RENÉ. 1957. Types of rural economy. Frederick A. Praeger, N.Y.

FAO. 1965. The state of food and agriculture, 1965, review of the second postwar decade. Food and Agr. Org. of the United Nations, Rome.

———. 1966. Production Yearbook, 1965. Vol. 19, Rome.

FRANKEL, S. HERBERT. 1952. 'Psychic' and 'accounting' concepts of income and welfare. Oxford Econ. Papers (1): 1-17.

GOVT. OF PAKISTAN. 1957. The first five year plan. National Planning Board. Govt. of Pakistan Press, Karachi.

HENDRIX, WILLIAM E. 1965. The experience of more rapidly developing countries, p. 12-24. *In* Iowa State University Center for Agricultural and Economic Development, Economic development of agriculture. Iowa State Univ. Press, Ames.

HICKS, J. R. 1940. The valuation of the social income. Economica (New Ser.) VII(May): 105-124.

IBRD AND IDA. 1963-64. Annual Report. Washington, D.C.

JOHNSTON, BRUCE F. 1958. The staple food economies of western tropical Africa. Stanford Univ. Press, Stanford, Calif.

JONES, WILLIAM O. 1957. Manioc: an example of innovation in African economies. Econ. Dev. and Cultural Change V(2): 97-117.

———. 1959. Manioc in Africa. Stanford Univ. Press, Stanford, Calif.

———. 1965. Environment, technical knowledge and economic development in tropical Africa. Food Research Institute Studies V(2): 101-116.

KIRK, DUDLEY, and NORTMAN, DOROTHY. 1967. Population policies in developing countries. Economic Development and Cultural Change 15(2) part 1: 129-142.

KUZNETS, SIMON. 1947. Measurement of economic growth, p. 10-34. *In* Economic growth—a symposium. J. Econ. Hist. Supplement VII.

———. 1948. On the valuation of social income—reflections on Professor Hicks' article. Economica (New Ser.) XV(Feb.): 1-16; (May): 116-131.

———. 1956. Some conceptual problems of measurement. Econ. Dev. and Cultural Change V(1): 6-9. Reprinted with omissions, p. 237-241. *In* Bernard Okun and Richard W. Richardson [eds.], Studies in economic development. 1961. Holt, Rinehart and Winston, N.Y.

LEWIS, W. ARTHUR. 1955. The theory of economic growth. Richard D. Irwin, Inc., Homewood, Ill.

LITTLE, I. M. D. 1949. The valuation of social income. Economica (New Ser.) XVI(Feb.): 11-26.

McPHERSON, W. W. 1965. Input markets and economic development, p. 99-117. *In* Iowa State University Center for Agricultural and Economic Development, Economic development of agriculture. Iowa State Univ. Press, Ames.

McPHERSON, W. W., and JOHNSTON, BRUCE F. 1967. Distinctive features of agricultural development in the tropics, p. 184-230. *In* Herman M. Southworth and Bruce F. Johnston [eds.], Agricultural development and economic growth. Cornell Univ. Press, Ithaca, N.Y.

MILLIKAN, MAX F. 1956. Statement, p. 13-29. *In* Hearings before the subcommittee on Foreign Economic Policy of the Joint Committee on the Economic Report, 84th Cong. 1st. Sess., Nov. 9-17, 1955. Washington, D.C.

NUTTER, G. WARREN. 1957. On measuring economic growth. J. Political Econ. LXV(1): 51-63. Reprinted 1963, p. 25-38. *In* Theodore Morgan, George W. Betz, and N. K. Choudhry [eds.], Readings in economic development. Wadsworth Publishing Co., Belmont, Calif.

NYE, P. H., and GREENLAND, D. J. 1960. The soil under shifting cultivation. Tech. Communication No. 51, Commonwealth Agric. Bureaux. Farnham Royal, Bucks, England.

PAGLIN, MORTON. 1965. "Surplus" agricultural labor and development: facts and theories. Am. Econ. Rev. LV(4): 815-834.

REYNDERS, J. J. 1961. Some remarks about shifting cultivation in Netherlands New Guinea. Netherlands J. Agr. Sci. 9(1): 36-40.

Robock, Stefan H. 1963. Brazil's developing northeast: a study of regional planning and foreign aid. The Brookings Institution, Washington, D.C.

Schumpeter, Joseph A. 1947. Theoretical problems, p. 1-9. *In* Economic growth—a symposium. J. Econ. Hist. Supplement VII.

Terra, G. J. A. 1958. Farm systems in Southeast Asia. Netherlands J. Agr. Sci. 6(3): 157-182.

———. 1959. Agriculture in economically underdeveloped countries, especially in equatorial and subtropical regions. Netherlands J. Agr. Sci. 7(Aug.): 216-231.

UN. 1964. World economic survey, 1963. Part I, trade and development: trends, needs, and policies. N.Y.

———. 1965. Statistical yearbook, 1964. N.Y.

———. 1966a Demographic yearbook, 1965. N.Y.

———. 1966b. Statistical yearbook, 1965. N.Y.

———. 1966c. Yearbook of national accounts statistics, 1965. N.Y.

USDA. 1964. The world food budget, 1970. For. Agr. Econ. Rep. 19. ERS, For. Reg. Analysis Div., Washington, D.C.

———. 1965. Changes in agriculture in 26 developing nations, 1948 to 1963. ERS, For. Agr. Econ. Rep. 27. Washington, D.C.

———. 1967. The world agricultural situation, review of 1966 and outlook for 1967. For. Agr. Econ. Rep. 33. Washington, D.C.

Usher, Dan. 1963. The transport bias in comparisons of national income. Economica (New Ser.) 30(118): 140-158.

Wickizer, V. D. 1960. The smallholder in tropical export-crop production. Stanford Univ., Food Research Institute Studies. I(1): 49-99.

Additional References

Green, L. P., and Fair, T. J. D. 1962. Development in Africa. Witwatersrand Univ. Press, Johannesburg, South Africa.

Kamarck, Andrew M. 1967. The economics of African development. Frederick A. Praeger, N.Y.

Lewis, W. Arthur. 1950. Developing colonial agriculture. Tropical Agr. XXVII(4-6, Apr.-June): 63-73.

Mellor, John W. 1966. The economics of agricultural development. Cornell Univ. Press, Ithaca, N.Y.

Mosher, A. T. 1966. Getting agriculture moving. Frederick A. Praeger, N.Y. for the Agri. Dev. Council, N.Y.

Schultz, Theodore W. 1964. Transforming traditional agriculture. Yale Univ. Press, New Haven, Conn.

Waterson, Albert. 1965. Development planning, lessons of experience. The Johns Hopkins Press, Baltimore, Md.

2

The Fundamental Cause of
Economic Stagnation

John C. H. Fei
Alpha C. Chiang

I. INTRODUCTION

Economic stagnation is one of the most time-honored problems that has occupied the attention of economists. Almost at the very inception of the study of economics, students of the subject were concerned about the eventuality of the economic system coming to a halt at some point in the future. In recent years, the acute interest in the problem of economic growth, in both the developed and the developing nations, reflects a resurgence of the same type of concern about stagnation, despite the fact that the latter-day economists seem to prefer a positive statement of the problem (promotion of growth) to a negative one (avoidance of stagnation). This problem has naturally also come to the forefront of the attention of agricultural economists, as a consequence of rapidly growing populations and lagging food supplies and agricultural growth in many of the low-income countries. It is the purpose of this paper to inquire into the fundamental cause of economic stagnation.

THE MEANING OF STAGNATION

Although the concept of stagnation has had a prominent place in the history of economics, it has by no means acquired a universally accepted definition. In the classical theory, for instance, stagnation refers primarily to the cessation of the process of capital accumulation, although the other key variables in the economy will also cease to grow as a consequence. However, to a modern economist, the term stagnation may principally convey the idea of the failure of the economy to achieve steady increases in its gross national product (GNP). In fact, a multitude of other interpretations may be assigned to the term as well, and in view of this, we must first adopt a precise definition before we can embark upon a rigorous inquiry into the fundamental cause of economic stagnation.

In this regard, two points may be noted. First, the notion of stagnation is relevant mainly in the *long run*. So, we shall be concerned with the tendencies that will manifest themselves in the distant future. Secondly, since the objective of all economic activities is, in the long run, to raise the consumption standard in the economy, the concept of stagnation should in the final analysis be defined in terms of *consumption* more than anything else. That is, it should be principally viewed as a *welfare* concept. These considerations lead us directly to this definition: An economy is *stagnant* if it is incapable of achieving a *sustained* and *unbounded* increase in its per capita consumption stream through time.

In giving the concept of stagnation a distinctly welfare-oriented definition, we are by no means running counter to the classical view of stagnation (with emphasis on capital accumulation) or the more modern view (with emphasis on GNP); we are simply focusing attention on the ultimate implication of both of these views. For, if an economy cannot raise its consumption standard at all, or can only raise it within limits in the long run, it surely does not qualify for the descriptive label "progressive" or "non-stagnant," regardless of the situation with respect to capital accumulation and/or the level of its GNP. Conversely, as long as an economy is capable of achieving sustained and unbounded increases in the consumption standard, then, regardless of the status of capital formation and GNP, it must not be considered stagnant.

A GEOMETRIC INTERPRETATION

The two words *sustained* and *unbounded* in the above definition are of crucial importance; let us amplify on their meaning graphically. By plotting per capita consumption, C^*, against time, t, as in Figure 2.1a, we may consider the curves A, B, L_1, L_2, and L_3 as exemplary time paths of the long-run per capita consumption standard. The last three of these, being horizontal straight lines, show no increases whatever in C^* through time. Curve B, on the other hand, does exhibit a sustained increase in C^*; i.e., we find $dC^*/dt > 0$ (positive slope) everywhere on the curve. That increase, however, is not unbounded, because curve B approaches L_1 asymptotically. The only time path in Figure 2.1a showing a sustained as well as unbounded increase in C^* is curve A. On that curve, not only is dC^*/dt positive throughout (hence, sustained), but C^* can exceed any arbitrary number we choose if given sufficient time to grow (hence, unbounded). Thus, under our definition, a non-stagnant economy should be characterized by a time path of consumption standard such as curve A.

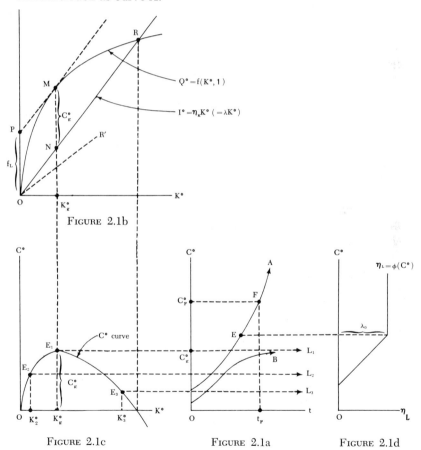

FIGURE 2.1b

FIGURE 2.1c   FIGURE 2.1a   FIGURE 2.1d

Note that, according to our definition, the level or magnitude of the per capita consumption stream is, as such, irrelevant to the notion of stagnation. An economy is to be considered stagnant even if it can attain, and maintain, a "high" level of C^*, such as indicated by the L_1 line. Indeed, it is even possible for a stagnant economy to achieve a sustained increase in C^*, as exemplified by curve B, provided that C^* will converge to some fixed magnitude—for then the increment in C^* will become quantitatively negligible in the long run. Such a definition is perfectly compatible with the traditional view of stagnation, which stresses only the *long-run* inevitability of the cessation in economic progress.

II. A THEORY OF STAGNATION

The aim of a rigorous theory of economic stagnation is to uncover the fundamental structural characteristics of an economy which render a sustained and unbounded C^* path impossible. That is, we must prove an *impossibility thorem* to the effect that whenever a particular set of structural characteristics is present in an economy, then a path such as curve A cannot possibly exist.

In the history of economic thinking, a variety of factors have been proposed as explanations for the phenomenon of stagnation. The classical school, for instance, explained stagnation on the strength of the fixity of land, in combination with the forces of the law of diminishing returns, a savings behavior based on the classical theory of distribution, and an endogenous demographic theory linking population growth to the wage rate. In the modern literature on underdeveloped countries, one finds as explanations of stagnation of such countries not only many economic factors, but also a host of cultural, political, and other non-economic forces found in those economies. From among such explanations, two structural characteristics can be singled out as being fundamental, in the sense that, together, they constitute a sufficient condition for stagnation. These two characteristics are: a persistent population pressure and the lack of technological progess.

THE FRAMEWORK

To examine this idea rigorously, let us assume a static production function $Q = f(K, L)$ of the neoclassical type, with positive marginal products ($f_K > 0$, $f_L > 0$), diminishing returns ($f_{KK} < 0$,

$f_{LL} < 0$), and constant returns to scale. Let the labor force L (identified in this paper with the population) be growing at a constant rate λ. Since the output Q at any point in time is divided into consumption C (which determines the per capita consumption standard $C^* \equiv C/L$) and investment I (which determines the rate of growth of capital I/K), we may write

(1) $\qquad Q = f(K, L)$ $\qquad\qquad$ [production function]

(2) $\qquad Q \equiv C + I$ $\qquad\qquad\;\;$ [division of total output]

(3) $\qquad \eta_K \equiv \dfrac{dK/dt}{K} = \dfrac{I}{K}$ $\qquad$ [rate of growth of capital]

(4) $\qquad \eta_L \equiv \dfrac{dL/dt}{L} = \lambda$ $\qquad$ [rate of growth of population].

Here we have four equations in five variables (Q, K, L, C, I). When a savings rule is added, the system will become closed;[1]† as they stand, however, these four equations constitute a savings-rule-free system.

Because of the assumption of constant returns to scale, we can rewrite (1) in the form of $Q^* = f(K^*, 1)$, where $Q^* \equiv Q/L$ is output per head (average product of labor), and $K^* \equiv K/L$ is capital per head (capital-labor ratio). Moreover, by dividing (2) throughout by L, we can obtain

$$Q^* = C^* + I^* = C^* + \eta_K K^* \qquad [\text{by } (3)].$$

Hence, the per capita consumption C^* can be expressed as

(5) $\qquad\qquad C^* = f(K^*, 1) - \eta_K K^*.$

This equation, central to the present discussion, admits of an easy graphic interpretation.

In Figure 2.1b where the horizontal axis measures the capital-labor ratio, K^*, the output per head $Q^* = f(K^*, 1)$ can be represented by the positively-sloped curve OMR which is concave from below. For any given constant value of η_K (rate of growth of capital), the $\eta_K K^*$ term in (5) plots as a straight line with slope equal to η_K, as exemplified by the line ONR. By virtue of (5), the vertical gap between the two curves at any level of K^* measures the consumption per head C^*, and when duly transplotted into the vertically aligned Figure 2.1c, such vertical gaps give rise to the in-

†Notes for this chapter begin on page 44.

verse-U-shaped C^* curve. Of course, given a lower value of η_K, line ONR must shift to a less steep position (such as OR'), and as a consequence a higher C^* curve will result.

THE VON NEUMANN STATES AND THE GOLDEN RULE OF ACCUMULATION

In the special event that the value of η_K is exactly equal to the constant population growth rate λ:

(6) $$\eta_K = \eta_L = \lambda$$

the capital-labor ratio K^* will remain stationary through time, so that there will be neither capital deepening nor capital shallowing. Such a state of affairs is known as a *von Neumann state*. The reader will note that, in a von Neumann state, a specific rule of savings is implied; namely, $S(= I) = \lambda K$, for only then will we find $\eta_K = \lambda$.

The constancy of K^* characterizes a von Neumann state, but since K^* can remain constant at various levels, there are various von Neumann states, each associated with a particular constant value of K^*. If the ONR line in Figure 2.1b is assumed to satisfy (6), i.e., if the slope of ONR is λ, then we have constancy in K^*, and each value of K^* on the horizontal axis corresponds to a distinct von Neumann state, and the consumption standard pertaining to each von Neumann state can be read from the C^* curve in Figure 2.1c. If K^* is constant at the level of K_2^*, for example, the consumption standard, also constant in the von Neumann state, will be the height of the point E_2, and the time path of C^* will be depicted by line L_2 in Figure 2.1a. Similarly, the capital-labor ratio K_3^* corresponds to the time path L_3.

According to the well-known "golden-rule theorem" (Phelps, 1961 and Robinson, 1962) there exists among all the von Neumann states one that yields the maximum consumption standard. In Figure 2.1c, the maximal value of C^* is C_g^*, attained when the value of K^* is K_g^*; in terms of Figure 2.1a, the corresponding time path is line L_1. To attain K_g^* (and hence, C_g^*), the economy must adopt the so-called golden rule of accumulation, namely, to set the rate of growth of capital equal to the marginal product of capital:

(7) $$\eta_K = f_K .$$

The rationale behind this rule can be explained with the help of Figure 2.1b. To maximize the vertical gap between the Q^* and I^* curves, we must find the value of K^* such that the slope of the Q^* curve and the slope of the I^* curve are identical. This condition is satisfied at K_g^* where the tangential line PM is parallel to line ONR, giving $MN = C_g^*$ as the maximum value of C^*. Since the slope of Q^* curve measures the marginal product of capital,[2] and the slope of I^* curve is η_K, the golden rule must indeed take the form of (7).

It is easily verifiable that, under the golden rule, the consumption standard, C_g^* must be equal to the marginal product of labor, f_L. For, by Euler's Theorem, we have

$$Q = f_K K + f_L L.$$

Thus, after dividing through by L, we can write

$$f_L = Q^* - f_K K^* = Q^* - I^* \quad \text{[by (7) and (3)].}$$

In Figure 2.1b, this means that the golden rule will give us

$$f_L = \text{distance } K_g^* M \text{ minus distance } K_g^* N = C_g^*.$$

(It may be noted that, since PM is parallel to ON, f_L can be graphically represented by the distance OP as well.) Consequently, the golden rule of accumulation is seen to imply the so-called classical savings rule, namely, that all the competitive wages be consumed, whereas all the competitive profits be saved and invested:

$$(8) \qquad\qquad C = f_L L \text{ and } I(= S) = f_K K.$$

When (8) is satisfied, we have consumption standard $C/L = f_L$, and growth rate of capital $I/K = f_K$, as shown in (7).

To sum up: (a) when capital and labor are growing at the same rate, by fulfilling condition (6) which implies a von Neumann savings rule, a von Neumann state will result, and (b) the particular von Neumann state which satisfies the golden rule (7)—or, what amounts to the same thing, the classical savings rule (8)—yields the maximum per capita consumption standard among all possible von Neumann states.[3] It follows that, in the consumption-maximizing von Neumann state, both the von Neumann savings rule and the classical savings rule are satisfied. That is to say, the two savings rules coincide, and we have $\eta_K = f_K = \eta_L = \lambda$. These notions are the analytical tools which we shall use to prove our impossibility theorem.

THE IMPOSSIBILITY THEOREM

The basic theorem we intend to prove is that, regardless of the savings rule adopted in the economy, economic stagnation is inevitable when a persistent population pressure exists along with a static production function; i.e., the savings-rule-free system represented by Equations (1) to (4) cannot possibly give rise to a sustained and unbounded increase in C^*.

Let us start by postulating a growth path of C^* such as curve A in Figure 2.1a. This curve is monotonically increasing and unbounded, and hence, must contain a point (e.g., point F) such that all the points on the curve beyond F will lie entirely above line L_1. That is, $C^*(t) > C_g^*$ for all $t > t_F$ in Figure 2.1a. With reference to such a point F, we may ask: Is there some constant η_K value which is consistent with the consumption standard associated with $F(C_F^*)$? The answer is yes, but such an η_K value must be *less than* the population growth rate λ. This is because if the capital growth rate is *equal to* λ, so that a von Neumann state obtains, the consumption standard can at most be $C_g^* < C_F^*$, whereas if the capital growth rate *exceeds* λ, the I^* curve in Figure 2.1b must become steeper than line ONR, and hence, by narrowing the vertical gap between the Q^* and I^* curves, must shift the C^* curve downward from the position shown in Figure 2.1c. On the other hand, if the capital growth rate is *less than* λ, a less steep I^* curve (such as OR') will result, and the C^* curve will shift upward.

Although a sufficiently low level of η_K will make the consumption standard C_F^* attainable, such a situation will involve a continual process of capital shallowing, since η_K falls short of $\eta_L = \lambda$ in this case. That is, K^* must decrease through time. Indeed, capital shallowing will occur not only at F, but also at all points beyond F. Now, consider two possible outcomes regarding the value of K^*. First, K^* may finally coverage to some positive value $K_0^* > 0$. In that event, the economy will ultimately grow in the manner of a von Neumann state; if so, curve A will not be able to rise above the horizontal line L_1 in Figure 2.1a. Secondly, K^* may continue to decrease all the way to zero. If so, an ever-rising consumption stream obviously cannot be maintained. Thus, the growth path A is contradicted in either of these two possible cases, proving the following:

Theorem: Under assumptions (1) to (4), all monotonically increasing time series of C^* will be bounded by C_g^*.

It is to be noted that although the proof of the above theorem is based on the *four* equations (1) to (4), only (1) and (4) actually represent behavioral assumptions. Thus, the economic interpretation of the theorem is that, as long as the technology of production (subject to diminishing returns and constant returns to scale) remains static, and as long as population pressure is persistent, the best per capita consumption stream the economy can hope for in the long run is the type exemplified by curve B in Figure 2.1a. Under our definition, such an economy is stagnant.

III. A RECONSIDERATION OF THE CLASSICAL THEORY OF STAGNATION

From the preceding discussion, it is clear that the twin conditions of static technology and persistent population growth are *sufficient* cause of stagnation. This suggests that, when the above two conditions are present, many other explanatory factors that have been proposed—be they economic, cultural, social, or political—may be only incidental, or even redundant. It is also possible that these other factors may become relevant primarily by operating through the two factors enumerated in our theorem. To demonstrate the point in question, let us briefly examine the classical theory of stagnation as an illustration.

THE CLASSICAL THEORY

The classical theory, as embodied in the writings of such classicists as Ricardo, McCulloch, and Senior,[4] envisages the phenomenon of stagnation as a consequence principally of the following attributes of an economy: (a) a production process involving three inputs: capital K, labor L, and land N, with emphasis on the fact that land is fixed; (b) a static technology with diminishing returns; (c) a rule of savings based on the Ricardian theory of income distribution and the assumption that all profits are saved and all other incomes are consumed; and (d) an endogenous theory of population growth, in which the population growth rate is an increasing or nondecreasing function of real wage or consumption per head (Iron Law of Wages). It is possible to show, however, that the fixity of land, the particular rule of savings assumed, and the endogenous theory of population growth are all nonessential as far as causation of economic stagnation is concerned.

THE ANALYSIS

The fixity-of-land attribute is generally believed to be the most important bottleneck factor responsible for stagnation. Let us see what happens when this attribute is deleted from the model. The classical production function takes the form of

$$Q = F(K, L, N) \quad \text{with } N = \bar{N}.$$

When the fixity-of-land assumption ($N = \bar{N}$) is relaxed as much as it can be relaxed, we have the opposite situation of unlimited land. In that case, since land becomes a free good, the above production function reduces to the form of (1).

The model which we investigated earlier, Equations (1) to (4), may now be viewed as a modified version of the classical model in which: (a) land is free instead of fixed; (b) the population growth rate is constant rather than a function of the real wage; and (c) the savings rule is unspecified. Our impossibility theorem then leads immediately to the conclusion that stagnation is unavoidable even when the amount of land is infinite. Hence, the classical fixity-of-land explanation is nonessential. Furthermore, the savings-rule-free nature of our impossibility theorem clearly implies that the particular savings rule of the classical model is also irrelevant. Finally, inasmuch as a constant population growth rate already implies the impossibility of a sustained and unbounded increase in the consumption standard, the effect of the Iron Law of Wages is merely to strengthen the force of stagnation by making it more difficult to increase per capita consumption.[5] This means that the Iron Law of Wages is also a dispensable explanatory factor.

IV. Generalization to a Two-Sector Economy

The impossibility theorem of Section II was proved in the framework of a one-sector economy. In the present section, we shall attempt to show that the impossibility theorem holds even when the technological horizon is broadened to include differentiated production functions in different sectors of the economy. For simplicity, however, we shall restrict ourselves to a two-sector framework.

A somewhat more general mathematical proof is given in the Appendix. Here we shall rely mainly on the graphic method.

The two sectors

Let there be in the economy a consumer-goods sector and an investment-goods sector, each with its own production function. In every time period, given the total amount of capital K and labor L, the economy must allocate the two inputs between the two sectors in some way. The allocation may be depicted by means of the familiar Edgeworth box OABC in Figure 2.2, where OA and OC are, respectively, the total available L and K. By plotting the isoquants for the investment-goods industry (such as i_0, i_1) with origin at point 0, and the isoquants for the consumer-goods industry (such as c_0, c_1) with origin at point B, we can obtain an allocation curve (contract curve) OPRB. If point P is a typical point on the alloca-

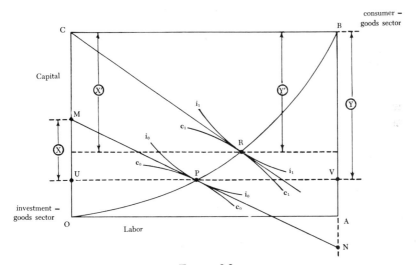

FIGURE 2.2

tion curve, the slope of the tangential line MN to the isoquants at P (i_0 and c_0) is the factor-price ratio (wage/profit). Similarly, at point R, the factor-price ratio is equal to the slope of line CR.

At any point in time, the available quantities of K and L in the economy will specify the dimensions of the Edgeworth box, and the production functions in the two sectors (as reflected in the two sets of isoquants) will determine an allocation curve. The choice of a rule of savings will then fix an "equilibrium point" on the allocation curve, thereby specifying the output of consumer goods C (hence, the consumption standard C^*) and the output of investment goods I (hence, the capital available for the next point in time). If population, L, is assumed to be growing at a given constant rate λ, as in Section II, then the available labor for the next point in time will also become known. In this manner, the dimensions of a *new* Edgeworth box can be found. Thus, as soon as a definite savings rule is chosen, the entire growth path of the economy becomes determinate, and that path can be represented by a *sequence* of Edgeworth boxes.

It is our objective to prove that, given static production functions in both sectors and a constant population growth rate, the same impossibility theorem holds in the present context. That is, regardless of the savings rule adopted through time, any monotonically

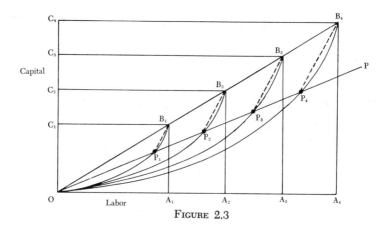

FIGURE 2.3

increasing per capita consumption stream C^* will always be bounded by some fixed magnitude. For this proof, we shall again employ as an analytical device the notion of von Neumann states.

THE VON NEUMANN SAVINGS RULE

In the present context, a von Neumann state is defined as a growth situation characterized by the constancy of K^*—the factor-endowment ratio—for the economy as a whole, i.e., by $\eta_K = \eta_L = \lambda$. Since K and L will grow at the same rate, the sequence of Edgeworth boxes pertaining to a von Neumann state must share a common diagonal, as exemplified by the boxes $OA_1B_1C_1$, $OA_2B_2C_2$, $OA_3B_3C_3$, ... in Figure 2.3.

As before, a von Neumann state implies a specific savings rule, namely that which enables the economy to maintain the same K^* at a given population growth rate. The observance of the von Neumann savings rule will fix a particular point on the allocation curve of each box. This is illustrated in Figure 2.3 by the points P_1, P_2, P_3, and P_4, which respectively lie on the allocation curves of the successive boxes of the von Neumann state depicted. It should be noted that the sequence of points P_1, P_2, . . . must lie on the same straight line OP, and that the lines B_1P_1, B_2P_2, . . . must be parallel. These facts signify that the input ratio in the investment-goods sector remains the same in all boxes, and so does the input ratio in the consumer-goods sector.[6] In short, any larger box in a von Neumann state is just a "blow up" of any smaller box. For example, referring to the first two boxes $OA_1B_1C_1$ and $OA_2B_2C_2$, the values of the following ratios are all identical: OA_2/OA_1 (population multiple), OC_2/OC_1 (capital multiple), OP_2/OP_1 (investment-goods output multiple), and B_2P_2/B_1P_1 (consumer-goods output multiple). It is then clear that, in a von Neumann state, a constant level of C^* is also maintained through time.

In the two-sector model, therefore, each von Neumann state is (as before) characterized by a fixed K^*, leading to a particular constant value of C^*. It will be our next task to show that the relationship between C^* and K^* can again be depicted by an inverse-U-shaped curve similar to the one in Figure 2.1c; i.e., the golden-rule theorem of Section II can be generalized to the two-sector context.

THE CLASSICAL SAVINGS RULE

The golden-rule theorem of Section II specifies that, among all the von Neumann states, the one which satisfies the classical savings rule—that all competitive profits be saved and invested—yields the maximum C^*. The choice of that savings rule entails, in the one-sector model, the search for the capital-labor ratio K_g^* in Figure 2.1b. What does the adoption of the classical savings rule mean in the two-sector framework?

Since all competitive profits are to be saved (and invested) under this rule, the total output of investment goods (new capital) must have the same exchange value as the total competitive profit income in both sectors. Equivalently, the exchange value of the wage income in the investment-goods sector must be identical with that of the profit income in the consumer-goods sector. In terms of Figure 2.2, the fulfillment of the classical savings rule will lead us to point R on the allocation curve, which has the property that the tangential line CR *passes through the upper-left corner of the box.*

To see why this is so, let us take a typical point P on the allocation curve, for which the tangential line MN (together with the horizontal line UV through point P) delineates two distances labelled X and Y on the two vertical sides of the box. Since the slope of MN is the factor-price ratio, the wage income of UP units of labor in the investment-goods sector has an exchange value of X units of capital. On the other hand, the profit income of BV units of capital in the consumer-goods sector has an exchange value of Y units of capital. To satisfy the classical savings rule, it is necessary that X=Y. This latter condition is satisfied only by point R, which gives the result that X′=Y′. This proves our claim. A point such as R may be referred to as the "classical allocation point."

Given an Edgeworth box and a population growth rate λ, the output of investment goods called for under the classical savings rule may or may not be equal to that required by the von Neumann savings rule. If, for example, the output of capital goods required by the von Neumann savings rule is i_0 units, which is less than i_1 units as determined by the classical savings rule at point R, then the von Neumann allocation point will be at the lower point P.

THE GOLDEN-RULE THEOREM GENERALIZED

To generalize the golden-rule theorem to the two-sector context, it needs to be demonstrated that, among all the von Neumann states, the one in which point P (von Neumann allocation point) and point R (classical allocation point) *coincide* will yield the highest consumption standard.

To begin with, let us prove the existence of a von Neumann state in which points P and R do coincide, i.e., a von Neumann state in which the classical savings rule does prevail. In Figure 2.4, let the isoquant map for investment goods be given. If the size of capital stock at time t is $\overline{K}$, we can fix the point C on the vertical axis as the upper-left corner of any Edgeworth box we intend to draw. Now, with a population growth rate λ, the von Neumann savings rule requires the output of investment goods to be $i_0 = \lambda\overline{K}$ units; this will uniquely specify the isoquant labelled i_0 as relevant for the von Neumann state. It is obvious that we can always construct a tangential line to isoquant i_0 that passes through the point C. In Figure 2.4, the point of tangency occurs at P. We are of course not yet certain that point P will lie on the allocation curve of some Edgeworth box. However, it is easy to show that it indeed will. By keeping the capital stock constant at $\overline{K}$, while varying the labor endowment, we can construct an infinite number of boxes with OC as the common left side, although only two—OABC and OA'B'C— are actually shown. Inasmuch as the slope of the isoquants of the consumer-goods sector varies continuously from point to point, it is clear that, when viewed from a point of origin lying somewhere on the line CBB', there must be an input ratio in the consumer-goods sector at which the slope of the consumer-goods isoquants will be

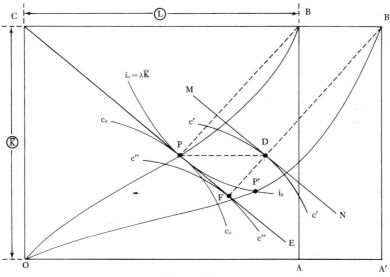

FIGURE 2.4

equal to the slope of line CP. Let that input ratio be indicated by the slope of line BP; then we can take point B as the upper-right corner of our box. In that case, we shall find the isoquant c_0 tangential to i_0 at P, and point P must be a point on the allocation curve of box OABC. If that input ratio had been different, then we would have obtained another point on the line CBB' as the upper-right corner of the desired box. The conclusion is that point P must lie on the allocation curve of *some* box among the infinite number of them that we can draw. In the present case of the box OABC, point P is at once the classical allocation point (its tangential line CP passes through the upper-left corner of the box) and the von Neumann allocation point (it lies on the isoquant $i_0 = \lambda\overline{K}$). This completes the existence proof.

It remains to show that the consumption standard of the box OABC is higher than that of any other box with the same amount of capital K, such as OA′B′C.[7] For this purpose, let us:

(a) construct a parallelogram B′BPD, thus defining a point D;

(b) draw a straight line MN through D, parallel to CE;

(c) extend line B′D to intersect CE at point F;

(d) draw the consumer-goods isoquants c′ and c″ (with origin at B′) passing through points D and F, respectively;

(e) let the i_0 isoquant intersect the allocation curve OB′ of box OA′B′C at point P′, thus pinpointing P′ as the von Neumann allocation point of box OA′B′C.

Then we may reason as follows: by the parallelogram construction B′BPD, the c′ isoquant is merely a transplant of the c_0 isoquant when the origin is shifted from B to B′. Hence, the slope of c′ at D is identical with the slope of c_0 at P. Furthermore, by the assumption of constant returns to scale, the slope of c″ at F is the same as the slope of c′ at D, because points D and F lie on the same ray emanating from the origin B′. Thus, the isoquant c′ is tangential to MN at D, and c″ is tangential to CE at F. Now, the capital-goods isoquant, i_0, and the consumer-goods isoquant, c″, obviously cannot be tangential to each other, as they are in fact tangential to the same straight line, CE, at two different points, P and F. The point P′— the intersection between i_0 and the allocation curve of the box OA′B′C—must accordingly be located to the northeast of c″; i.e., P′ must lie on a consumer-goods isoquant with a smaller output than c″. However, in view of the fact that PBC and FB′C are two similar triangles, we have BP/CB=B′F/CB′. This means—recalling the assumption of constant returns to scale—that, in order to maintain the per capita consumption standard of box OABC, namely c_0/CB, the consumer-goods output in box OA′B′C should be set at c″ units (see point F), in which case the per capita consumption standard will be c″/CB′ ($=c_0$/CB). Since P′ involves a lower consumer-goods output than point F, however, P′ must entail an inferior consumption standard to that of point P. This completes the proof of the two-sector version of the golden-rule theorem: The von Neumann state in which the classical savings rule prevails, as exemplified by box OABC, is the one with the highest consumption standard C*.

THE IMPOSSIBILITY THEOREM

The fact that one particular von Neumann state, with a specific value of K^*, is associated with the maximum C^* attainable in all von Neumann states in the two-sector economy means that, when C^* is plotted against K^*, we will again obtain an inverse-U-shaped C^* curve similar to the one in Figure 2.1c. Then, by the same argument employed in Section II, the impossibility theorem there stated can be shown to apply with equal force to the two-sector model.

V. CONCLUSION

In this chapter, we have presented a theory of economic stagnation in the form of an impossibility theorem. Specifically, it has been demonstrated that when a static technology subject to the law of diminishing returns is coupled with a persistent population pressure, economic stagnation is bound to result, in the sense that per capita consumption standard cannot rise in an unbounded manner. This theorem was proved first for the case of a one-sector economy, and then generalized to the two-sector framework. Of course, we have not given specific consideration to the more complicated case of an economy with more than two sectors, but it would seem intuitively clear that the same impossibility theorem will remain valid even then.

Since a static production function and a persistent population pressure are *sufficient* cause for economic stagnation, it follows that, in order to enjoy economic progress, it is *necessary* to have either a steady improvement in technology, or population control, or both. This constitutes the long-run policy implication of our analysis. In this connection, it should be noted that even a once-and-for-all change in technology would be incapable of preventing stagnation, for as soon as such a technological change is completed, the economy will simply find itself in a new milieu of static technology. Rather, what is needed is a continual process of technological improvement over time, and hence, a continual upward shift of the production function.

APPENDIX

In this appendix, we shall prove a theorem which is slightly more general than the golden-rule theorem of Section IV. For a two-sector economy of the neoclassical type, let the two commodities be an industrial good (first commodity) and an agricultural good (second commodity). If K and L represent capital stock and labor force for the economy as a whole, the defining property of an Edgeworth box is:

(A1a) $I = f^{(1)}(K_1, L_1)$ [industrial production function]

(A1b) $Q = f^{(2)}(K_2, L_2)$ [agricultural production function]

(A1c) $K \equiv K_1 + K_2$ [allocation of capital]

(A1d) $L \equiv L_1 + L_2$ [allocation of labor]

(A1e) $\dfrac{f_{L_1}^{(1)}}{f_{K_1}^{(1)}} = \dfrac{f_{L_2}^{(2)}}{f_{K_2}^{(2)}}$ [optimum allocation condition],

where (A1e) stipulates the equality of the marginal rates of technical substitution of the two sectors, thereby defining the optimum allocation curve of the box. We shall assume (A1a) and (A1b) to satisfy all the conventional properties of the neoclassical production function.

Let us assume that the agricultural good, $f^{(2)}$, can be used only for consumption, whereas the industrial good, $f^{(1)}$, can be used either for investment or consumption. By denoting industrial consumer good by I_c and investment good by I_i, we have

(A2) $f^{(1)} \equiv I_c + I_i.$

It shall be further assumed that the consumption demand for I_c is proportional to the consumption demand for the agricultural good $f^{(2)}$, i.e.,

(A3) $I_c = \gamma f^{(2)}$ $(\gamma > 0).$

If $\gamma = 0$, the situation will reduce to the special case where the industrial good is not consumable—the case investigated in Section IV above. It is by allowing γ to take a non-zero value that the theorem proved in this appendix is something of a generalization of the theorem of Section IV. The assumption of complementarity in consumer preference in (A3) is, of course, not entirely realistic, but it has the advantage of permitting us to deal with the per capita consumption of the agricultural good alone, rather than of both goods, because the maximization of the per capita consumption of *both* goods is attained (under the condition of complementarity) when we maximize the per capita consumption of the *agricultural* good alone. In this light, we shall simply define

(A4)
$$C^* = \frac{f^{(2)}}{L} \; .$$

Let the rate of growth of population be λ. Then the defining property of a von Neumann state is that $I_i/K = \lambda$, or

(A5)
$$I_i = \lambda K.$$

Now consider the vector $V = (K, L, K_1, L_1, K_2, L_2, I, Q, I_c, I_i)$, whose ten elements are the ten variables in the above model, and another vector $\beta V = (\beta K, \beta L, \ldots, \beta I_i)$, which is a scalar multiple of V by the constant β. In view of the homogeneity of all the functions in (A1), (A2), (A3), and (A5), it is obvious that if V is a solution (i.e., if the variables in V satisfy all these equations) then βV will also be a solution. Thus, if V_0 stands for the vector of variables at time $t=0$, then the vector of the time series $V_0 e^{\lambda t}$ represents a von Neumann state which expands at the same rate as the population growth rate λ. Furthermore, as can be seen from (A4), the value of C^* is constant through time in a von Neumann state.

The mathematical problem of the golden-rule theorem is to find that particular solution vector V which maximizes C^* as defined in (A4). However, in view of the homogeneity property of the system, we may set K to be constant ($K = \bar{K}$), and maximize C^* subject to the conditions of (A1), (A2), (A3), (A5), and the condition $K = \bar{K}$.[8] There are ten variables—the variable C^* and the nine variables in V when constant K is excluded—and nine equations. Thus, one of the variables, say L, can be viewed as exogenous, the specification of which would determine the values of every other variable in the system. For purposes of maximization, we must now focus our attention on the derivative dC^*/dL.

From (A4), we have

$$\frac{dC^*}{dL} = \frac{1}{L} \left[f^{(2)}_{K_2} \frac{dK_2}{dL} + f^{(2)}_{L_2} \frac{dL_2}{dL} \right] - \frac{f^{(2)}}{L_2} \; .$$

Hence,

(A6) $\dfrac{dC^*}{dL} \gtreqless 0$ if and only if $f^{(2)}_{K_2} \dfrac{dK_2}{dL} + f^{(2)}_{L_2} \dfrac{dL_2}{dL} \gtreqless \dfrac{f^{(2)}}{L} \; .$

The expressions dK_2/dL and dL_2/dL can be evaluated as follows. From (A1a) and (A1b), we have

$$dI = f_{K_1}^{(1)} \, dK_1 + f_{L_1}^{(1)} \, dL_1 \, ; \, dQ = f_{K_2}^{(2)} \, dK_2 + f_{L_2}^{(2)} \, dL_2 \, .$$

However, from (A2) and (A5), we see that

$$dI = dI_c + dI_i \, ; \, dI_i = \lambda \, dK = 0.$$

Thus, $dI = dI_c$.

Moreover, we know from (A3) that

$$dI_c = \gamma df^{(2)} \equiv \gamma dQ.$$

Therefore, we have $dI = \gamma dQ$, or, by using the dI and dQ expressions derived earlier:

(A7a) $f_{K_1}^{(1)} \, dK_1 + f_{L_1}^{(1)} \, dL_1 - \gamma \left[f_{K_2}^{(2)} \, dK_2 + f_{L_2}^{(2)} \, dL_2 \right] = 0.$

Next, we can write

(A7b) $dK_1 = -dK_2$ [by (A1c)]
(A7c) $dL_1 = dL - dL_2$ [by (A1d)]
(A7d) $f_{L_1}^{(1)} = \rho \, f_{L_2}^{(2)} \, ; \, f_{K_1}^{(1)} = \rho \, f_{K_2}^{(2)}$ [by (A1e)],

where

(A7e) $\rho \equiv f_{L_1}^{(1)} / f_{L_2}^{(2)} = $ ratio of MPP$_L$ in the two sectors.

By substituting (A7b) − (A7e) into (A7a), and simplifying, we obtain

(A8) $f_{K_2}^{(2)} \dfrac{dK_2}{dL} + f_{L_2}^{(2)} \dfrac{dL_2}{dL} = \dfrac{\rho}{\rho + \gamma} f_{L_2}^{(2)} \, .$

Finally, the substitution of (A8) into (A6) yields the desired information that

(A9) $\dfrac{dC^*}{dL} \gtreqless 0$ if and only if $\dfrac{\rho L}{\rho + \gamma} f_{L_2}^{(2)} \gtreqless f^{(2)} \, .$

This mathematical result must now be given an economic interpretation. For this purpose, let P_1 and P_2 be the dollar prices of the two commodities. Then,

(A10a)   value of investment good $= P_1 I_i = P_1 f^{(1)} - P_1 \gamma f^{(2)}$

(A10b)   capitalists' total income $= P_1 K_1 f_{K_1}^{(1)} + P_2 K_2 f_{K_2}^{(2)}$.

The equalization of the wage rate (and also of the profit rate) between the two sectors under competitive conditions implies

(A11a) $\qquad\qquad P_1 f_{L_1}^{(1)} = P_2 f_{L_2}^{(2)}$ [wage-rate equalization]

(A11b) $\qquad\qquad P_1 f_{K_1}^{(1)} = P_2 f_{K_2}^{(2)}$ [profit-rate equalization],

with the result that

(A11c) $\qquad\qquad \rho = \dfrac{P_2}{P_1}$ $\qquad$ [by (A7e)].

By comparing the value of investment good (A10a) with capitalists' total income (A10b), we see that (A10a) $\gtreqless$ (A10b) if and only if:

$$f^{(1)} - \gamma f^{(2)} \gtreqless K_1 f_{K_1}^{(1)} + \rho K_2 f_{K_2}^{(2)} \quad \text{[by (A11c)],}$$

or

$$f^{(1)} - K_1 f_{K_1}^{(1)} \gtreqless \rho K_2 f_{K_2}^{(2)} + \gamma f^{(2)},$$

or

$$f^{(1)} - K_1 f_{K_1}^{(1)} \gtreqless \rho \left[f^{(2)} - L_2 f_{L_2}^{(2)} \right] + \gamma f^{(2)} \text{ [Euler's Theorem],}$$

or

$$L_1 f_{L_1}^{(1)} \gtreqless (\rho + \gamma)\, f^{(2)} - \rho L_2 f_{L_2}^{(2)} \quad \text{[Euler's Theorem],}$$

or

$$\rho L_1 f_{L_2}^{(2)} + \rho L_2 f_{L_2}^{(2)} \gtreqless (\rho + \gamma)\, f^{(2)} \quad \text{[by (A7d)],}$$

or

$$\rho L f_{L_2}^{(2)} \gtreqless (\rho + \gamma)\, f^{(2)},$$

or

$$\frac{\rho L}{\rho + \gamma}\, f_{L_2}^{(2)} \gtreqless f^{(2)} .$$

Therefore, Equation (A9) can be interpreted to mean: $\dfrac{dC^*}{dL} \gtreqless 0$

if and only if the value of investment good $\gtreqless$ capitalists' total income. To maximize C^*, it is necessary that $dC^*/dL = 0$; this means that all the capitalists' income must be saved and invested, i.e., the classical savings rule must be followed:

$$(A12) \qquad\qquad \frac{\rho L}{\rho + \gamma} f_{L_2}^{(2)} = f^{(2)}.$$

We then have a total of eleven equations (A1), (A2), (A3), (A4), (A5), (A7e), and (A12) to determine the values of the eleven variables—C^*, ρ, and all the variables in V excluding K.

As a final note, it may be pointed out that, for the aggregate one-sector model of Section II, various authors have proved that if the classical savings rule is chosen consistently through time, the value of capital-labor ratio K^* will converge to that value of K^* which maximizes C^*, i.e., K_g^* (see Fei, 1965). A similar question arises in the two-sector model as to whether the value of K^* will also converge to such a C^*—maximizing value, if the classical savings rule is consistently observed through time. The answer is in the affirmative. As Uzawa (1961) has shown, the value of K^* will, in the two-sector model, always converge to some value K_0^*. The results of this appendix now indicate that Uzawa's K_0^* must indeed be the K_g^* value as determined by the golden rule of accumulation.

Notes

1. If, for example the Keynesian savings rule ($I = sQ$, where s represents the propensity to consume) is added, the result will be the Solow (1956) growth model.

2. By the appropriate choice of units, we can let $L = 1$. Then $K^* = K/L = K$, and the $f(K^*, 1)$ curve in Figure 2.1b becomes the total product curve as a function of capital alone, and therefore, its slope must be the marginal product of capital.

3. It should be pointed out that, in the case of certain special production functions (which fulfill the constant returns to scale and diminishing-returns conditions), the golden-rule theorem may not hold; i.e., there may *not* exist a K^* which maximizes C^*. Given the production function

$$Q = AK^\alpha L^{1-\alpha} + BK,$$

for instance, output per head is

$$Q^* = A(K^*)^\alpha + BK^*,$$

and the slope of the Q^* curve (Fig. 2.1b) is

$$\frac{dQ^*}{dK^*} = \alpha A(K^*)^{\alpha-1} + B.$$

If the population growth rate λ is less than B, then nowhere on the Q^* curve will we be able to find a point (such as M) such that the slope of Q^* is equal to that of the I^* curve.

In our analysis below, we shall assume that the golden-rule theorem does hold.

4. For a succinct synopsis of the theory, see Baumol (1959, 13-21).

5. The Iron Law of Wages can be represented by the η_L curve in Figure 2.1d, which shows the population growth rate as a non-decreasing function of the consumption standard C^*. For this type of curve, it is reasonable to postulate a maximum biological reproduction rate λ_0 for all sufficiently high consumption standards. As we did in the proof of our impossibility theorem, let us postulate a monotonically increasing consumption path such as curve A in Figure 2.1a. It is clear that, sooner or later (e.g., after point E on curve A), the maximum population growth rate, λ_0, will prevail. The constancy of the population growth rate will then imply that all the arguments in our impossibility theorem become applicable.

6. This fact, which follows from the constant returns to scale assumption, is well known in the proof of the factor-price equalization theorem in neoclassical international trade theory.

7. As drawn, the alternative Edgeworth box OA'B'C has a lower capital-labor ratio than box OABC. It is not difficult to reconstruct the diagram and to prove the same theorem for the case where OA'B'C involves a higher capital-labor ratio.

8. This is due to the fact that if $V = (K_0, L_0, \ldots, I_{c0})$ is a solution to (A1), (A2), (A3), and (A5), then $(\bar{K}/K_0)V$ is also a solution with the same value of C^*, such that the K_0 term in V is replaced by $(\bar{K}/K_0)K_0 = \bar{K}$. Alternatively, the reader may think of this procedure of holding K constant as an analytical device by which we can let the variations in L alone reflect changes in K^*. This was of course essentially what was done in the analysis of Figure 2.4.

Note that, strictly speaking, the tangency condition in (A1e) need not be postulated at the open end in this maximization problem, as it can be deduced from the maximization problem itself. It is included here for the sake of conforming to the exposition in the text.

Literature Cited

Baumol, W. J. 1959. Economic dynamics. (2d ed.). Macmillan, N.Y.

Fei, John C. H. 1965. Per capita consumption and growth. Quart. J. Econ. LXXIX(1): 52-72.

Phelps, Edmund. 1961. The golden rule of accumulation: a fable for growthmen. Am. Econ. Rev. LI(4): 638-643.

Robinson, Joan. 1962. A neoclassical theorem. Rev. Econ. Studies XXIX (3)no. 80: 219-226.

Solow, Robert M. 1956. A contribution to the theory of economic growth. Quart. J. Econ. LXX(1): 65-94.

Uzawa, Hirofumi. 1961. On a two-sector model of economic growth. Rev. Econ. Studies XXIX(1)no. 78: 40-47.

3

Importance of Agriculture
in Economic Development

Arthur Gaitskell

The purpose of this chapter is to consider whether, and if so, why, agriculture is important as a subject in economic development, what significance should be attached to it, and how it fits in with other aspects of such development.

A Preference for Industry

The condition of agriculture in many developing countries indicates that, until recently, it has had a very low priority of attention. It has, in fact, been rated unimportant. The derision in the phrase "country cousin" epitomizes a common human attitude towards agriculture, and it is desirable first to consider the reasons for this attitude.

The most obvious reason is that the richest countries in the world are the industrial countries. A clear relationship exists between the amount of power installed and the amount of wealth per head of population. It follows that the road to wealth seems to be through industry. The very word "developed" implies industrially developed, while the word "backward" suggests a rural subsistence economy. In such a context, it would seem that breaking away from the grip of mere agriculture is the first step towards breaking away from poverty.

This inclination to emphasize industry is also connected with a feeling that industrialized countries have, in the past, tended to use underdeveloped countries as sources of raw material and as markets for the sale of their manufactures; they have grown rich in the process, while the underdeveloped countries have remained poor. This pattern of development is criticized for having broken up the cohesion and diversity of occupation in the village life of the poorer countries while the benefit of change—the stimulation of forward links providing jobs in a new diversity of occupations—has all occurred in the richer countries. Psychologically, resentment at just being "hewers of wood and drawers of water" for other people's benefit has been a powerful spur to develop one's own industries.

This sense of being at the wrong end of the terms of trade was powerfully accentuated before World War II, and is frequently so again today, by the very low prices obtainable for agricultural primary products and often by the great difficulty of being able to sell them at all. In such circumstances, again, industrialization seems to be the only means of liberation from poverty.

In countries subject to political colonialism before independence, and indeed to economic "colonialism" even when independent, the pattern of development was usually one in which such economic development as there was, whether agricultural in the sense of plantations or by extraction of minerals, by industry, or by import and export trade, was largely one of private investment for profit by expatriate capitalists. Local inhabitants tended simply to continue a traditional subsistence way of life in a separate sphere and only entered the market economy as labor. Often, the colonial power pursued a policy of encouraging the preservation of the local people's way of life according to traditional law and custom, particularly in regard to land. This was done partly to protect them from exploitation, partly from convenience and cheapness of administration through traditional channels, and partly from some distrust of modern influences on them. Only since World War II and, to a great extent, since independence, has the concept of actively developing the country come to the forefront of state policy as opposed to leaving this to the vagaries of expatriate private enterprise profit.

It is also apparent that, quite apart from colonialism, traditional values persist and frequently form impediments to economic growth. Not everybody gives this top priority in their lives. Many find greater happiness in, or put greater value on, leisure, status and caste, religious precepts, or the traditional methods of their ancestors. Such people, no doubt, are thorns in the flesh of "developers."

Nevertheless, since World War II, pressures inclining to the gospel of economic growth have impinged on developing countries from many directions, and most of these are promoters of industrialization. It is in the agricultural sector that the resisters and traditionalists live. One great stimulus to industry immediately resulting from the war was the need to replace shortages. Import substitution started in necessity. The war also widened horizons, but mainly towards values only obtainable in urban conditions, increasing thereby the country-cousin image of rural life. Thousands for the first time saw what the world was like beyond their village and beyond their country. The comparison created the disturbing needle of rising expectations, later sharpened by literacy, radio, journalism, and travel.

The galloping race to independence left new political leaders with the task of meeting these expectations, and external contacts tended to confirm their own inclinations that the solution lay in industrialization. Russian communism continuously gave it priority and urged developing countries to follow their example as the only way to escape exploitation by Western capitalism; but industrial promotion was equally powerfully abetted by Western world salesmen. Apart from sales of machinery, industrialists in developed countries could still see profit for themselves by setting up industries in underdeveloped countries, and they had the organization and capital to do so. No such external organization or such interest arose in the case of agriculture, except for plantations, and the local attitude to these was increasingly hostile. Industrial promotion has also been abetted from within by the fact that enterprising individuals from the local community have frequently seen much better opportunities for personal enrichment by investment of their capital in a protected industry rather than in the agricultural field.

Finally, decision-makers in developing countries have usually come from the educated elite, which has inclined to make them urban oriented. For politicians, the risk of subversion seems much closer in urban crowds, and cheap food for the citizen and the industrial worker has often seemed more immediately important than raising farmers' incomes. The risk of an inflationary wage spiral has tended to support this viewpoint.

There are also other reasons which push people into a preference for industry. In a general way, industry has a much greater appeal than agriculture to a developing country. Industry suggests the modern world, and people are more willing to learn new skills in it. Ready-made machinery can be imported and erected and, subject to learning how to use it, the thing works. Nothing has to be discovered. By contrast, agriculture is old, and most people think they already know all about it. It suggests drudgery and poverty, and to alter this state of affairs usually does involve local discovery. It also involves changing the traditions of the poorest, most conservative, and illiterate elements in the country, not by bringing them into a new environment like a factory, but by persuading them to alter their real sheet anchor, i.e., the way they use their land. Paying wages to employees who can be dismissed if unsatisfactory and getting more from the sale of the products than is paid out in wages seems a much easier operation than persuading farmers, who cannot be dismissed, to learn how to pay themselves more wages. Organization of industry seems largely a matter of the management making a plan and the machines and the labor following it. In indigenous agriculture every little farmer is his own manager, and getting them organized at all is a major problem.

All this suggests that pursuing industry is a much tidier, easier process. Turnover of capital in industry is more rapid than in agriculture, so it can stand high interest rates more easily and thereby attract finance. There seems to be less uncertainty about industry, and there is a uniformity in an industrial process, whatever the locality, which helps to predict profitability. By contrast, agriculture involves enormous variations from crop to crop and country to country, and this is accentuated by the fact that anything organized about agriculture is anyway liable to be upset by climatic effects beyond human control.

Finally, if one looks at the developed world today from a developing country's viewpoint, one sees that the majority are employed in industry, commerce, and services and that only a small minority are actually engaged in farming. Industry seems the obvious target for which to aim. Indeed, one sees a great deal of progress, not merely in industry, but also in agricultural production in developed countries. One notes, however, that the technological success in agriculture has been closely linked with subsidies made possible by surpluses derived from industry. In developing countries no such surpluses exist. It is very easy to conclude, therefore, that the only way to stimulate the development of agriculture is to develop industries first.

I have set out all these arguments which favor a preference for industry in order to bring out one of the facts of life which confronts agricultural development today in poor countries; namely, that there exists an underground bias towards interest in industry and urban life. It is a bias which is extraordinarily difficult to shift, for many of the above arguments are quite valid.

COMPLEMENTARITY BETWEEN AGRICULTURE AND INDUSTRY

In spite of all the above arguments, there has recently been a swing-over in many developing countries (and let us realize that this phrase includes regions in apparently developed continents like Europe, for example, Spain, Italy, and Greece) to complementary growth of agriculture and industry, and, in places, a swing-over to priority for agriculture because of previous neglect. There appear to be various reasons for this change, among which the following are prominent.

One basic cause is that today a central purpose for encouraging development at all is the existence of widespread undernourishment and poverty. This is a comparatively new reason since hitherto the main spur to development has simply been private profit. However, in today's world undernourishment is a very powerful reason. The East/West conflict, the *raison d'être* of international and bilateral aid agencies, and local political leadership all generate an urge to raise the standard of living. Whereas a generation ago an attitude of indifference prevailed towards materially backward areas and few countries felt it obligatory or desirable to worry about their neighbors, today a sense of moral obligation, ideological conflict, fear of an unbalanced world, and a need for markets for the products of richer countries combine to make the raising of everyone's standard of living a common world objective. Within many developing countries perspective planning for a minimum income is a conscious, if illusive, target.

The chief centers of undernourishment and poverty in developing countries are, however, the rural areas. This is where most of the population still live and where rapidly increasing population exerts its greatest pressure, making their standards lower. If the way of life of the majority is to be improved, it is essential that agriculture be improved.

In this connection I listened recently to Professor Arthur Lewis, who raised a very vital question, especially for Western world policy. "Is the emphasis on growth rate alone right?" he asked. "Should there not also be attention to the misery rate, even if the growth rate is slower?" He quoted India as having the highest percentage of misery per thousand people in the world in spite of a high rate of industrial development. He mentioned Jamaica, which has had a fantastic increase in gross national product in the last ten years, but which still has a 14 per cent rate of unemployment and great misery. One might add the case of Mexico, often described as a model to follow for dynamic growth in recent years, but where 50 per cent of the population is still in rural areas, hungry and poor and underemployed. One could apply the warning to Pakistan, now fashionably quoted as a prototype for Asia in rapid growth, but where 50 per cent of the population lives on small subsistence holdings on only 9 per cent of the land.

The point is that the imbalance is not only between rich and poor countries, but between rich and poor and urban and rural sectors, within developing countries. It is precisely on the inequality in this imbalance that the communist faith imparts its greatest propaganda and with great validity. If misery is to be overcome, more must be done to improve conditions in rural areas. A major reason for land reform is that far too many have no sense of citizenship and a great sense of contrast in wealth. The political risk has to be weighed, or it may destroy the growth. We in the Western world often project our own experience and ideology and advocate growth through the dynamism of private enterprise. Do we forget sometimes that in developing countries conditions are far more difficult, that there is far less time for the spontaneous acquisition of skills, far greater population pressure, far less scope to invade other countries by force, and far less tolerance of inequality than was available in these respects in our history of growth? In advocating growth in our pattern are we paying anywhere near enough attention to the "left-outs"?

The problem of the "left-outs" hits many developing countries in the phenomenon of urban drift. Those countries which have started development from a mineral and industrial nexus have frequently found that this results in a lopsided economy which puts a considerable strain on local society. This particularly affects young people. Education, radio, and newspapers all depict a softer, more fashionable life in towns. The young people who go beyond the standard 8 years of schooling drift to towns for administrative, commercial, or factory jobs which simply do not exist. The resultant overcrowding, slum conditions, and disappointment at unemployment lead to delinquency and discontent and to high social costs in housing and police. These circumstances also form a serious threat of subversion to ruling political regimes. The discontent is often equally felt in the countryside where those who remain not only suffer economically from the departure of the young, but feel themselves a despised and neglected element not sharing in the national progress around them.

The rural discontent is often accentuated by the price ratio between agricultural and industrial products. Import substitution and industrialization behind tariffs, although it has developed skills and an urban sector, has frequently meant high cost manufactures and low agricultural prices. Moreover, the poverty in the countryside, when the majority still live there or in urban slums, affords a very narrow home market. This in turn leads to under-utilized capacity and higher cost industry, making competition in international trade harder. Thus, derelict agriculture is coming to be recognized as a major constraint on industrial growth.

The need for concurrent prosperous agriculture is also becoming increasingly evident as more and more countries are finding that it is impossible to solve the employment situation by industrialization alone. Modern industry is capital intensive, seldom labor intensive, and can only deal in tens of thousands, whereas the problem of raising the standard of living runs into hundreds of thousands. Let me illustrate this from recent studies of job opportunities in East Africa. In Tanzania, the 1964-69 Development Plan postulates a 7 per cent growth rate in industry, thereby providing an estimated 116,000 new jobs in the period. However, the estimated number of new entrants seeking jobs is 1,150,000. In a single year for a typical age group of 250,000 youngsters, of whom 47 per cent get no schooling, only 23,000 jobs will be available in organized employment. The rest must live off the land.

Analogous figures are available for Kenya. There the estimated annual number of those who complete the 8-year standard school program is 150,000; 15,000 of these can find places in secondary schools, and the rest must compete for 35,000 paid jobs arising per annum in the economy. The remaining 100,000 must find self-employment; the only place is on the land. If these are representative figures for Africa, what can be the position in overcrowded countries in Asia?

The problem of job opportunity raises an awkward dilemma in regard to education, so demanded by developing countries and so popular as aid from the developed world. Of course, literacy and skills are essential to growth, and education should provide them. However, what kind of education and for how many, at what period in a country's development may be as important to growth as a general conviction that education is good. The Food and Agriculture Organization of the United Nations in its African Survey pointed out bluntly that most current curricula educated children to leave the land where, as the above statistics suggest, most of them must find self-employment. Recently I heard Professor Arthur Lewis suggest that, for many developing countries, about 3 per cent of persons entering secondary schools would provide the country's need for skilled personnel. To exceed this figure might provide literacy, but might not be a wise investment. In other words, over a certain level, expenditure on education might simply become consumption. The expenditure might have been better directed to investment for growth in the real backward sector—agriculture. These are awkward, challenging ideas, but it may well be that some of the most significant aid currently being provided in the world is that arising from the Freedom from Hunger Campaign in its attempts to create agricultural schools and farm institutes. Education to obtain a better income from farming may help more people to jobs at a certain stage of development than any other investment.

You may feel that some of these arguments are still theoretical and have not yet led to much practical change in the attitude towards agriculture. Let us turn to a very practical subject which certainly does keep the need for improved agriculture in the forefront. I refer to the problem of foreign exchange earnings. Such earnings are, of course, essential to buy the basic imports necessary to growth and particularly to industrialization. Exploitations of minerals, oil, copper, tin, bauxite, gold, diamonds, and so on probably provide the quickest answer and in time may develop around them processing and supply industries. A great many countries, however, are not blessed with these assets and are dependent on ecologically suitable crops, whether raw or processed, as major foreign exchange earners. Admittedly, the market is very competitive and is overloaded by synthetics and by production in developed countries of more universally grown crops. However, those countries which, for this reason, have neglected their agricultural export opportunities and put all their money into industrialization —for instance the Argentine—have not escaped the problem of how to sell the products of their high cost industries. Other countries have found that their traditional primary agricultural exports need expansion, not neglect, and there can be little doubt that the resulting need for market outlets is a compelling reason for trading with the communist world. There seems little doubt, also, that if we really want to help developing countries, or indeed prevent their collapse, we must ease the tariffs and quotas which impede their sales of primary products and expand this trade. The converse view, that they can get by on industrialization alone, has not been vindicated.

Perhaps the most pressing practical problem which is bringing agriculture to the forefront is the plain need for food. The increase in the population as a whole, the increase in the numbers who no longer grow their own food because they have joined the urban and industrial sectors, and the increasingly sophisticated type of food which higher incomes and better nutrition demand, are all placing more and more strain on many developing countries. Unless their own agriculture can supply these needs, the countries must import or run a serious risk of inflation and possibly famine. Thus, the situation is not only that agricultural exports are desirable to earn more foreign exchange, but that agricultural improvement is essential to stop an increasing drain on foreign exchange. In this sense also, apart from the fact that derelict agriculture provides no internal market, it begins to strangle industrial development. The classic current example is again India, where in 1966 no less than 11 million tons of food had to be imported merely to keep people alive. Admittedly, Public Law 480 supplies have eased this situation in many lands, but these supplies are far from inexhaustible and are, in the long run, an unreliable solution. Some might even consider it a dangerous solution on the grounds that the donation of food is conducive to sloth in improving agriculture locally. Even in Europe, in Spain, the question of food imports is one of the foremost problems of the economy today. In 1965, Spain had to spend 570 million dollars of foreign exchange on this drain out of the 1,000 million dollars which she earned from a phenomenal figure of 14 million tourists, a catastrophic waste of resources needed for other purposes. It is significant also that even in Russia, for all its emphasis on growth by industrialization, the main burden of Secretary Brezhnev's 1965 report to the Central Committee of the Soviet Union was on urgent measures for the further development of agriculture, measures which largely consisted of doubling the price of many agricultural products and decentralizing the authority for production.

I have called this section the case for complementary development of agriculture and industry. I hope that in stating the above arguments, I have not given the impression that I think industry is unimportant. This is not what the arguments suggest to me. What they do suggest is that if agriculture is neglected, the chances of progress are very heavily restricted, and grave social, political, and economic tensions may occur. They also suggest that the optimum pattern is not haphazard investment in industry according to the whims, ideological or otherwise, of individual politicians and competing salesmen, but rather a deliberate complementary advance of agriculture and industry, with agriculture supplying the food and many raw materials for local processing industries and industry supplying the inputs for modernizing agriculture plus the consumer goods to liven up the rural areas. I heard Walt Rostow once say that all businessmen ought to regard the rural areas as potential customers. *Laissez-faire* policies alone will not accomplish this. Rostow went on to say that the revolutionary public-private partnership in the rural life of the U.S.A. was the partnership between the knowledge imparted to the farmer by the Agricultural County Agent and the stimulus to effort imparted by the mail-order catalogue. I believe that it is this public-private partnership that we need in our strategy for growth in developing countries, adding, if you like, the incentive of higher and more reliable agricultural prices practiced so long in the West and recently in Russia, and adding, if you like, deliberate decentralization of industry to rural areas as in Israel and Japan.

You may feel that a complementary advance of agriculture and industry is too cozy a concept to work in practice. Yet, because of the imbalance created by haphazard industrialization in the past, this in fact is what countries like Spain and Italy are trying to implement in their national plans through a series of regional development poles.

You may rightly say that people in developing countries are suspicious of advisers who point out the importance of agriculture, fearing an implication of the old "hewers of wood and drawers of water" position. It is difficult today for such people to believe that development in the Western world itself started with agriculture. In England, it was the wool trade which first created a society of diversified skills and preceded industrialization. In Japan, it was the silk trade, and in the United States, Canada, and Australia the basis of progress began in agriculture. We need to get away from the belief that attention to agriculture implies subservience and backwardness and into an understanding well-phrased recently by Sir Ronald Prain, Chairman of Rhodesian Selection Trust. I have chosen this statement particularly because it comes from an industrial magnate in the great copper belt in Zambia. He said that improved agriculture offers the best prospect of a major contribution to employment. Behind the farmer stands an army of ancillary trades and professions: road and rail transport, fertilizers, textiles, food processing, stock feed, starch, paper, canning, power, timber, tobacco, cement, steel, leather, and all the services stimulated by them.

Are Prain, Rostow, and Lewis all talking nonsense? Which do you think in its ramifications is the biggest industry and the biggest employer of labor in the most developed country in the world? No, it is not petrochemicals, steel, or space rockets. It is agriculture. Agriculture in the United States in all its ramifications is a science, a business, a profession, and an industry. In 1962, of 65 million people employed in the United States, 25 million produced for and serviced farmers, 9 million processed and distributed farm products, and 250,000 scientists directly served agriculture. The career demand generated by agriculture was for 15,000 graduates per annum—2,000 on the actual farms and ranches and 13,000 in research, extension, conservation, and commercial operations. Forty per cent of all jobs in the United States were in 500 distinct occupations relying on agriculture (FAO, 1962).

A PLEA FOR URGENCY

In this chapter I have tried to express the importance of agriculture in economic development from two opposite poles. From the proton pole, or end of the road picture just described, I have sought to illustrate what an enormous contribution the ramifications of investment in improved agriculture have made in developed countries and, correspondingly, could make in developing countries. From the neutron pole, and I understand that this is the boiling, explosive element in science, I have suggested some of the dangers we face if we do not pursue agricultural development: the backwardness of the rural sector in most developing countries, the constraint that this implies on progress, and the tensions likely to arise.

I would like to add one point more: the formidable nature of the task confronting us. Statisticians tell us that the world population is likely to double in the next 35 years, from 3,000 million to 6,000 million. Merely to feed this increase at present low nutrition standards will be quite a problem. To turn them into consumers with purchasing power and a decent standard of living will be a gigantic task.

I expect, like myself, you find that the bigger the statistics, the more difficult they are to grasp. To make them more realistic, let me break them down in two examples. The estimated additional population in India alone between now and 1985, say 20 years, is about equivalent to the present population of the whole United States. The United States currently uses 80 pounds of fertilizer per capita. Asia uses 3 pounds. To raise this figure to 30 pounds, merely to keep people decently alive, means increasing the usage tenfold in 20 years. Karl Olsen, longtime in the Food and Agriculture Organization of the United Nations, speaking at a conference on this very subject at the Massachusetts Institute of Technology in 1964, underlined the difficulty of getting people to realize the urgency of the need to improve agriculture in developing countries. He likened mankind to people drifting in a canoe downriver to the brink of a great waterfall, mesmerized by the sound of it getting clearer every year, but doing little to avert the disaster ahead of them.

Have any of these arguments persuaded you of the urgency for action about agriculture? I doubt it, and this for an additional reason that puts people off the subject. I would like to express this in the form of a story I once heard from the United States economist Alvyn Maine. "There was once a man," he said, "who sold himself to the devil in order to get rich. The pact was an unusually simple one. The devil undertook to supply him annually with 100 million dollars on condition that he spend the whole lot in a single year. If he failed he would die on the 31st of December. Joyfully he embarked on a life of wine, women, and song, but they made but a small dent in his bank balance. He went in for risky investments, but they turned out successful and merely added to his pile. In despair, as Christmas drew near, he consulted his friend, the Governor of a developing country, and explained his approaching predicament. To his intense relief the Governor had a solution. 'Give it to me,' he said, 'to spend on agricultural development and I'll get rid of the whole lot in a week.' "

The story well illustrates the attitude of most treasury officials, bankers, and all the hierarchy of money to investment in agriculture in the underdeveloped world. Their fears are right. It is risky. The rate of return, especially from the vast numbers of small holders who comprise the world's most difficult development task, is uncertain. Curiously enough, we seldom check the rate of return from our investments in defense or education. The money goes and we assume it is worthwhile. Have we reached the stage when the improvement of agriculture in the developing world is rapidly becoming a problem of defense for all mankind?

This is not a plea for excusing a blind eye on the economics of integrating rural areas in development. However, it is a plea for realizing that this is our greatest task, because in it we are dealing with two-thirds of the world's population whose condition is steadily deteriorating. It is also a claim that this task is the most exciting, demanding, creative, urgent, and baffling challenge facing our generation.

Literature Cited

FAO. 1962. Increasing food production through education, research and extension. FAO Basic Study No. 9, published for the Freedom from Hunger Campaign. Rome.

4

Processes and Priorities
in Agricultural Development

Earl O. Heady

To join the search for the mysteries explaining the economic development of agriculture has become rather fashionable in recent years. Why these mysteries exist is itself a mystery. I would argue that the process need not be shrouded in mystery. The knowledge is already at hand, theoretically and practically, in explaining the development of agriculture. The variables which are important to the process are rather obvious, and those which should be manipulated, aside from other restraining forces, are intuitively evident.

I am referring to the variables relating to the endogenous process per se of the structure and economic growth of agriculture. What is less obvious is how to overcome the political, cultural, intellectual, and similar restraints, largely exogenous to the agricultural development process, which prevent "getting on with the job" where it has great marginal urgency and productivity. The voids in agricultural development are to be overcome by explaining and diverting these outside conditions which prevent changing price relatives, supplying knowledge, capital, and other resources, and by improving the tenure and other economic environment within which agriculture functions.

Theoretically, we already have the framework or models for specifying the variables which result in economic development of agriculture. Highly consistent with the framework, we also have ample evidence that the framework, model, or system functions at various levels of farmer education and intellect. Of course, we have to add a structure which accounts for the distributed lag with which farmers and cultivators react or adjust to improved conditions in factor supplies, factor and commodity prices, knowledge, and changes in the cost and profit structure of the firm. It is too much to expect, as some almost do, that agriculture should react instantaneously to changes in the variables and environment which may be consistent with the theory of development, or that it should simply improve the food supply because officials wish it would do so. There are no examples of "an overnight transformation" of agriculture. Even in the United States, sometimes taken as the hallmark of agricultural development, adjustment to the variables and structure conducive to economic development has been in a distributed lag fashion. It took a good twenty-five years for the industry to accomplish mechanization after tractors and complementary equipment of an efficient nature were developed. It took almost fifty years, after the creation of the facilities and a moderate increase in the supply of knowledge, for United States agriculture to step up to a high level of scientific orientation. This process will be distributed over another twenty years before existing knowledge is fully exploited. The process of mechanization in Japan was somewhat shorter. However, there exist in all countries conditions which contribute to a lagged reaction to manipulation of growth variables. Most typically, the restrained reaction stems from resources which are fixed or have highly inelastic supplies to agriculture. As a result of their low reservation prices to farming, they remain in use rather than being replaced by new capital technology or migrating to other economic sectors. New technology replaces them only when the supply conditions surrounding them are altered or their productive life and services are depleted.

As mentioned previously, no new theory is required to explain the conditions which will cause the firms of agriculture to use more and different resources and to increase supply of products. The theory is already at hand, and practical examples of attainment abound. Sum the actions of firms, if enough of them are encouraged to react, and economic development is accomplished for the agricultural sector. The economic development of agriculture is nothing more than the use of more capital resources, in substituting one form of capital for another or for land or labor, and in increasing output. These changes in resource demand and product supply are encouraged only if the prices of resources and products are favorable, the supply quantity of resources (usually reflected through supply prices) is conducive, the revenue and cost structure (the economic expression of tenure conditions) of its farm firms are appropriate, and the degree of certainty or the planning horizon promises a sufficient payoff on durable investment. Increase the support prices for United States farmers and they increase resource commitment and output; supply knowledge and attain satisfactory price relationships for Japanese farmers and they use more fertilizer and invest in tractors; provide a favorable price outlook and Greek cultivators convert from cereals to long-term investments in citrus groves; provide an adequate investment horizon and degree of certainty and Polish cultivators invest in orchards and buildings in the midst of a socialized economy; provide packing facilities with a market and Ethiopians sell off cows which they have long "hoarded"; provide a supply of resources and adequate price incentives and selected villages of Indian cultivators move towards Japanese farming technology. At every point over the world where sufficient time series data are available, computation of supply functions shows farmers to be responsive to prices of factors and products. The mysteries of agricultural development are small indeed. More mysterious and complex are the "outside" policy, planning, political, and cultural processes which provide restraints to appropriate changes in the "growth variables" or policies which relate to agriculture.

THE UNITED STATES AS AN EXAMPLE MODEL

If one wanted to find the most efficient model or plan for the development of agriculture, he would look to the United States. The structure of American agriculture is partly and importantly a function of the state of economic development and should not be entirely used as the model for other agricultures. The foremost stage of economic development of the United States economy results in resource prices which favor the substitution of capital for both land and labor. Hence, mechanical technology is favored over labor technology and scale economies specify fewer but larger farms. Yet the instruments employed by the public to draw forth the development of the industry are those highly consistent both with theory for specifying economic development and with the manipulations needed in any agriculture to attain development. Although the United States is not noted for planning, the long stretch of public policies for American agriculture represents the most consistent and successful set of plans implemented over the entire world—including those socialist countries where the crux of life is government plans. United States planning for development has often been unwitting, the public not always knowing that the instruments being used were those highly adapted to the progress of agriculture. In this bundle of instruments, the following policies, all conducive to a flow of resources into agriculture and a greater output of farm products, were emphasized. At first, the supply of resources was kept large and resource prices were kept low. Up to the point spatially feasible, additional land was acquired and distributed to farmers at zero or low prices. Farmers responded to this supply-price incentive, and labor and land resources were continually brought into the agricultural transformation process. Once against the spatial restraint of land supply, the nation turned in other directions for increasing resource supplies and lowering their real prices. Public development of research and educational facilities extended the knowledge resource and encouraged more of it to be used along with the capital technologies which complement it. Creation of public facilities to increase the supply and lower the price of capital and credit greatly encouraged the use of this resource. The lowering of prices through subsidization of the cost of irrigation, fertilizer and lime, and similar specific capital items, under the Bureau of Reclamation and the Soil Conservation Programs of the Federal Government, caused some spurt in the use of these inputs or technologies and helped to increase output. Outstanding among other instruments have been programs to raise the levels and increase the stability of farm product prices. Rather than dampen trends towards a growing output, these price measures have been just as important as those on the resource side in encouraging farmers to use more resources and new capital technologies. Added to these instruments of prices and resource supplies were tenure systems which were not ideal, but were generally conducive to a firm set of cost and return relationships providing profit motivation. Of course, the rate of development of agriculture has not been consistent over the United States in the last half of this century, but has generally varied in proportion to incentives provided through resource and capital prices, knowledge availability, tenure restraints or farm cost/return structures, and product prices.

So here is the recipe, if some must still seek it. Lower prices and increase availability of resources, add certainty and greater quantity to product prices, blend with knowledge and a firm or tenure structure which relates input productivities appropriately with resource/product price ratios. This mixture can be brought to a developmental boil in a container of commercial farming, if not successfully in a purely subsistence environment which is outside the market economy. It will have a delayed or lagged maturity, depending upon the dosage of the above variables and the extent to which a very few specific cultural factors exist. These factors include (1) creating a new "state of mind" for cultivators who have previously been oriented to production best guaranteeing food for subsistence in the year ahead, and who must now look to expansion towards the market, and (2) acquainting families with the mysteries of managing credit and capital in order to convert them from subsistence operations.

This recipe has been tested and proven successful over many parts of the world; so much so that it is doubtful that anyone will ever come up with a better one. Hence, the creation of the conditions implied above is one of the priorities for bringing economic development to agriculture. There is no mystery to the process. If a mystery exists, it is to explain those exogenous conditions which prevent governments and planning agencies, which wish agricultural development, from manipulating the above instruments and going forward with the recipe.

Agriculture has failed to respond as hoped or expected in many countries, but the reasons are often obvious. Too frequently agricultural development has not been given an appropriate priority. The leap to a modern industrial economy, including steel mills and an international airline operated at a deficit, has been given precedence over farm improvement. Just as frequently, a price structure has not been provided which is conducive to the use of new and more capital resources such as fertilizer, insecticides, and improved seed varieties. Input prices have been kept too high and output prices have been kept too low. Capital has not been moved into the hands of subsistence farmers to convert them to a market economy. Input prices have been too high because the planning of industrial development has given insufficient attention to inputs such as fertilizer for agriculture, and the importance of an industry scale and prices which favor their use in agriculture have been overlooked. Frequently, the absolute supply and the facilities to move and store inputs are lacking.

Industrial inputs for agriculture also have been discouraged through trade policy which has excluded imports at low prices to favor national industrial development or to preserve foreign exchange for industrial development. Output prices have been too low for a number of reasons. One has been the emphasis on low prices for the consumer. Although this may be needed, a better policy would be producer prices which favor growth in output, but subsidize consumers at lower prices—somewhat along the lines of British price policy. The acceptance of foreign loans or aid funds tied to the import of cheap farm commodities has acted in a similar manner to dampen prices and lower the payoff from internal agricultural development in many countries. United States surpluses shipped under various labels have served in a similar manner, although frequently these surpluses have been needed as "an ace in the hole" to bridge bad weather and other short-run disasters. In a few notable cases, export taxes, which serve as a major source of government revenue, deprive the farmer of the portion of the world market price he would otherwise receive. Ethiopia, where the bulk of exports is represented by farm commodities, is an example.

The argument is not against adequate and cheap food for consumers; it is against inadequate prices and low-grade incentives for farmers. It is not against industrialization; it is against an inadequate supply of industrial inputs representing modern technology and a high payoff. It is against systems that fail to incorporate the generation and supplying of knowledge with the extension of other inputs. For development of tardy agricultures, the inputs necessary in the mix typically are complementary. It is rather futile, as many countries have done, to establish an extension education machine when there is no new or adapted research knowledge to go with it. It is unproductive to supply credit when fertilizer, insecticides, and improved seeds are not physically available; or to supply fertilizer when adapted crop varieties are lacking. It takes no new theories, or mysterious explanations of the agricultural development process, to know that at some level these resources are technical complements and any one as a limitational input restrains the productivity of others.

In these respects, the United States needs to invert its policy and aids to many developing countries, just as the developing countries also need to invert the aids which they accept from the United States and other countries. The supply price of resources is so low in the United States that its agriculture burdens the nation with output. A much greater portion of these resources, including both physical materials and the persons containing the "know-how" to generate and to communicate knowledge, should be diverted to other countries. The result could be higher supply prices for these resources in the United States and lower prices elsewhere. While United States agricultural policy balances the market mechanism in the direction of higher commodity prices and output at home and lower commodity prices and output abroad, the shift to export subsidized or low-cost resources would be in the opposite direction for inputs, and it would have the opposite effects of United States farm products exported under subsidy. In general, less-developed countries need to turn more in the direction of the input sectors and knowledge supplies which are so highly advanced and low in costs in Western countries. It is certainly necessary for this to have priority over "home development of industry" for numerous countries over the next decade.

There is, of course, a relation between the development of non-farm sectors, which fabricate farm inputs at low prices, and the economic progress of agriculture. The supply price of these inputs can be low only if the structure of agriculture provides a sufficiently large market for capital items. At the outset in many countries, the small market for capital inputs can be supplied initially at lower prices from foreign sources. Development of local industrial sources on a sufficient scale then can come at a later time when agricultural advancement in technology and in capitalization merits such development.

PRIORITIES IN THE AGRICULTURAL SECTOR

Mention of development and relative resource prices also suggests some other priorities in the economic development of agriculture. Situations can be outlined which help specify when agriculture should be given priority over industry in development and vice versa. Let us examine some cases.

Case I.—Farm output is low, diets are miserable, hunger prevails, both agricultural and industrial sectors are characterized by labor unemployment or underemployment, and export possibilities are unfavorable for farm products. Priority needs to be given to the development of agriculture, but not to all facets of it. Crop biology should be given precedence. The capital items required are improved seeds, fertilizer, insecticides, and irrigation where it is uncostly and has a high short-run payoff. These capital inputs serve as substitutes for land. Emphasis should not be given to mechanization and labor substitutes. Criteria for investment might almost correspond to staples with lowest demand elasticities, as these are weighted with resources committed to them. Little priority would be given to investment in types of livestock or other products which are characterized as the consumption items of high-income elasticities and high-income consumers. A good many nations fit this category, particularly those nations which face another decade or two of increases in farm labor and population because industrialization cannot be rapid enough to keep pace with the birth rate. More countries would fall in this category if the world food crisis ever moved to the intensity now being projected by numerous people.

Case II.—Food supplies are adequate for the basic items of diet; agricultural labor is highly underemployed. Labor migration to other countries may even exist. Here, no priority should be given to any aspect of agricultural development, except as the marginal productivity of investment in farming stands at a level with that of non-farm sectors and export potentials exist. Otherwise, priority should be given to industrial development to create employment for absorbing the unemployed of both farms and towns. Examples of this category may include regions such as Southern Italy.

Case III.—Food supplies are adequate, a high level of employment exists in non-agricultural sectors, underemployment abounds, and incomes are relatively low in agriculture. Industrial development should be further emphasized to expand non-farm employment opportunities for migrants from farms. However, some special emphasis can be given to certain aspects of the development of agriculture. These include mechanization to replace labor as factor prices are drawn into a favorable ratio, and production of livestock and other products which are consistent with high income elasticities of demand and high level consumer incomes. A most important investment may also be in mobility of human resources in agriculture. There are many examples of countries which fit into this category in various degrees in Southern Europe, Eastern Europe, and a majority of the countries in Western Europe. Even included here are broad reaches of American farming.

Additional Remarks.—Other categories could be presented, but the number given is sufficient to indicate that there is no universal rule or condition which can specify all priorities for industrial development over agriculture or vice versa. In a very few cases, no priorities should exist for agriculture. In others, the urgency is to employ resources and exports which further the output of food from basic plant food sources or export crops. At other stages of development, the urgency steps up to livestock and mechanization. The important thing is to "get at" the development of agriculture. There are few, if any, good examples of a nation having invested too much in agricultural development relative to industrialization. True, there have been large mistakes in agricultural investment: extension services without research knowledge to communicate, fertilizer plants without distribution and storage facilities, machines without spare parts, mechanization in countries where relative factor prices specify labor technology, and unfeasible irrigation projects. However, as a whole, overinvestment in sensible agricultural development is hard to find. The danger and fact is more in the opposite direction. True, what is needed is balanced development. If we have sufficient knowledge of the production and supply functions of major economic sectors, of resource demand functions peculiar to each industry, of consumer demand and welfare functions, we can build up a system which gives an empirical specification of balanced development. However, in the absence of these functions, details, and facts, the possibility of error certainly is in the direction of underinvestment in agricultural development relative to industrial development. Perhaps the United States provides the single clear-cut example of overinvestment or policy formulation drawing forth too much agricultural development. Countries on the other side of the food supply pinch would prefer this type of error to their own type of underinvestment and insufficient policies for agriculture.

Research Priorities.—In the realm of knowledge generation, research in the less-developed countries should emphasize the applied, except where fundamental knowledge is lacking for conditions unique to the country. Fundamental knowledge is the least-cost import and requires only a good set of journals and translators. On the other hand, good applied research, which adapts modern technologies to the conditions of the country, is too often lacking. This distortion between fundamental and applied research not infrequently stems from the returning graduate student who finds greater status in speaking to his colleagues abroad through the scientific journals than in developing applied technologies for his country.

In the realm of knowledge priorities, we have already mentioned that distorted investment occurs when elaborate extension or advisory services are established in the absence of knowledge to extend. Again, "balance" is required in the investment of these two activities. And, at low stages of development, the public or governmental agency must give priority to research. This is true because the major inputs of agriculture are land and labor. Capital represents too small a proportion of the total to provide an adequate market for capital inputs. Hence, research of the private sector on behalf of agriculture is minimal. At high stages of development, as the major input becomes capital items from non-farm sources, industry turns heavily to agricultural research as a means of further expanding the demand for new farm technologies. These new technologies are chemicals in the form of fertilizers, improved seeds, steel in the form of machines, pest and disease control materials, and other inputs. At this stage, the public sector can lower its priorities for agricultural research, since the momentum will be carried forward by the private sector.

At low levels of development, following our earlier categorization, priority should be given to crop biology. Farm engineering must be emphasized at a later stage of economic development where labor/capital price ratios specify mechanization. Similarly, improvement of the livestock sector through research would generally receive the high priority label only at higher stages of development when per capita income levels are higher.

Farm Scale Priorities.—Structural changes of agriculture, as expressed in the scale of farms, also should be a function of economic growth. The massive units of Eastern Europe are consistent neither with the stage of economic development in those countries nor with the structure of resource prices in the underdeveloped countries. Large-scale units should have no particular priority at low stages of economic development. There may be management scale economies as there are fewer and larger farms to which knowledge can be communicated. Aside from this, however, economy of scale is, in a sense, a function of economic development and relative factor prices. At low stages of development when capital is in short supply and has a high price relative to labor, the optimum resource mix in farming is one which calls for a large amount of the labor resource in relation to capital. Under labor technology, scale or cost economies do not extend far over the land area. Major cost economies in the use of modest capital items are largely exhausted as soon as relatively full employment is reached for the bullock team, horse, or camel which provides the power. High stages of development, where capital prices are low relative to labor prices, call for a resource mix which is made up largely of capital. Scale economies then extend much further, and larger farms are in order. In this sense, the economic development of farming, starting from low stages, does not call for structural reorganization which amalgamates farms into large individual units for the possibility of high levels of mechanization.

Commercial versus Subsistence Farms.—In establishing priorities for the development of agriculture, several other facets of the industry and its environment must be given consideration. If we wished most rapid development and could neglect welfare, we would concentrate effort on commercial farmers who participate in the market and leave aside those who operate as subsistence family units. In some countries, of course, the majority of farmers are in the latter category, and the only hope for massive improvement is to convert them to participation in economic activity through the market. Their scale of operations must be extended so that they produce beyond family requirements. Their product must enter the market so that they are influenced by price and related variables. A generation may be required before many "traditional subsistence farmers" are converted to the "market state of mind," but their sons may react much more rapidly.

In almost the same context, the supplies of the consumer goods which trickle out to remote villages often need to be changed materially. If the goods are not there, or if their distribution prices are too high, the incentive for farm commercialization is much less. Typically, modern consumer goods sell at extremely high prices in the village as compared to the city.

If growth in the food supply were to take precedent over all else, other emphases could be established. Governments could develop their own farm operations and put them on a commercial basis. Then farms should be able to operate at a profit; otherwise the price and other variables are inconsistent with economic development of farming in general. These farms also could serve as an "inductive or empirical example" for the rank and file of cultivators. Persons with little education tend to act on the basis of inductive or quantitative evidence rather than on the basis of deductive or theoretical evidence. Similarly, the government might "hire" a large "sample" of farmers to follow prescribed farm plans and improved technology. If the development posed really has a payoff, it should allow a surplus to increase the income of the cultivator plus the salary of a managerial supervisor who leads a group of farms. If the development suggested will not cover these two returns or costs, it undoubtedly has too low a payoff to be considered in a developing country, or has input and output prices which are at inappropriate levels. Finally, for a rapid spurt in output, the possibility of giving franchises to experienced foreign farmers could be considered where land supply does not provide a prohibiting restraint. Given a franchise of five, ten, or whatever number of years is necessary to provide a sufficient payoff under an appropriate set of prices, food supply could be increased while the "know-how" of farming is brought to the midst of the country's cultivators. A good example of the latter possibility is in Ethiopia where Dutch farmers have developed highly efficient sugar operations. Although the technology used may not be adapted to large numbers of the country's farmers, the operations have been successful in rapidly increasing the output of one commodity. Other countries have sufficient land to borrow the technique. A franchise with short-run termination can prevent all concerns and complexities of colonialism.

PRIORITIES IN MEETING WORLD FOOD NEEDS

The food crisis being so widely discussed poses the possibility that both developed and underdeveloped countries will have to place greater priority on food production. Some popular discussions suggest that this priority should be established for the developed countries, with food then shipped to the underdeveloped countries. Since highly misleading policy could arise from these popular demands and the broad humanitarian desire to prevent hunger and starvation, we need to examine this complex set of possibilities in terms of priorities which are realistic and logical.

It is obvious, of course, that the world must face up to this pending food crisis. At current compound rates of growth, world population is projected to double in less than thirty-five years. World population took 1,500 years to double from the advent of the Christian era to the year 1600. It took three more centuries, from 1600 to 1900, for world population to triple to 1.5 billion persons. However, at current rates of increase, it will double again in thirty-five years; in Central and South America it will double in twenty-five years. Obviously, this rate of growth cannot go forward unabated. Even if food could be supplied, standing space would soon expire, a point which seems to have escaped those who extend the conventional wisdom that the solution to the world's pending food crisis is simply that of increasing food output.

A worsening of the food position prevails mainly in the underdeveloped countries. Food production has moved ahead much more rapidly than population and food demand in highly developed countries. Accordingly, the import-export pattern in food has been reversed between highly developed and underdeveloped countries. Prior to World War II, there was one general trade pattern: Western Europe was the only importing region, and the rest of the world exported to it. There were six grain-exporting areas: North America, about 5 million tons; Latin America, about 9 million tons; Eastern Europe, 5 million tons; and small quantities for Asia, Africa, and Oceania (New Zealand and Australia). Western Europe has maintained its position as an importer; it buys about the same amount of grain now as it did in the immediate prewar period to meet greater population needs. However, mammoth changes have taken place in trade among other world regions. Only North America and Oceania remain as major exporters. Asia and Africa have become net importers, along with Latin America and Eastern Europe. Prior to World War II, the net annual flow of grains from the less-developed regions was about 11 million tons. Now, annual shipments of grain from developed countries to less-developed countries are close to 25 million tons.

Given current rates and projections of population growth, and without alternative solutions, the world's food situation could deteriorate materially in another dozen years. Then, should not the United States plow up the land idled under various programs, develop more irrigated land, and put it to crops to ship to the countries with deficit diets and rapidly growing populations? Will not the mushrooming world population cause food to be high priced and in short quantity even in the United States? Without a deep study of the situation, the answer to these questions would appear to be an unconditional "yes." The answer to the world's population and food crisis is more complex than this, however. Even to produce surplus food and give it away throughout the world is not an easy task. Although the world food situation will help lessen the problem of surplus capacity in the United States, our agricultural capacity is not the answer to the world's pending food and population problem. Universally, people and societies abhor suffering through hunger and malnutrition. All possible efficient steps should be taken to eliminate these problems on a world-wide basis. However, it also is possible to use rash policies which discourage development of food production and bring later misery to populations.

In advanced countries, population growth, if it is a problem, is one of the distant future. Knowledge and technology have been able to hold birth rates in check and to boost the rate of increase in food output to levels exceeding population growth. Investments in capital processes and technical knowledge may give emergence to large food supplies from non-agricultural resources before farm resources place a restraint on output and raise the real price of food within these countries. The pressing short-run problem, a span of the next three decades, is in the less-developed countries. The majority, but not all, of these countries are only recently independent entities able to determine their own national policies. The balancing of growth in population or demand and supply of food is one of the major problems that most of them must solve in the next decade or so. The posed world crisis, before population growth rates thrust sharply above food growth rates, is perhaps three decades away. However, for individual countries in the above category, it is only a decade or so away. The balancing of food needs or demand and food supply involves appropriate investment in farm technological improvement and in population management.

Actually, the problem is not one of balance. Food output and consumption will be balanced in three decades even if it means twice as many people subsisting on a miserable 2,000 calories per day. The basic problem is more nearly one of management of food supplies and populations in a manner that will balance them at levels of adequate diets and human welfare. Investments of both types are required; that in knowledge and technology of birth control is no less important, and certainly would pay a much higher return on investment in the long-run balancing process, than investment in expanded food supply.

How do the agricultures of highly developed countries fit into this complex? Cannot the abundance of food and the potential of greater output in these countries be channeled to the food-deficit countries, thus warding off the crisis and even helping to lift the level of human well-being? This would be a simple solution, if it were possible. It would also satisfy the sincere humanitarian interests and intentions of the many individuals, groups, organizations, and nations. However, it is unrealistic as the major answer to the world's pending food crisis.

To be certain, the agricultural resources of the United States and other developed nations have an important and significant role in this complex of food and population. It is not, however, in providing the increment of food required for an uncontrolled increase in the world's population over the next half century. It is obvious that world population cannot go forward forever unchecked. Present rates of increases would soon absorb all of the untapped food-producing potential of both developed and underdeveloped countries. Then, when the final restraints of food production were reached, there would be even greater masses of people to starve or to live in hunger and misery. Human disutility and suffering would be multiplied, and the negative effect could well be greater than if excess food stocks were withheld as a check against population growth. Ethical questions even arise as to whether societies should provide more and improved health and medical services which decrease mortality rates, without parallel investments and intensity of effort to increase food supply for the greater number of persons who are thus present to consume.

Blind increases in production in developed countries, to be converted to food handouts for less-developed nations, do not provide the solution to the world's population problem. To an extent, they can even discourage the endogenous improvement of agriculture and growth of food supplies in less-developed countries as they lower world prices and those for local cultivators. Thrown into the market without price safeguards, they can lower the profitability of improvement by cultivators and farmers in countries where population is large and food production is small. They can lessen the urgency and lower the intensity of motivation of internal improvement in food output by less-developed countries. In the last decade, food aid from the United States has diverted too much of the appropriate attention and investment from the more fundamental long-run problems of birth control and population management and from basic agricultural knowledge and improvement in developing countries.

As mentioned previously, to produce farm products in developed countries and to send them as gifts or handouts is not the long-run answer to the world population and food problems. This approach would only postpone the "day of reckoning" by ten or fifteen years. First, on the side of food supply, the developed countries do not have a large enough land area to meet an unlimited increase in food needs resulting from an increase in future world population. It is more important, in terms of available land area and unexploited production potential, that agriculture of the less-advanced world regions be developed for these purposes. This approach not only provides a greater food production base, but also gives the developing countries greater certainty of food supplies under the ever unpredictable tides of world politics, and greater freedom in selecting their own destiny. Even apart from political considerations, food production should be developed in both the short-run and long-run where it is most economical and where it returns the greatest payoff on investment. In the short-run, the payoff often will be greater in countries, such as the United States, with highly developed agriculture and underutilized capacity. This is true because of the educational and organizational restraints involved in short-term adjustment of the agricultural structure in most less-developed countries. However, over the long-run, the payoff is almost certain to be greater in improvement of agriculture in developing countries with favorable resource endowments and tardy technological developments. These countries are using resources or inputs at such low levels that their marginal response should be much greater than in developed nations where resource combinations more nearly approach the optimum systems. Of course, for some developed nations with a clear long-run comparative advantage in food production, and in some less-developed countries with clear advantages in industry over agriculture, further developments should follow these lines with trade catalyzed by appropriate international, commercial, fiscal, and investment policies.

It is high time that a proper priority be given to progress of agriculture in developing countries where resources are favorable and populations are pressing. They must commit greater investment to the complex of resources needed to provide an enlarged and economic supply of food products. They must develop realistic plans which recognize the hard facts before them. This is true even if the goal and need were only one of lifting diets for current populations to humanitarian levels. Too many countries, as history is beginning to reveal, have minimized agricultural investment in attempting to leap-frog into advanced industrialization.

However, investments, even in agricultural development, will not ward off a pending long-run world food crisis stemming from population growth. Only investments in knowledge and technology of birth control can do so. This investment is basic if calamity is to be averted. Not only is it the sole long-run solution to the problem of population relative to food supply, but it will return much more on the investment than will agricultural development in bringing population and food requirements into a realistic and humanitarian balance with future food supply. It, too, is an investment which does not have immediate payoff. Effective population control programs lag considerably in effectiveness and will provide the appropriate payoff only after sufficient time and effort have been devoted to bringing knowledge to less literate parents, to overcoming fears and superstitions, and to providing birth control technology with certainty and an economic cost level.

Excess production capacity of the United States and other developed countries can be used effectively to meet short-run emergency problems in world food supplies. As mentioned previously, the payoff in the short-run from investment in more seed, fertilizer, and tractors, and fuel for these purposes, will be quicker and greater in developed countries where farmers already have the "know-how" and only need to have their abilities unleashed. The short-run return is much lower in countries where this environment of knowledge and effective decision acts with a lag of up to ten years or more. Even then, the emphasis should be on stocks to meet weather emergencies and similar calamities, and on helping to lift a few countries out of the "squeeze" in which they now find themselves. The major efforts should be directed toward the urgent matter of "getting the show under way" in the less-developed countries. Food aid from the United States perhaps should be used only where recipient countries agree to invest appropriately both in development of their own agriculture and in birth control.

Here is exactly where the agricultural resources of the United States can make their large and basic contribution to the world food problem. There is greater opportunity and necessity for furnishing the resources which serve as ingredients in getting development under way than there is for producing food to ship as gifts to less-developed countries. These resources may include fertilizer, seeds, insecticides, and similar inputs, or the plants and other resources to produce these inputs. In some cases they include investment funds, although international aids have caused this restraint to fall in importance relative to the resources mentioned below. More important than these classes of resources are those intellectual resources of research, education, management, and organization which can uncover adapted knowledge and get new technical capital adopted in developing countries. This category is one in which the United States has excelled. It is hard to find planning and policy which has been more appropriate in promoting agricultural development. This nation increased the supply and lowered the prices of resources. Simultaneously, it bolstered commodity prices against input prices and sometimes subsidized the cost of inputs; both price forces encouraged the use of inputs, extension of output, and development of agriculture. These and related steps, including the provision of capital and the organization of a system to channel advanced technical knowledge to producers, are the effective economic elements of agricultural development anywhere in the world. It is this set of tools, if they can be effectively transplanted, which will serve most in aiding the development of agriculture in less-developed countries. Part of this mix is necessarily that of managerial and organizational ability to implement successfully action programs and knowledge. Organizational and management experience and ability are perhaps even more scarce as resources than is capital in typical less-developed countries.

These intellectual resources, rather than food, are the large contributions which can be made from the experiences and capabilities of our agriculture. We have growing opportunity to divert some of our public resources accordingly since, as pointed out previously, the stage of economic development is causing private industry to assume more of the responsibility of research and knowledge communication to agriculture.

It is essential that underdeveloped countries develop their own agriculture if they are to meet their food needs in the next ten to fifteen years. It is imperative that they develop population control if they are to meet their food problem of the next quarter century. Our food can help meet the emergency in the first case, but it can have little bearing on the second.

5

Product Markets
and Economic Development

Richard A. King

Relatively little attention has been paid to the role of product markets in the economic development process. There can be no doubt that inefficiency in the marketing of agricultural products is characteristic of many developing areas of the world. The cause for concern about this inefficiency is suggested by the basic premise on which this paper rests. The premise has been clearly stated by Earl Heady (1966, 3) when he writes that, "At every point over the world where sufficient data are available it has been found that farmers respond to changing farm product prices and farm input prices." Farm product prices are transmitted by, and reflect the efficiency of, the marketing system.

How do farmers respond to prices and income? Heady (1966, 2) argues that: "No new scientific breakthroughs are required to explain the conditions which will cause farmers to use more and different resources and to increase farm productivity. . . . Increasing the productivity of agriculture means using more capital; it means substituting one form of capital for another or for land or labor; it means increasing total farm output. These changes are encouraged only if certain conditions exist: the prices of the productive resources and of farm products, and the farmer's tenure situation must be favorable—and the farmer must be promised sufficient payoff from a long-run investment in his enterprise." This set of conditions is entirely reasonable.

Why is it desirable that farmers respond to price and income incentives? The answer must be phrased in terms of the desire to reach some more or less well-defined goal. Three possible goals might be considered. First would be a nutritional goal. Clearly, there is need to improve the poor diets that presently exist in many tropical regions of the world. A second possibility is a price stability goal. Some of the political unrest in the world stems from the instability of food prices and, in particular, from the rapid increase which has occurred in the prices of basic foodstuffs. A third possibility is a growth goal. There may be a desire to release resources now used in agriculture in order to increase the output of non-farm goods and services. Thus, any one of these three goals would be sufficient to justify investigating how product markets may encourage or discourage the desired response on the part of growers.

Inefficiencies in product markets interfere with the achievement of such goals. There are two types of inefficiencies: one is in the production of marketing services and the other is in the pricing system. For example, wholesale food marketing facilities that have been used for decades in Lima, Peru, are unsatisfactory from a health standpoint. They are inefficient because of the large amount of labor that is required to move products for sale into the market and out again; this arises from the necessity of using wheeled hand carts for moving products from incoming trucks to sales stalls. These procedures are inefficient because of the excessive spoilage of products that occurs during the marketing process, not to mention the tremendous time delays involved.

The second type of economic inefficiency occurs in the pricing system. One may observe frozen beef being flown into the city of Arequipa, Peru, from Argentina while live cattle are being shipped from Arequipa to Lima for slaughter and sale. This type of cross haul is typical of areas where the pricing system does not effectively allocate food supplies.

We assume, then, that product markets through the transmission of relative product prices do play an important role in farmers' response in terms of output. However, what kinds of changes in product markets are called for in order to stimulate the desired output of farm products and to entice into the market economy many producers who are now outside commercial agriculture—and indeed outside the money economy—in many nations of the world? This chapter is concerned with some possible answers to this question.

MEANING OF DEVELOPMENT AND GROWTH

Do we have models which explain how producers respond to various schemes that might be designed to achieve the goals that have been established? Much of the literature which deals with economic development is quite general and of relatively little help in charting a course for rapid agricultural development. A hypothetical conversation between a county agent and a Florida orange grove operator will illustrate this point. After spending the morning studying the operations of the grove our county agent has the following suggestions: "Joe, you should get rid of some of the underemployed labor you have on the place. You need to invest more capital, and your use of purchased inputs is far too low. What you need is more non-farm inputs. You should also get that input quality up. I believe if you apply more indigenous innovations you would find your earnings would increase substantially. But the thing that would be of most help is to get yourself a good education."

Now this conversation may seem a little far-fetched, but it is not too different from the type of recommendations we find in much of the literature. Although the recommendations are basically sound, one must admit that they are not especially helpful in their present form. The problem of how to translate such general concepts into specific development decisions is largely untouched.

A variety of growth models has been developed in recent years. Although many growth models were designed primarily to deal with problems of growth or stagnation in the advanced countries, they have been applied in much of the planning for underdeveloped countries. Hirschman (1958, 30) makes the following comment on such attempts: "Now, there is no harm in making these computations if all they are expected to yield is an approximate idea of the amount of capital that is likely to be used in the course of the growth process. But if one thinks that the functional relationships assumed in the model are a meaningful description of the development process, a point may be reached at which the model becomes a hindrance rather than a help in the understanding of the reality of underdeveloped countries."

The relationship between growth models and the development process is not clear-cut. The confusion which exists in the literature is illustrated by Bruton (1965, iii) when he writes: "Terms such as low income, nongrowing, and underdeveloped may be used interchangeably to refer essentially to an economy the past history of which suggests that there are forces at work that prevent growth from occurring."

Some authors have concentrated on the characteristics of the economy under discussion. For example, Hirschman (1958, 29) distinguishes between economics of growth and economics of development in terms of the answer to the question: Is the economy developed or underdeveloped? For economically advanced economies he uses the term economics of growth. For underdeveloped countries he uses the term economics of development. For him, economics of growth is the analysis of the growth process of advanced industrial countries, whereas economics of development is the analysis of the growth process of underdeveloped countries.

An alternative distinction between development and growth is made by Maurice Byé (1962, 110) in "The Role of Capital in Economic Development": "The growth of a quantity is its increase. Growth of national per capita income is increase of national per capita income. The growth of an economy is generally characterized by growth of net national income per capita. Any economic system, for example a national economy, may experience growth either while its structure remains unaltered or while its structure changes. The development of an economy is its growth in conditions of changing structure. . . . An economy is fully developed when its structure is such that per capita productivity is as high as it can be with given national and world resources and given technical knowledge. In the contrary case we speak of an underdeveloped economy."

This terminology still leaves something to be desired. In order to identify a developing nation, it is necessary to know whether or not the economic structure is changing, however defined. Furthermore, before classifying an economy as underdeveloped, one must investigate whether or not with given resources and technical knowledge higher per capita productivity would be possible. With a literal application of this criterion, the group of developed countries would constitute a null set. Leibenstein (1966) supports this conjecture.

A third alternative, which has more appeal to me, draws the distinction between economics of growth and economics of development in terms of the type of statements we wish to make. Economics of growth is concerned with "if-then" statements, whereas economics of development deals with the evaluation of "either-or" choices. A simple growth model would be one which describes the functional relationship between certain independent variables and a selected dependent variable such as per capita income or rates of change in per capita income. Development models, on the other hand, must be formulated in such a way as to deal with the problem of selecting the best among alternative strategies.

A strategy has been defined as any of the courses of action open to a participant in a conflict situation (Dorfman *et al.*, 1958, 433). Game theory is defined as the attempt to determine optimal strategies explicitly (Dorfman *et al.*, 1958, 445). The choice of a strategy depends upon the payoff from alternative courses of action. For example, using this terminology we might define the payoff to development strategies in terms of level of economic activity or in terms of rate of growth.

To summarize, we may regard economics of development as the evaluation of alternative strategies. This evaluation can be carried out only where the alternatives are clearly specified and where the payoff associated with each is well defined. These strategies have as their goal the modification either of the level of economic activity or the rate of economic growth or both. Although theories of growth may provide some insights into general relationships among the variables associated with growing economies, as a whole they are quite unsuited to specific decision-making situations experienced by individual firms, regional development groups, or national planners.

ANALYTICAL MODEL

Among the models which are available for evaluating alternative strategies for product market development, we find that the perfect market in space, time, and form is a useful framework. By using this model it is possible to study the existing situation and to plan specific development proposals. This perfect market model can be described briefly as follows. Prices in different geographic areas of a country will differ by not more than the cost of transfer from one point to another. Within a given market area, prices will differ exactly by transfer cost from point of production to point of consumption. Where this condition does not hold, multiple markets are said to exist. Similarly, prices at one point in time will not exceed prices in a previous point in time by more than the cost of storage. Failure of this condition to hold is evidence of distinct markets in the time dimension. Finally, the price of a product will differ from the price of another product derived from the same raw product by no more than the cost of processing. We thus have a model which describes price relationships among geographically separated points in space, among different points in time, and among alternative forms of a common raw product.

Is this model an adequate representation of the product markets observed in developing areas of the world? It is possible that the decision-making process of producers and marketers may not be price-oriented. It is clear, for example, that a self-sufficient agriculture is substantially different from an agriculture in which farm products are produced primarily for exchange. Similarly, in a handicraft industry artisan goods may be sold on order instead of being mass-produced for the general purchaser. In these two situations it is quite possible that market price would play a minor role in short-run decisions.

Another factor that might affect the role of price is the pattern of ownership of production facilities. We may find, for example, that absentee ownership or communal ownership will result in decision-making procedures different from those found where owner-operators predominate. It is also possible that public policy builds certain types of inefficiency into the market price system. For example, prices paid to producers of Peruvian rice may be fixed at a uniform level throughout the country as a result of public price policy decisions. Finally, we may find that discontinuities exist in market price relationships, and it will be necessary to investigate the sources of these imperfections in order to make recommendations as to how they might be eliminated.

A recent study of regional rice supply and demand relations in Peru will illustrate how the perfect market model might be used to measure the importance of location and the relation between transfer costs and regional price behavior. The approximate locations of rice surpluses and deficits are shown in Table 5.1. Marketable surpluses are concentrated on the north coast, the

TABLE 5.1.—Approximate location of excess rice supply and demand, 1963-64[a].   *(Metric tons)*

Economic area	Supply	Demand	Net
1. North coast	89,900	14,656	75,244
2. Central coast	0	72,087[b]	—72,087
3. South coast	12,820	12,482	338
4. North sierra	0	3,476	— 3,476
5-8. Central sierra	0	13,865	—13,865
6-9. South sierra	0	6,099	— 6,099
7. High jungle	18,400	40	18,360
10. Low jungle	4,350	2,765	1,585
Total	125,470	125,470	0

a. Based on Mathia and Coffey (1965, 14).
b. Does not include imports of 49,178 metric tons.

south coast, and in the high jungle while the rest of the country is largely deficit. In addition to the domestic supply of 125,470 metric tons, imports of nearly 50,000 tons were purchased from abroad. If we assume that all imported rice was consumed in Lima, the domestic supply would be allocated as shown in Figure 5.1, given the transfer costs shown in Table 5.2.

Rice prices in each area can be expressed in terms of premiums or discounts relative to the Lima price. In Area 1 the price would be Lima less 171 soles per ton or S/3829. In Area 7 the price would be S/3542 and in Area 10, S/3906. Although Area 3 is slightly surplus, the price in Camaná is S/4229. In the deficit areas prices are S/3857 in Area 4, S/4372 in Area 5, and S/4642 in Area 6. Under perfect market conditions prices would rise sharply from north to south, reflecting greater distances from major surplus areas.

TABLE 5.2—Transportation cost matrix

Markets	Supply areas			
	Jaen-Bagua	Pacasmayo	Pucallpa	Camaná
	(Soles per metric ton)			
Cajamarca	315	118	1,074	1,038
Lima	458	171	504	229
Huancayo	830	579	466	714
Cuzco	1,100	813	980	413

Source: Based on Mathia and Coffey (1965, 12).

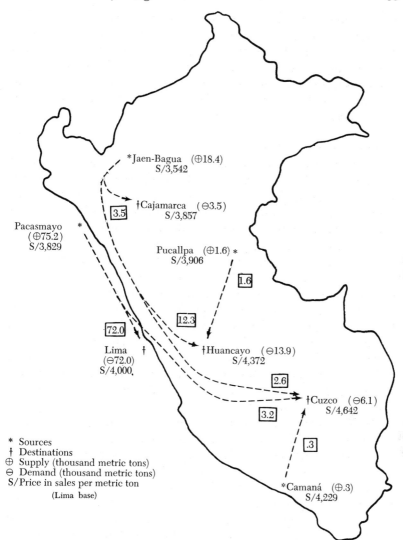

FIGURE 5.1. Allocation of rice supplies and regional price differentials, Peru.

In this example we have shown how transfer costs may be used to identify optimum shipping patterns for rice. We can, however, go further than this to show the price relationships which can be expected to exist given the fact that prices in consuming and producing areas are tied together through transfer costs. Should prices differ by more than transfer costs, there would be an incentive for new shippers to buy in the production area and sell in consumer centers. This reorganization would influence market supplies, raising prices in the market from which the supplies were withdrawn. Equilibrium would be achieved as prices in that market rose, and the heavier supplies on the first market depressed prices there.

Development Strategy

We turn next to the question of strategy for product market development. Three facets of development strategy must be considered—planning, implementation, and evaluation—"PIE." The best starting place often will be an evaluation of the present situation. Some of the reasons why the perfect market model may not be consistent with the existing situation were discussed above. It is important to evaluate the reasons for the failure of the two to coincide, before action is prescribed. For example, if the decision-making process of producers and marketers is not price-oriented or if the ownership of production facilities has an important role to play in determining the effect of a price change, a completely different set of recommendations may be in order than if the reason for the discrepancy is a specific public policy decision, lack of knowledge, or imperfections in the operation of the pricing system itself. Evaluation, then, is a first step in the development of a product market strategy.

The second step is that of planning. In the case of a product market problem the planning process would begin with identification of marketing regions. For each of these regions it is necessary to develop projected prices in form, time, and space dimensions as described above. Given these projected price relationships, regional development plans can be prepared. Some plans will be of a short-run variety in which existing plant capacity is regarded as fixed, whereas others will be of a long-run type with expansion or complete reorganization of existing marketing facilities under consideration.

The third and equally important component of strategy is the implementation of these plans. This may be the responsibility of the public sector or the private sector, but in any case plans must be sufficiently specific so that the implementation process is clearly spelled out.

Product market development strategy will include the three steps of planning, implementing, and evaluating. The best point at which to cut into this cycle will vary with time and place. The three steps represent a continuous series of operations that are never fully completed but, when successful, lead to the upward revision of goals and improvements in the execution of the revised plans.

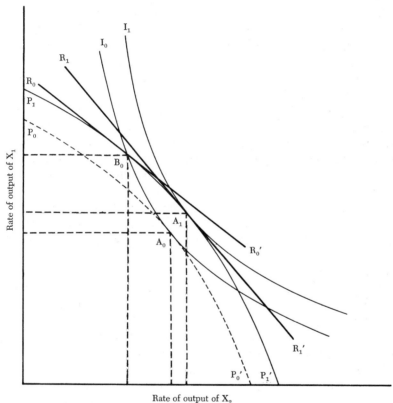

FIGURE 5.2. Production possibility curves, community indifference curves and relative prices lines; the two-commodity case.

A simple diagram may clarify the evaluation and planning steps. Suppose we have a region producing two products, X_1 and X_2 (Fig. 5.2). The production possibilities curve P_1P_1' indicates the alternative combinations of X_1 and X_2 which may be produced in this region. Now let us suppose that there is a community indifference map represented by indifference curves I_0 and I_1. The optimum rates of output of X_1 and X_2 are indicated by the point of tangency of the production possibilities curve and the curve I_1 at point A_1. Suppose, however, that this region has failed to make full use of its production potential and that instead of achieving a product combination lying on line P_1P_1', the product combination lies on line P_0P_0'. In this case the output combination of X_1 and X_2 is represented by A_0.

There are a number of reasons why a region might fail to make full use of its production potential. Among these are an inadequate transportation system, lack of know-how on the part of producers, or the inability to obtain the inputs needed at the proper time. Another possibility would be the failure of the marketing system to operate effectively.

Another type of difficulty is the failure of the price system to reflect the "true" relative product prices. Given our initial situation, the "true" relative product price line is represented by line R_1R_1'. However, suppose the pricing system produces instead the set of relative prices represented by line R_0R_0'. The response of producers to this set of prices is represented by point B_0. Again the region has failed to produce the highest level of satisfaction which is attainable. In many regions the pricing system does, in fact, distort consumer preferences among products. The net effect is to reduce the level of well-being of the community at large.

Now suppose we consider the expansion of the production possibilities for a region such as that indicated by the movement from P_1P_1' to P_2P_2' (Fig. 5.3). The shaded area reflects the new production possibilities that are now attainable. Clearly, this new production possibilities curve is the result of an added bundle of new inputs which may include new marketing facilities, new price support or price maintenance programs, or additional credit which makes it possible for producers to hold their product for sale at a time when prices are more favorable. The shift will vary with the region which has been selected for development—in some areas a large shift might be achieved, whereas in others only a small shift in the production possibilities curve is possible. In any case, the result of this new production potential is to make possible the output of X_1 and X_2 represented by point C lying on indifference curve I_2 instead of point A_1 on indifference curve I_1.

Obviously, it is impossible for producers to "see" indifference curves such as I_1 and I_2. Producers respond instead to relative prices which, ideally, in this new situation would be the tangent to the production possibilities curve at point C. The problem which faces economic development specialists is to select the "best" new

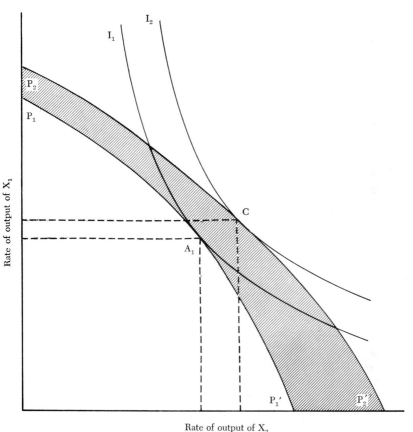

FIGURE 5.3. Expansion of production possibilities.

bundle to introduce and the "best" area in which to make this introduction. For this purpose it is necessary to have relative price projections such as those which can be developed using the perfect market model.

In a recent paper, Nelson (1966) offers a useful framework for considering the specific ingredients of a product market development scheme. First, it is necessary to identify the advance which is sought. In the case of the Peruvian agricultural sector, this might be a given quantitative expansion in the food supply or a specified increase in the incomes of persons in the agricultural sector. After having identified the advance, it is then necessary to weigh the effects of: (1) introducing new components, (2) introducing changes in the system within which these components are combined, and (3) developing new knowledge. These three parts—components, systems, and the supply of new knowledge—must be woven together in such a way that product market development moves forward in the most efficient manner possible.

In the event that small changes in the present situation are sought, it might be feasible to concentrate entirely on providing new components. On the other hand, if major changes are desired, it may be necessary to introduce whole new systems of marketing. The problem is to select those projects for which the payoff will be highest, given the advance which has been set as the goal of the development effort.

Differences in product characteristics must be considered in preparing market development plans. Industrial crops such as cotton, sugar, coffee, tea, and perhaps wool and manufactured milk are marketed under arrangements quite different from those for storable foods such as potatoes, beans, rice, and corn and from the handling of perishable foods such as vegetables, fruit, and fresh milk. In the initial stages of development, efforts may be concentrated upon the storable foods in order that unreasonable seasonal variations in prices of beans or corn may be eliminated through more satisfactory storage plans. Or it may be that a wholesale food market needs to be constructed in order to reduce drastically the cost of marketing perishable fruits and vegetables. For many industrial crops it may be found that the marketing system is already reasonably efficient as compared with other nations of the world, and these crops might well be left for consideration at a later date.

Another characteristic of agricultural products to be considered is the time dimension of the production process. There are certain crops such as tea, coffee, bananas, cacao, and fruit for which long-run planning of marketing methods and facilities is necessary. For products such as beef cattle, dairy, and poultry, a shorter planning period may be relevant, whereas for annual crops such as potatoes, rice, and vegetables, short-run decisions with regard to production and marketing methods must be examined.

There will be situations where relatively little is needed in the way of marketing facilities. McPherson (1965) reports that the construction of an all-weather road north from Quevedo, Ecuador, was sufficient to encourage rapid expansion in banana production, not only along the newly-built road, but in areas well ahead of its completion. Since neither irrigation nor drainage investment was necessary, individual families were able to make the entire investment that was required, upon being assured that the road would be completed by harvest time.

In any case, it will be necessary to identify marketing regions for the commodities selected for the initial attack. Price projections for these regions must be developed in form, time, and space dimensions, and the specific projects to be considered must be spelled out. It is also clear that there may be some substitution involved in making a decision to develop the marketing system for industrial products before that for storable foods or perishable foods. Such decisions turn on the desired advance.

Conclusions

The improvement of product markets should be an important component of any plan which seeks to accelerate the rate of economic growth in a region. The plan for product market development must be short-run in nature, consistent with long-run goals, subject to frequent revision, acceptable to government, acceptable to private marketing firms, and acceptable to producer groups. Considerable effort will be required to insure proper implementation of the plan once the plan itself has been prepared and adopted. Evaluation must be recognized as a vital step in the threefold process for achieving product market development—planning, implementing, and evaluating.

Literature Cited

Bruton, H. J. 1965. Principles of development economics. Prentice-Hall, Inc., Englewood Cliffs, N.J.

Byé, M. 1962. The role of capital in economic development, p. 110-131. *In* Howard S. Ellis and Henry C. Wallach [eds.], Economic development for Latin America. Macmillan and Co., London.

DORFMAN, R., SAMUELSON, P. A., and SOLOW, R. M. 1958. Linear programming and economic analysis. McGraw-Hill Book Company, Inc., N.Y.

HEADY, E. O. 1966. A recipe for meeting the world food crisis. CAED Report 28, Center for Agricultural and Economic Development. Iowa State Univ., Ames.

HIRSCHMAN, A. O. 1958. The strategy of economic development. Yale Univ. Press, New Haven, Conn.

LEIBENSTEIN, H. 1966. Allocative efficiency vs. "X-efficiency." Am. Econ. Rev. LVI(3): 392-415.

MATHIA, G. A., and COFFEY, J. D. 1965. Analysis of interregional competition in the rice industry (mimeo). Faculty of Social Sciences, Universidad Agraria, La Molina, Lima, Peru. Published in Spanish as: Analisis de la competencia interregional en la industria del arroz. Anales Científicos II (3): 292-312.

MCPHERSON, W. W. 1965. Input markets and economic development, p. 99-117. *In* Iowa State Univ. Center for Agricultural and Economic Development, Economic development of agriculture. Iowa State Univ. Press, Ames.

NELSON, R. R. 1966. The efficient achievement of rapid technological progress: a major new problem in public finance. Am. Econ. Rev. LVI(2): 232-241.

6

Factor Markets
and Economic Development

Glenn L. Johnson

This discussion of factor markets is an aspect of the more general problem of bringing about economic development in an emerging nation. Despite the current very unsettled conditions in Nigeria, I am going to discuss the problems from a Nigerian setting because I want very much to make use of knowledge of a concrete situation.

My early experience in Nigeria was in connection with the Economic Development Institute at the University of Nigeria, which I directed for an eighteen-month period. The past fifteen months have been devoted, on a 40 per cent basis, to serving as the director of the Consortium for the Study of Nigerian Rural Development. This consortium includes the University of Wisconsin, Colorado State University, Kansas State University, Michigan State University, the Research Triangle Institute in North Carolina, the United States Department of Agriculture, and the United States Department of the Interior. All of these universities and governmental agencies are contractors, carrying out agricultural development projects which deal in a fundamental way with the factor markets in Nigerian agriculture.

MARKET OPERATIONS AND
CHANGES IN MARKET STRUCTURE

At the onset, it seems advantageous to distinguish between the *operation* of a given market structure and *changes in the structure* of markets. Persons concerned with agricultural development and progress are always concerned with the effectiveness with which markets operate. This concern involves given market structures. The problems of agricultural development in most emerging nations, however, often involve more basic problems than the efficiency with which a given market structure operates. These problems involve possible changes in market structure which would affect the welfare of people and the entire nature of their society.

There is a continuous spectrum of problems ranging between these two types, and it is advantageous to compare them by means of rather extreme examples. In eastern Nigeria, we can ask if the traditional native markets and the transportation system effectively distribute native-grown rice to the urban population. If they do, there is no problem of efficiency in distributing rice within the present market structure. If, however, this market structure does not distribute rice effectively, the problem may not be structural at all but merely one of getting the market itself to operate more effectively. At an opposite extreme is the market for land, which involves familial, tribal, and governmental restrictions which appear to serve to impede the sale and purchase of land as well as to reduce the value of land in exchange. Even if such a market operates efficiently, it has undesirable characteristics. The correction of these characteristics involves major changes in the institutional structure of the Nigerian land market and, for that matter, of the entire Nigerian society and economy.

In the remainder of this chapter, I am going to consider: (1) the operation of existing markets in Nigeria; (2) structural changes under way or needed in Nigerian factor markets; (3) tendencies toward overuse of factors of production in Nigeria; (4) needed revision in the development policies of Nigeria which would improve the structure and operation of Nigeria's agricultural factor markets; and (5) some of the conceptual and methodological problems encountered in doing such research.

OPERATION OF THE EXISTING
FACTOR MARKETS IN NIGERIA

The existing factor markets for Nigerian agriculture handle traditional factors, imported and improved factors, and credit. Each of these will be discussed below.

Markets for Traditional Factors.—There is little concrete evidence that the markets for the traditional factors of production (land, native labor, and native supplies and equipment) are operating so ineffectively as to be a problem.

Land, by and large, carries little value, and there does not seem to be a well established price for land for agricultural purposes. In my view, this is evidence that the market is working effectively rather than that it is working poorly. The low value of land appears to be the consequence of having the government tax away the value of land used for the production of export crops, while subsistence crops seem to compete with jungle or bush fallow at near zero marginal returns. In other areas of poor land and/or high population, subsistence crops compete with heavily-taxed export crops at above zero marginal values.

In the case of cattle, there is some evidence that local leaders and semi-governmental officials derive income from streams of cattle on the way to market in such a way as to reduce the value of grazing rights of the nomadic herders to virtually zero.

In the case of labor, as a factor of production, we find that native labor is hired from one farm to the next. Also, there has been in the past a significant migration of itinerant Ibo rubber tappers from the east into the midwest rubber-producing regions. Anschel (1965) questions whether the method of paying itinerant tappers provides proper incentives for long-term care and maintenance of the rubber trees. Anyone who has been on the public highways of Nigeria is aware of the nomadic laborers used to drive cattle from the northern ranges to the southern population centers. Nigerian labor responds quickly to employment opportunities in the non-farm economy and to the lack of employment opportunities in farming. One must conclude that perhaps the labor market operates effectively, and that the main problems are likely to be structural rather than operational.

Not many native supplies and/or items of native equipment used in agricultural production have to be transported any significant distance. The simple hoes, cutlasses, knives, cutting hooks, and other items which are used in agricultural production are manufactured, for the most part, locally and used locally, as evidenced by the wide interregional variation in the design of this equipment. The local markets provide for rather effective ready exchange of these items, with money as the usual medium of exchange.

Markets for Imported and Improved Factors.—The apparent fact that markets for land, native labor, and native supplies and equipment are operating fairly well in Nigeria does not preclude the possibility of substantial imperfections or inefficiencies in the markets for money and for the imported and modern factors of production, such as petroleum, fertilizers, simple imported tools, large-scale equipment, expatriate technicians, baby chicks, and improved planting materials for cocoa, rubber, and oil palm.

The petroleum marketing system is growing rapidly with assistance from expatriate investment firms. Although very few gasoline-powered pieces of farm equipment are used in Nigeria, there is no difficulty in obtaining the petroleum products to operate those pieces which are present. Furthermore, a new refinery to process plentiful Nigerian crude oil is now coming into operation. In the case of fertilizers, only small amounts are used, and there are no Nigerian manufacturing facilities. The high cost of importing and distributing fertilizer has been offset in the north by a subsidy which places fertilizer prices at about the same level as they are in the United States. However, since farmers in the northern provinces receive about 6 cents per pound for their cotton whereas United States farmers receive about 30 cents, it is not surprising that Nigerian cotton farmers use fertilizer sparingly.

Simple tools, machetes, rubber-tapping knives, lanterns, and other items are imported and passed through the native marketing systems to even the most remote villages. For instance, one is continually amazed at the flow of goods through the Onitsha market, where the market women serve as brokers for distributing the merchandise throughout central Nigeria via the Niger and Benue Rivers or via "mammy-wagons" over the existing partially developed highway system.

Little heavy farm equipment is imported. Most of the heavy work involved in preparing the land is done manually with a short-handled hoe. Earlier, equipment for processing palm fruit was imported and set up in "pioneer oil mills" on government account. Some of the pioneer oil mills were sold to private operators. More recently, the government imported one thousand hydraulic hand Stork mills to use in processing palm fruit. Only about forty of these one thousand mills have left the government warehouse in Port Harcourt for installation. This failure of a government attempt to place an important factor of production into use appears to result from difficulties in the product market, rather than in the factor market. The government, via the oil palm marketing board, levies a substantial "tax" on palm oil. This tax was imposed originally to stabilize prices to producers by withholding revenue in years of high prices for distribution in years of low prices. However, the price stabilization scheme has been converted into a source of government revenue for use in many developmental projects, part of which are in agriculture. Currently, the levy is running in the neighborhood of 50 to 60 per cent of the world price of palm oil. Three years ago, the tax ran at about 40 per cent. At such rates of taxation, private investors find it difficult to spend large amounts of money for hydraulic Stork presses to process palm fruit.

Miller (1965) indicates that the hand screw-press, the hydraulic hand-press, and the pioneer oil mill processing technologies do not vary greatly in efficiency, though the hydraulic hand-presses tend to be somewhat more efficient than hand and screw-press processing methods. Higher palm oil prices would increase labor returns for the production of palm fruit, thereby making it less important to families and villagers to engage in hand processing as a source of income. Instead, family members would find it more beneficial to produce fruit, and the production of a larger quantity of fruit would make it advantageous to shift to the hydraulic hand-presses. Thus, it appears that the low demand for hydraulic Stork presses is traceable to the marketing board taxation.[1*]

There is no real effective demand for expatriate technicians to assist in rubber, oil palm, cocoa, and livestock production in Nigeria. The institutional structure of the land market prevents expatriate firms from establishing plantations without being subjected to substantial Nigerian control, while the marketing board taxes remove the incentive to establish such holdings. Similarly, marketing board taxes discourage Nigerians from establishing plantations and importing expatriate technicians to operate them. In the past, the competitive position in the world market of Nigerian rubber, which is not taxed by the marketing boards, has not been strong 'enough to encourage the establishment of large-scale rubber plantations by Nigerians employing expatriate technicians. However, some institutional structures are being changed, which may permit such operations to be profitable.

*Notes for this chapter begin on page 111.

Both government and private agencies are busy supplying baby chicks for poultry producers in the southern part of Nigeria. Given the existing marketing facilities for eggs and the per capita income of the population, it appears that overinvestment in poultry production has taken place.

In the case of rice, improved seeds and equipment have moved in freely, and, as is true for poultry, there is much evidence that Nigerian rice producers and millers have overinvested relative to investment costs in equipment to handle rice (Welsch, 1964). The incentive for investment comes from the fact that, as a net importer of rice, Nigerian rice producers receive the world price for rice plus the cost of transporting the rice to Nigeria for the country as a whole.

On the other hand, and in sharp contrast, large-scale subsidized production of improved oil-palm seeds and planting material for rubber and cocoa has not resulted in sufficient use of these materials from a national viewpoint, though apparently individual producers are overinvested in oil palm. The record appears to be better for cocoa than for palm. Earlier, heavy plantings were encouraged by higher prices. However, lower world prices and marketing board operations appear to have left the individual cocoa farmer in a position of overinvestment. Thus, though cocoa producers have made better use of the planting material than have palm producers, they, too, are overinvested. As mentioned previously, Nigerian rubber production is in a relatively weak world position competitively, and there is little incentive for rubber producers to utilize the improved planting materials provided by government subsidy. Even so, the reduction of revenue from palm oil by the marketing boards has made rubber competitive with oil palm. It is a reasonable hypothesis to conclude that, from the standpoints of both individual producers and society, Nigerian smallholders have overinvested in the kind of rubber plantings they traditionally make.

As in the case of the traditional factors of production, the markets for imported and improved factors of production seem to be working fairly well. The difficulties encountered appear to this observer to be largely those of inadequate demand. Inadequate demand for these factors is traceable, in turn, to governmental policies which depress prices received by Nigerian producers for export products to a point at which it is not advantageous for them to utilize imported and modern factors of production.

The Credit Market.—We now turn to the traditional credit markets. There is a widespread feeling that these markets are not operating efficiently. While in Nigeria, I became aware, however, that money had moved from Onitsha to the Abakaliki area to be invested in rice mills for milling rice produced in that and in even more distant localities. Similarly, I know that the very extensive north-south movement of cattle is financed privately and that this financing is integrated vertically, in some instances all the way to the slaughter block in the southern cities. To my knowledge, no one knows the cost of providing this credit. However, the jealousy with which this credit market is guarded would indicate that substantial earnings are being made by the persons providing it.

Historically, the United Africa Company and other expatriate buyers of Nigerian palm oil, cocoa, rubber, and groundnuts have provided a substantial amount of capital to finance the consolidation, storage, and transportation of these commodities to the seaports. Since independence, these functions have been taken over, in some instances, by private Nigerians. *Time* magazine (1965) listed and showed pictures of a number of new Nigerian millionaires, some of whom have made their fortunes in this trade and who, most likely, derive substantial revenues from financing domestic trade in the export commodities.

One central bank and a number of other banks which operate regionally have rather substantial investments in agricultural marketing firms and, in a few instances, in the production of crops. As noted above, the conviction is widespread that the Nigerian agricultural credit "system" is not working efficiently. Some persons holding this conviction feel that it is not worthwhile to try to make the present market run efficiently; instead, they feel that a basic structural overhaul of the agricultural credit market is required. Presently, the Consortium for the Study of Nigerian Rural Development is starting a research project to determine the extent of the agricultural credit problem and to investigate what the United States Agency for International Development (USAID) might do to alleviate the problem if alleviation is needed.[2]

Summary of Operation of Existing Factor Markets.—This brief survey of problems in the existing factor market structures in Nigeria indicates that the problems are probably three in number.

1. There appears to be unequal bargaining power between

buyers and sellers. (a) Within the country, unequal bargaining power appears to exist between nomadic cattlemen of the north and chiefs and semi-officials in local semi-governments. Similar inequalities are probably to be found in the operation of the markets for export crops. Some of the effect of these inequalities on the factor markets is indirect, as these inequalities lower income and, hence, the demand for factors of production. (b) Some inequalities may be external to the country. These involve the operations of expatriate purchasing firms and expatriate firms marketing modern factors of production in Nigeria.

2. The biggest problem in the operation of the existing markets appears to be the local governments of Nigeria, which are, in effect, landlords. Landownership is not concentrated in the hands of a few large individual owners, as is common in many South American countries; instead, it is in effect concentrated in the hands of the government, which taxes the export crops so heavily that it probably extracts most of the economic rent of land, making it (the government) the principal landowner of the country. These heavy rates of taxation have reduced the effective price of land to the point where crops return low wages, leaving virtually no income to purchase capital equipment other than the small amounts of locally manufactured supplies and equipment absolutely necessary to produce the crops.

3. There is a tendency towards overinvestment throughout Nigerian agriculture. In the case of rice and poultry production, where initial prices were favorable, this tendency towards overproduction showed up very quickly in excess capacity. In the cases of the palm and cocoa, which have been heavily taxed for a long period of time, the excess commitment of resources is in the form of labor, land, and trees. The excess is *relative to prices received* by farmers for the product. At world prices for palm oil and cocoa, there is considerable evidence to justify expansion However, in view of the prices which producers actually receive, there is much evidence that they feel they have invested too much of their time, land, and resources in the production of these commodities, a conviction borne out by the rapid rate of migration from agricultural work to urban slums and by the low demand for improved oil palm seeds, improved oil palm seedlings, improved rubber planting material, and, for that matter, improved planting material for cocoa. Although it is often asserted that the migration to

urban slums is sociological, not economic, this explanation is far from satisfying.

Again, this survey of existing factor markets does not indicate large-scale inefficiencies in the operation of the markets. Instead, it indicates need for substantial structural changes with respect, mainly, to the role of government.

STRUCTURAL CHANGES IN NIGERIA'S AGRICULTURAL FACTOR MARKETS

In this section, I am going to discuss some of the structural changes indicated to be taking place in the money, land, and labor markets. The efforts of institutions either to improve the human agent or to control population would be regarded as a structural change in the labor market. I am also going to discuss structural changes needed in the production and the importation of factors of production embodying new technologies and in the creation of industries to supply new factors of production. I shall also have something to say about the distribution of income as it conditions the demand for factors of production in Nigeria.

Needed Structural Changes in the Agricultural Credit Market.— As indicated above, all does not seem to be well in the operation of the money market for Nigerian agriculture. Each of the regional governments has taken steps designed, hopefully, to reduce the costs of acquiring money and of distributing it to and collecting it from agricultural producers. As yet, no federal action has been taken. There appears to be a need for a federal agricultural credit institution to make money available to Nigerian agriculture from the central money markets in Nigeria and abroad. Undoubtedly it is expensive to extend and to collect rural credit in Nigeria. Despite such costs, however, it has been possible in some countries to establish governmental agricultural credit systems which become self-sustaining at lower interest rates. However, it would be unrealistic to conclude that a reduction in the cost of credit would be sufficient to modernize Nigerian agriculture, as there are important problems on the income side which must be solved before the potential demand for modern factors of production will be released fully, even with cheaper credit.

Needed Structural Changes in the Land Market.—The basic structural changes in the land market required to modernize

Nigerian agriculture appear to be less drastic than in many countries. The ownership of such private land values as the governments let develop is widespread, although individual Nigerians are often unable to identify the land which they own or would pledge as collateral for a loan. However, as members of families and tribes, they have rights to the use of land and to improvements which they make on it. Though it is commonly said that Nigeria has a difficult land tenure problem, growing out of tribal and community ownership of land, it is my observation that the extended family and community ownership of land is not the main problem. Wherever, to my knowledge, it has been profitable for land to pass into individual ownership, Nigerian institutions have been flexible enough to permit this, as evidenced by the large-scale housing developments growing up around the centers of high-income population. As I pointed out earlier, Nigeria is unlike many countries of the world in that it is not private landowners who exploit the Nigerian farmer; instead, if the Nigerian farmer is exploited by those who control income from land, it must be by the government which would be doing so via marketing board levies on the economic rent of land. It is in this area that changed market structures should be considered.

Another structural reform needed in the land market involves land reclamation and development. The first dam is now being constructed on the Niger River. In addition to providing power, it will provide some irrigation water and flood control along the Niger River bottom. Full-scale development of the Niger and Benue rivers under some valley developmental scheme would do much to make additional land available for production and to improve the productivity of land now in the valley by providing irrigation water and protection from flooding. The introduction of a developmental scheme such as the Tennessee Valley Authority would be a major structural change in the Nigerian land market. In the Cross River valley to the east of the Niger valley, one finds a large amount of land inadequately utilized because the water supply problem has not been solved to permit humans to live in this area on a year-round basis. There are structural institutional changes which would help provide both drinking and irrigation water in substantial parts of the Cross River valley. Further, in the lowland areas along the main streams, there are large areas of land which would be well-adapted to rice production provided certain engineering and disease-control problems were solved. One of the structural reforms needed in the Cross River land market is construction of flood control and drainage facilities for these areas. Before such operations can take place, there will have to be a major restructuring of the institutions controlling the use of land, as well as a medical or mechanical breakthrough on the control of the snail which spreads schistosomiasis to rice laborers working in irrigation water.

Needed Structural Changes in the Rural Labor Market.—The labor market in Nigerian agriculture is working fairly well, viewed in isolation. From the perspective of the total economy, however, serious problems of a structural nature become apparent. Governmental and business labor is unionized and has been able to enforce wage demands with general strikes to the extent of causing per capita money income to rise to levels creating inflation.

This tendency to overpay governmental and business labor has combined with the government's heavy taxation of agricultural export crops to create what appears to be a premature, mass exodus of labor from agriculture. Although it is true that there is too much labor in agriculture, given the prices which the government permits producers to receive, there is also evidence that much of the labor now leaving agriculture to become unemployed in the urban slums could have been profitably employed in agriculture, had internal agricultural prices been permitted to reflect world market conditions. Thus, the basic problems with the rural labor market appear to grow out of the inadequate returns to labor which grow, in turn, out of the taxation of the agricultural export commodities.

Perhaps the most basic structural change needed in the labor market in Nigeria is population control. With the rate of population growth estimated at between 2 and 4 per cent, it is extremely difficult for Nigerian productivity to increase enough to provide for an improvement in per capita real incomes. Still further, it is extremely difficult to find the revenue to finance the institutions required to educate such a large quantity of human beings.

Another important structural change which is taking place very rapidly in the labor market is occurring in educational institutions. Eastern and western Nigeria have long had rather extensive primary educational facilities. Although serious questions can be raised about the quality of the secondary schools in the southern regions, there are substantial numbers of secondary graduates available to go to the universities. In the more feudalistic Moslem north, ideas on education are modernizing rapidly. The University of Wisconsin has a major teacher-training project in the north which will provide teachers for raising the level of general education in that area. At the sub-university level, agricultural training takes place mainly in government agricultural schools designed to train extension workers who commonly have three to six years of education. This method of improving the quality of the human agent is being pushed very rapidly, and the products of these government training schools are, in turn, improving the technical know-how of Nigerian farmers. At the university level, three additional agricultural faculties have been established in the last six years, bringing the total number to four for Nigeria's 55 million people. These rapidly growing faculties have high priority in public investment schemes of the regional and federal governments.

A basic difficulty encountered in getting qualified persons into agriculture continues to be the low earnings in that sector. The income level is largely a result of government policy, which depresses prices received by farmers and, hence, the income of the human agent in agriculture—educated or uneducated.

Needed Structural Changes in the Production and Importation of New Technology.—One of the most basic, but unutilized, structural changes occurring in Nigeria's factor markets is taking place with respect to her research facilities for producing new technologies and for testing importable ones. There have been major, highly productive experiment stations working on oil palm, cocoa, and rice. In addition, there are stations working on the subsistence crops, and a new station is being established for rubber. In the north, there are major research stations which are devoted to livestock production and which also include the control of the tsetse fly and rinderpest. Still further, each of the four agricultural faculties is developing a research program and each of the regional ministries dealing with agriculture operates research facilities. At the federal level, there is a newly created Ministry of Natural Resources and Research which is, in effect, a ministry of agriculture as mines, power, and water transportation are handled in other ministries. There is also the proposed Ford Foundation/Rockefeller Foundation Institute of Tropical Agriculture which will cost about 25 million dollars.

The structural changes which have established and are establishing these research facilities have been expensive to Nigerian governments and to foreign donor governments. The effectiveness of these research agencies in producing new technologies has been substantial in the past, as witnessed by the highly improved strains of oil palm, the new rinderpest vaccines, techniques for clearing the tsetse fly, and disease controls for cocoa. However, the discouraging note is the slow rate of adoption of these technologies. Some critics have blamed inadequate extension services and have called for further structural changes in facilities for distributing technical information to farmers. However, I doubt that the primary difficulty has been with the extension services, though they have been inadequate, for similarly inadequate extension activities have paid off handsomely where there have been substantial benefits to be gained from adoption. The rinderpest control program has been operated very effectively. There have been substantial payoffs to small amounts of research and extension work on rice, and the rate of adoption has been rapid. The same has been true in the poultry industry. However, adoption has been slow for oil palm, cocoa, and rubber where economic incentives are low for adopting the results of research. In a real sense, agricultural taxation policies have counteracted the effectiveness of money raised by these taxes and devoted to the production and dissemination of new agricultural technologies.

The Creation of Industrial Facilities to Supply New Factors of Production.—So far, few industries, other than those operated by government, have been established to supply new factors of production to Nigerian agriculture. Cement manufacturing is rather well developed, mainly in the hands of the government. Similarly, the government produces asbestos sheets and roofing materials. The creation of a government-owned fertilizer industry is being studied by Nigerian governments, USAID, and possible foreign investors. A private jute mill is being established which should produce sacking material for the groundnut industry. To my knowledge, no tractors, gasoline motors, or major pieces of agricultural equipment are manufactured in anything approaching a modern factory, though some steel is processed for construction purposes, and plans are under way to start a steel smelting industry. There is large-scale government production of improved palm seeds, improved rubber planting material, improved cocoa material, and seed rice. In the case of rice, some evidence indicates that seed rice might better be propagated by associations of growers, empowered by government to license their membership (Welsch, 1964). By and large, the main deterrent to an expansion of industrial production of new factors of agricultural production appears to be low farm earnings and consequent low demand for factors. For the export crops, earnings are low because of government taxation problems. For the subsistence crops, earnings are low because per capita incomes prevent an expansion of domestic markets for the subsistence crops.

TENDENCIES TO OVERPRODUCTION

When an agricultural economist observes the operation of factor markets in a country like Nigeria, and compares it with other countries, such as the United States and with still other and different countries having highly centralized control over agriculture, he may ask himself about tendencies to over- and under-invest in agriculture. Agricultural economies characterized by private ownership tend to overinvest in agriculture, in contrast to the opposing tendency of agricultural economies operated by government to underinvest in agriculture. This question comes quickly to mind in comparing United States agriculture with the centralized agricultural economies of Russia and China. Initially, this question does not arise so quickly with respect to the Nigerian agricultural economy where the production decisions are made on a decentralized basis, mainly by private individuals, families, or local village councils. More recently, however, I have begun to see that there is an extensive overinvestment in agricultural production in Nigeria, given the *prices which the Nigerian producer receives for his products.* In a sense, I go beyond Schultz' (1964) transforming of traditional agriculture to conclude that Nigerian farmers have not only reached their economic margins, but have actually exceeded them.

In the case of both rice and poultry, it is evident that the private entrepreneurs of Nigeria have invested so much of their own time and resources that they produce an output so large that it has to be sold at prices which yield substandard returns relative to returns in the non-farm Nigerian economy. Though investments in oil palm production lag far behind what would be advantageous to individual producers if they received the world price, there is evidence from the standpoint of their personal accounts that the farmers themselves feel that they have overinvested at the present prices. The Nigerian palm oil producer, cocoa producer, rubber producer, and groundnut producer finds himself, like his American farmer counterpart, with substantial overcommitments of his own labor and resources to agricultural production at returns unsatisfactory in view of returns obtained from resources and effort in the non-farm sector. And, like the United States agricultural economy, returns to agricultural labor in Nigeria remain low despite extensive off-farm migration to the urban centers.

Nigerian governmental agencies, however, are slow to invest. Though the government taxes palm so heavily as to discourage private investment, it does not make sufficient investments itself. It seems to be difficult to get tax money from government to invest despite favorable returns to government which, of course, collects its own taxes (MacFarlane and Oworen, 1965).

In considering the structural changes with respect to factor markets of both Nigeria and the United States, we seem to be asking what kinds of structural changes should be made to get around the problem of overcommitment of resources to agricultural production. The problem is similar, yet different for both countries. Nigeria faces the task of correcting adverse governmental policies which, on balance, means that the economy as a whole *underinvests* in agricultural production. The United States faces the problem of correcting government policies, which means that the economy as a whole has *overinvested* in agricultural production. The similarity, however, exists with respect to the positions in which the individual producers of both countries find themselves. Given the prices which both receive as a result of the policies of their respective governments, the private agricultural entrepreneurs of both countries have overcommitted their labor and resources to agricultural production to such an extent that they receive substandard rates of return on their own labor and resources.

Needed Revisions in Government Policies as Aspects of Structural Adjustment of the Factor Markets

The above discussion should have made it abundantly clear that a major difficulty encountered in Nigerian factor markets for agriculture involves inappropriate governmental taxation policies, particularly with respect to the taxation of agriculture. These heavy taxation policies tend to negate the development of new technology in Nigerian research facilities and to nullify the efforts of extension workers and free markets to distribute these new technologies via the equipment, planting materials, and supplies in which these new technologies are embedded. A related difficulty involves the tendency to centralize the *production* of modern inputs in the hands of government. This preference for central control, despite the fact that the bulk of Nigerian agricultural production is in the hands of individual entrepreneurs, does tend to stultify the development of the industries which would service agriculture with modern factors of production.

Prior to and after the *coup d'état* on January 15, 1966 (though secret from January 15 to July 29), regionalism and tribalism have been important divisive factors which have kept the agricultural economy from integrating into a national economy. This grew out of the inability to establish national policies with respect to governmental support for the development of credit institutions, agricultural education, agricultural research, and extension. Whether or not this situation can be corrected remains to be seen.

CONCEPTUAL AND EMPIRICAL DIFFICULTIES OF
RESEARCH ON FACTOR MARKETS IN NIGERIA

Basic problems of structural reform in factor markets, as well as elsewhere, involve non-normative and normative investigations. Further, once the existing situation and possibilities are described and the values sought and avoided are equally well described, there remains the problem of devising decision-making rules and institutions for processing normative and non-normative information into solutions of the problems of structural reform.

In the recent *coups d'état*, the decision-making rules were changed from those set up in the federal constitution which had governed Nigeria since its independence. Decision-making rules, at the public level in Nigeria, are further complicated by the customary use of different decision-making rules in the different tribes. In the east, for instance, some villages make decisions on the basis of consensus among a group of elders or leaders. In the north, decision-making has been more centralized and more feudalistic in nature. Thus, in addition to doing normative and non-normative work, persons working on restructuring the factor markets in Nigeria are required to work with decision-making rules as endogenous variables.

I see little possibility that an aloof social scientist, concerned only with the positive or non-normative, would be able to enter into the process without being rejected by important Nigerian decision makers. Instead, it seems to me that agricultural development researchers in Nigeria must *help* hammer out the normative concepts, the non-normative concepts, and the decision-making rules on which solutions of factor market problems depend.

For more technically-minded economists, I should also point out that, in some instances, no possible adjustments in the Nigerian factor markets are Pareto-optimum; i.e., any possible policy will worsen the economic positions of some persons. Even if there are no Pareto-better policies, there may still be fairly strong evidence that certain solutions in which some persons lose and others gain are superior to other solutions in which some persons also gain and some also lose. Further, it must be taken as given that the Nigerians, like the Americans who set up the farm credit system, are not always seeking Pareto-optima solutions. They are not and simply will not always be satisfied merely with solutions which require that no one loses. Thus, the normative work of the researcher on problems of Nigeria's agricultural factor markets must go beyond ordinal utility measurements without interpersonal validity, to an attempt to get interpersonally valid utility measurements of some sort. Still further, a serious question exists as to whether all of the values sought and evils being avoided can be reduced to utiles and disutiles and summarized into a single variable to be maximized or minimized. For this reason, calculations involved in the maximization of a single function do not appear to be appropriate in handling many of the important factor market problems in Nigeria.

This problem is encountered in concrete form in connection with the Consortium for the Study of Nigerian Rural Development sub-projects on agricultural education, agricultural research, direct investments in agricultural production, and in agricultural factor markets (both public and private), the modernization of the northern livestock industry, agricultural credit, product markets, and on the interference of traditional structures with agricultural

development. The best amount of research and agricultural education to be supported depends on the demand for the products of
such investments from the agricultural economy of Nigeria. Ability
to support agricultural education and research depends, in turn, on
the revenue which can be extracted from the agricultural economy,
which also depends on international trade. Further, the kind of research needed depends on whether or not population control policies
are going to be put into effect. If such policies are put into effect,
research should concentrate on export commodities; if they are not
put into effect, there will be greater need for subsistence crops. One
way to solve such a problem is to carry out an input/output analysis
designed to maximize gross national product (GNP).

However, I cannot bring myself to believe that all of the values
sought and evils being avoided can be reduced to utiles, or to
GNP as measured in pounds, shillings, and pence as the least
common denominators.[3] Hence, my interest has turned away from
utility maximizing, profit maximizing, or GNP maximizing computations to the use (at least partially) of non-maximizing simulation
models in order to study the Nigerian agricultural economy. It is my
hope that simulation models can be used to trace some of the
interrelationships among: (1) the products of educational and
research agencies, (2) expenditures in support of educational and
research agencies, (3) the tax flows and their reinvestments, (4)
international trade, (5) balance of payments, and (6) population
growth. It is also my hope that we may be able to develop
simulation models which can be asked the consequences of commonly advocated policies in Nigerian development. I do not en-
vision these simulation models as being maximizing in nature, at
least not exclusively so. I hope, instead, that responsible Nigerian
administrators will be able to ask the model about the consequences
in terms of ten or fifteen different objectives of following a given
policy. After the model tells them the likely consequences, year by
year for the next fifteen years or so of following a given policy,
it may very well be that they will want to reformulate the question
and ask the simulation model a question about the consequence of
following an alternative and possibly better policy.

If we can provide non-maximization answers which do not pre-
tend to reduce all "goods and bads" into a single least common
denominator called utility or GNP, it may very well be that we can
help Nigerian administrators carry on better dialogues involving

the results of agricultural development research. Such answers can help them ask and obtain the answers to the important questions involved in restructuring Nigerian agricultural factor markets.

NOTES

1. Sylvester Ugoh, Deputy Director of the Economic Development Institute of the University of Nigeria, has pointed out that one of the main reasons why hydraulic Stork presses are not used at present is that people do not want to sell their palm fruits to the firms that would process them in these mills. According to custom, the man of the family gets the value of the fruit and the woman the value of the kernels. When the fruit is sold in the bunch, the man gets the whole value, leaving the wife out of the picture. However, the author of this paper notes that the independence of the Nigerian market woman and her pecuniary aggressiveness suggest that a more profitable situation for palm produce would lead to another division of monetary returns between man and wife which would be profitable to all concerned.

2. Since this paper has been written, the Consortium for the Study of Nigerian Rural Development has completed two studies on Agricultural Credit in Nigeria: Jones *et al.* (1966), and Bauman *et al.* (1966).

3. Further, I see no basis for believing that institutional, technological, and educational changes have consequences which meet the second order conditions mathematically necessary for the existence of a maximum.

LITERATURE CITED

ANSCHEL, KURT. 1965. Economic aspects of peasant rubber production in midwestern Nigeria. Ph.D. Thesis. Mich. State Univ., East Lansing. Univ. Mircrofilms. Ann Arbor.

BAUMAN, HAROLD, WHITNEY, JOHN, and CONNALLY, CHAN. 1966. A situation report on agricultural credit in Nigeria. Consortium for the Study of Nigerian Rural Development. Mich. State Univ., East Lansing.

JONES, TED, GANS, A. P., HOOVER, ROBERT G., MAXEY, RICHARD P., STONE-HAM, A. H., and SMITH, MERVIN G. 1966. A proposed agricultural credit program for Nigeria. Consortium for the Study of Nigerian Rural Development. Mich. State Univ., East Lansing.

MACFARLANE, DAVID L., and OWOREN, MARTIN A. 1965. Investment in oil palm plantation in Nigeria. Univ. Nigeria Econ. Dev. Institute, NSUKKU.

MILLER, WILLIAM L. 1965. An investigation of the economics of processing palm fruit in eastern Nigeria. Ph.D. Thesis. Mich. State Univ., East Lansing. Univ. Microfilms. Ann Arbor.

SCHULTZ, T. W. 1964. Transforming traditional agriculture. Yale Univ. Press, New Haven, Conn.

TIME MAGAZINE. 1965. 17 Sept.

WELSCH, DELANE. 1964. The rice industry in the Abakaliki area of eastern Nigeria. Ph.D. Thesis. Mich. State Univ., East Lansing. Univ. Microfilms. Ann Arbor.

7

Trade Preferences
and Developing Countries

Harry G. Johnson

The most original new idea on policies to further the economic development of the underdeveloped world—and the most seductive to the developing countries themselves—that emerged from the first United Nations Conference on Trade and Development (UNCTAD) at Geneva in 1964 was undoubtedly the proposal for temporary trade preferences in industrial products to be granted by the advanced countries.[1]*

This proposal, the brain-child of Dr. Raul Prebisch, Secretary-General of the conference, evoked sharp divisions among the leading industrial nations. The Americans adamantly opposed any consideration of preferential trading schemes.[2] The British indicated a willingness to generalize Commonwealth preferences to all less-developed countries, provided that other developed countries would grant similar preferences. The Common Market countries were divided between support of the "Brasseur Plan" for the organization of markets and advocacy of preferential arrangements of a "non-discriminatory" character (according to the General Agreement on Tariffs and Trade [GATT] concepts).

The less-developed countries themselves were divided in economic interests; those of them belonging to the British Commonwealth or to the Associated Overseas Territories of the European

*Notes for this chapter begin on page 131.

Economic Community enjoy a preferential advantage in these markets over their rivals in non-member developing countries. A united front in demanding preferences was achieved only by incorporating the proviso that developing countries which lost by the extension of preferences should be adequately compensated.

No Solution Through GATT

The divisions among the advanced countries over the trade-preference issue, and especially the obdurate opposition of the United States, prevented the conference from arriving at an agreed statement of principles concerning it. Nevertheless, the question of trade preferences for developing countries has since been receiving increasing attention.

The transformation of UNCTAD into a continuing organization of the United Nations, with Dr. Prebisch in charge under a Trade and Development Board, has created a new institution with a vested interest in the proposal and the facilities to promote it. Further, the Kennedy Round of GATT negotiations drags along interminably, as the result, first, of French reluctance to negotiate on the terms laid down by the United States Trade Expansion Act, then of the internal cleavage between France and her Common Market partners. This has destroyed any hope of heading off the demand for preferences by a massive liberalization of trade along GATT lines, designed to provide the special concessionary benefits for the developing countries envisaged in the GATT Action Programme of 1963 and the new GATT Chapter on Trade and Development. The danger, indeed, has been that negotiations will not be concluded before the Trade Expansion Act expires in 1967. Finally, the official United States position on the preference issue has been softening from dogmatism into pragmatism in response to pressure from the Latin American countries, a trend symbolized by the support given last November by the United States representatives in the Organization for Economic Co-operation and Development (OECD) for the initiation of a study by that organization of the issues raised by trade preferences for developing countries.

These developments suggest the need to take a fresh look at the issues raised by the proposal for trade preferences for developing countries, and particularly at the principles of commercial policy embodied in GATT and in the "conventional wisdom" concerning the seriousness of existing tariff barriers that has evolved among those concerned as officials or observers with tariff negotiations under GATT. That is the purpose of this article.

As a preliminary, it is essential to examine the respective contributions that aid and trade may make to the promotion of economic development, and the economic sense of the GATT principle of non-discrimination, since confusion on both subjects has befogged each side of the argument over preferences. The main body of the article discusses the case for and against trade preferences for developing countries, concentrating on the question of how far such preferences might serve to promote development. It is argued that preferences might have a far more powerful influence in promoting development than the conventional wisdom suggests. The reason is chiefly that the conventional method of evaluating the protective effect of national tariffs focuses wrongly on averages of the tariff rates applied to commodities, and fails to consider the really relevant barrier: the effective rates of protection of "value added" implicit in national tariff schedules. However, the policies of protection pursued by the less-developed countries themselves may be sufficiently serious barriers to their exports to prevent their deriving much benefit from preferences granted by the developed countries, unless they make major changes in their exchange-rate and protective policies. The conclusion discusses whether trade preferences could be used as a means of promoting trade liberalization along lines consistent with the ideals that lie behind the present GATT system governing tariffs and tariff negotiations.

TRADE AND AID

The primary purpose of the 1964 United Nations Conference on Trade and Development was to consider possibilities for new policies in the field of trade that would, by enlarging the export earnings of the developing countries, help to fill the prospective "foreign-exchange gap" between their growing import and debt-service requirements and the foreign exchange likely to become available from their relatively slower-growing exports and from the virtually stagnant volume of foreign aid from the developed countries. In much of the documentation of UNCTAD, and of the argument at and about the conference, there is a clear basic assumption that aid and trade are substitutes for one another. This assumption is consonant with the main lines of contemporary thinking on problems of development finance, which takes as its frame of reference the balance-of-payments constraint on policy. However, from a more fundamental point of view, one which concentrates on the real resource requirements of economic development, this assumption is not merely superficial, but erroneous in important respects.

Aid, properly defined, entails a transfer of real resources from the aid-giving developed country to the aid-receiving developing country. Such resources have the special attraction to the latter of being immediately usable externally, whereas domestic resources made available by saving and taxation have to be converted into external resources through exporting or import-substitution. The transfer involves a sacrifice by the aid-giving country, and a gain by the aid-receiving country.

This proposition, however, has to be qualified by recognition of the fact that what is officially catalogued as aid is a heterogeneous mixture of grants, loans, and transfers in kind, much of it tied to purchases at prices (or reckoned at notional values) above world market prices. When allowance is made for future repayments of interest and amortization on loans, and for excessive prices of aid-financed goods, the real resource transfers involved in foreign aid today probably run to no more than about half the nominal total.[3]

Trade, on the other hand, is the provision of better opportunities to sell in export markets goods whose production and export necessitate the expenditure of real resources and whose import provides additional real resources to the importing country. An explicit transfer is involved only if the trade opportunity enables the exporting country to charge, and obliges the importing country to pay, higher prices than would otherwise prevail. Significantly, it was trade opportunities of this kind that were sought in the demands voiced at the 1964 UNCTAD conference: for commodity agreements to raise the prices of primary products and for trade preferences in industrial products. If trade preferences had the expected effect of enabling exporters to charge the domestic price of the importing country, instead of the world market price, their effect would be simply to transfer tariff revenue from the government of the importing country to the producers of the exporting country. Expanded trade opportunities may, however, and frequently will, involve only the opportunity to sell more goods at about the same prices as previously prevailed (depending on the circumstances of international competition). In this case, there is no explicit transfer, and the effects have to be evaluated in terms of the theory of the gains from trade.

GAINS FROM TRADE

According to this theory, the exporting country gains to the extent that the goods purchased with the additional export proceeds are worth more than the goods that the resources required to produce the additional exports could have produced in other activities, such as in subsistence agriculture or in the import-substitution sector of the economy. For developing countries—which typically incur substantial excess costs in substituting for imports—this gain could be substantial. However, obviously, it could never be so great as to equal the value of the additional export proceeds if these were received as a gift. Thus, this kind of trade opportunity, which for practical purposes can be identified with non-discriminatory tariff reduction (and some types of preferential trading arrangements), cannot be a substitute for an equivalent flow of aid.

For its part, the importing country will gain in real terms if providing the trade opportunity enables it to substitute cheaper imports for more expensive domestic output (trade-creation). In this case, expanding the trade opportunities it offered to developing countries would enable it to give more aid without reducing its real income—in contradiction to the notion prevalent among developed countries that the "sacrifice" of more trade would excuse a policy of less aid. On the other hand, the importing country will lose in real terms if providing the trade opportunity involves switching imports to a higher-cost source of supply (trade diversion). This possibility of loss arises only with preferential (as opposed to non-discriminatory) tariff reduction; and, given that the tariff rates on which preferences would be based are almost universally less than 100 per cent, the loss involved could be only a fraction of the value of the trade switched.

To sum up, except where trade merely raises the prices received by the developing countries for their exports, trade and aid are *not* substitutes. In particular, trade may increase and not reduce the real resources available to the developed country, while trade may be substantially less useful than an equal flow of aid to the developing country. This last point, by itself, suggests pessimism with respect to the potential contribution of trade to development. Such pessimism, however, is not wholly black, for one must take account of the dynamic (as distinct from the financial) aspects of the development problem, and the possible differences between trade and aid in this respect.

The process of industrialization is not a matter merely of accumulating the capital necessary to establish the capital-to-output ratio required by an industrial economy. It is much more one of inculcating in those who manage and use the capital the habits of seeking constantly to improve efficiency, so that economic growth becomes a self-sustaining process. This is a matter of education and social psychology about which too little is known; however, historical and increasing contemporary evidence suggests that exposure to competition in a large market can play an important part in the process.

Observation of the industrial problems of the developing countries also suggests that, typically, their markets are too small for their efforts at industrialization on the basis of import-substitution to bring this force into play. This implies that aid, which characteristically—at least until very recently—has been devoted to supporting import-substituting industrialization policies, does little to stimulate the dynamic processes of growth, and may even reinforce the factors that tend to suppress them in small, highly protected economies. Trade, on the other hand, could evoke dynamic responses to competitive opportunities that would reinforce the growth process, and so be more fruitful in the longer run than aid. This would depend, however, on whether the trade opportunities proposed offered rewards to competitive ability, or merely provided limited monopolistic privileges in a closely controlled market.

IS NON-DISCRIMINATION
ECONOMICALLY SENSIBLE?

The principle of non-discrimination is the principle that the same rate of duty should apply to all imported goods, regardless of their country of origin. This principle is the foundation of the

GATT system of regulating international trade. The conviction that the principle represents an ideal for the conduct of international commercial diplomacy underlies much of the aversion with which commercial policy negotiators regard the trade preferences proposal.

As applied within GATT, however, the principle is inherently self-contradictory, owing to the exception allowed to it for free trade areas and customs unions. For this exception converts the principle into the rule that discriminatory tariffs are bad unless they go to the limit of 100 per cent discrimination. More fundamentally, as trade theorists have long been pointing out, non-discrimination between sources of supply of individual goods is by no means the same thing as non-discrimination between countries exporting to a particular national market. Tariff rates may be set high on goods of which one country is the preponderant supplier, and low on goods of which another country is the predominant supplier.

This possibility of discrimination between countries, by appropriate selection of commodities for favorable tariff treatment, has in fact been exploited in past rounds of negotiations under GATT. The negotiation machinery has perforce concentrated on bargaining between the large "dominant-supplier" countries, which can offer profitable access to markets and also benefit from the receipt of tariff concessions. The item-by-item approach has enabled these countries to concentrate tariff reductions on those goods in which they have an important trading interest.

The dominant-supplier authority of the United States Trade Expansion Act—since made irrelevant by Britain's failure to secure membership in the Common Market—was intended to allow exploitation of the same possibility of non-discriminatory discrimination by concentrating the largest tariff reductions on the industrial products in which the United States and Europe jointly dominated the world market. Although in principle the "linear" (or across the board) approach of the Kennedy Round precludes the discrimination possible under the earlier "item-by-item" method, in practice the exceptions lists granted to the bargainers, together with the complicated "tariff disparities" procedure, may leave plenty of room for discrimination against the smaller and less-developed countries.

There is, in fact, strong evidence (part of which is presented below) that the principle of non-discrimination as applied in GATT has in practice involved serious discrimination against the less-developed countries by the developed countries. There are two main reasons for this, apart from the biases inherent in the negotiating process just discussed.

The first is that although, as GATT was originally envisaged, trade in agricultural products was to be subject to the same rules as trade in industrial products, in fact GATT operates on the rule that domestic agricultural policies override international trading obligations. Agricultural products are relatively far more important in the trade of the less-developed countries than in the trade of the developed countries.

Second, the developed industrial countries—primarily Britain and the United States—have used GATT as a medium for the negotiation of special arrangements for trade in cotton textiles, nominally intended to regulate, but actually used to restrict, the growth of exports of such products by the developing countries. Cotton textiles are the main industry in which the developing countries have established an internationally competitive position, in spite of abnormally high tariff barriers.

Apart entirely from the question of how non-discrimination works in practice, there is the more fundamental question of whether non-discrimination is a sensible rule for dealings by one nation with others. Tariffs inherently involve discrimination in favor of resident producers as against foreigners. The presumption is that residents have some special claim on the nation, deriving from their political affiliations to it. If politics make a difference between residents and foreigners, what sense is there in insisting that politics should be allowed to make no difference between foreigners? Politics have, in fact, made such differences in the past, as evidenced by the Commonwealth preferential system and the association of the overseas territories with the Common Market. These arrangements rested on the special obligations of certain powers to their former colonial territories.

In the present-day world, it can be argued that the developed countries have recognized and assumed responsibility for an obligation to assist the less-developed countries to develop, and that this obligation sanctions the establishment of international trading arrangements discriminating in their favor. To put the point another way, it can be argued that the ethical principle embodied in the principle of non-discrimination is the principle that equals should be treated as equals, and that in international economic relations developed countries and less-developed countries are not equal.[4]

ARGUMENTS FOR TRADE PREFERENCES

In the documentation and proceedings of the first UNCTAD conference, the argument for trade preferences in industrial products for developing countries is presented as "a logical extension of the infant-industry argument." This orientation of the case for preferences is obviously aimed at exploiting the exception allowed by the GATT rules for infant-industry protection. It will not stand serious examination.

Essentially, this argument for preferences is that the markets of the developing countries are too small for the process of "learning by doing" posited by the infant-industry argument to work effectively. Consequently, it is argued, what is required to promote the development of industry in the developing countries is a temporarily protected position in a larger (world) market, such as preferences could give. The proposition that national markets are too small in most underdeveloped countries for protection to produce ultimately efficient production is probably correct. What is involved here, however, is not a logical extension of the infant-industry argument, but an empirical emendation of it. The traditional infant-industry argument contains no stipulation about the size of country required for the argument to be valid. The failure to make such a stipulation is undoubtedly due to the fact that the countries for which the argument was originally advanced—for the United States by Hamilton and for Germany by List—were potentially or actually comparable in size to the contemporary advanced industrial nations. This is not true of the great majority of underdeveloped countries today.

The proposition that most of the underdeveloped countries are too small to benefit from infant-industry protection, however, does not logically lead to the recommendation of preferences in the markets of the developed countries, at least in the generalized form of across-the-board preferences for a fixed period of time advocated at the first UNCTAD conference.

In the first place, the traditional infant-industry argument claims that the market process fails to take account of the full social returns from investment in a new industry, and thus sanctions a "social investment" in such industry; this investment is to be financed by charging the consumers of the nation a higher price than they would have to pay in the world market. In other words, it recommends a transfer from the consumers to the producers of the nation, a transfer deemed economically beneficial to the nation in the long run. By contrast, the argument for preferences is an argument for a transfer from the consumers (or taxpayers) of the developed countries to the producers of the less-developed countries—an international as contrasted with an intranational income transfer. Logically, the assumption that a market larger than the national market is necessary for the growth of industry into efficient production would lead to the recommendation of production subsidies, not preferences.

Secondly, the infant-industry argument, if fully worked out, implies that protection should be provided on the scale and for the time-period required for the protected industry to establish its competitiveness, if protection is justified at all. This is a very different principle from granting a preferential margin at a common rate and for a common period on the tariffs normally levied on imports of manufactures by developed countries. That principle would involve choosing the extent to which developing-country industries receive protection in developed-country markets, not by study of the infant-industry potentialities of the industries in question, but by the levels of protection the developed countries happen to accord to their existing industries. These are not at all closely related to the probable ability of the developing countries to become competitive in these industries.

Moreover, preferences based on existing tariff rates would give the maximum incentives to the establishment in the developing countries of those industries that are subject to the highest protective barriers in such countries, and that consequently would face the highest barriers to exports when the temporary protection given by preferences had ended. In this connection, too, it might be noted that, since the grant of protection generally reflects the political influence of the industry receiving it, basing preferences on existing tariff rates would entail the maximum threat to the most politically influential industries in the developed countries.

Thirdly, the strength of the argument depends on the reality and strength of the assumed possibilities of infant-industry development. Despite the popularity of the infant-industry (and infant-economy) concept in the conventional wisdom on economic development, no serious effort has been made to test and to prove it, or to show that the inability of less-developed countries to export the industrial products they produce is associated with unexploited infant-industry possibilities.

There is, on the contrary, a mounting volume of evidence to the effect that the difficulties of such countries in industrial exporting are attributable to the domestic policies of import-substitution-cum-currency-overvaluation they practice. It is an obvious truism that the economies of large-scale production cannot be realized in a small market. It is less obvious, but probably more important, that modern industry is an intricate network of input-output relationships between firms, and that the effort to force self-sufficiency by protection in a small, industrially backward economy renders the industry of that economy internationally uncompetitive by raising the costs of manufactured inputs above world levels. This effect of protectionism is not a consequence of the limited size of consumer markets, and could be offset only to a limited extent by trade preferences.

The infant-industry argument for preferences, therefore, carries little conviction. However, more cogent arguments can be advanced in their support. These arguments necessarily assume: (a) that the developed countries have accepted a real obligation to assist the development of the developing countries; (b) that, nevertheless, they are for various reasons unwilling to increase their foreign aid programs substantially; and (c) that any massive move towards trade liberalization is not politically feasible in the near future.

In these circumstances, it can be argued that an increase in aid given in the disguised form of trade preferences would be a desirable second-best, and could be sold to the public of the developed countries where a direct increase in aid could not. Moreover, greater exposure of the developing countries to the opportunities and pressures of competition in the world export market is desirable, and if multilateral non-discriminatory liberalization is politically impossible to negotiate, trade preferences might constitute a feasible second-best route to the more desirable objective. Incidentally, these two arguments point to quite different preferential systems, since the former stresses transfers of resources through higher prices, and the latter emphasizes the beneficent effects of competition in the market.

ARGUMENTS AGAINST TRADE PREFERENCES

Apart from ideological objections deriving from the principle of non-discrimination discussed above, the arguments against the preference proposal are of two broad sorts: that preferences would do relatively little to promote the exports of the developing countries, and that they would involve serious costs. The strength of the second argument obviously depends heavily on the validity of the first (which is discussed in the next section). For, clearly, costs can be considered high or low only in relation to benefits. Nevertheless, the nature of the costs deserves some independent discussion, since the argument from costs so frequently serves as an excuse for doing nothing.

Two kinds of cost have been advanced in argument against preferences: the administrative costs of operating a preferential system, and what may be called the "moral risks" of introducing the preferential principle.

The administrative costs would depend on the type of preferential system adopted, and would clearly increase with the degree to which preferences discriminated among developing countries and with the extent to which quotas were used to control trade. The addition to administrative costs entailed by preferences, however, may easily be exaggerated, given the overhead costs inherent in any customs system and the complexity of present tariff legislation. In this connection, it is worth recalling that in 1958 an expert group from the Organization of the European Economic Community (OEEC) found that it would be administratively feasible to associate the other European countries with the Common Market in a European Free Trade Area, in spite of the alleged insuperability of the "trade-deflection" problem.

The alleged moral risks are that preferences would create a strong vested interest against further multilateral trade liberalization, and that a preferential scheme would have to be approved by the United States Congress, which might take the opportunity to indulge in an orgy of domestic protectionism, favoritism towards particular developing countries, and retaliation against particular developed countries. The vested-interest argument is not very persuasive, since the developing countries having the interest would not be directly represented in the policy-making of the developed countries giving the preferences; and once the preferences were established the economic foolishness of discriminating against efficient producers in developed countries in favor of inefficient producers in developing countries might generate public pressure for lower tariffs all around. Further, the establishment of preferences would probably have to be accompanied by the development of adjustment assistance techniques for the domestic producers adversely affected by the new competition, and so pave the way for a bolder assault on tariff barriers.

The fear of what the United States Congress might do if offered the chance to jettison the principle of non-discrimination is a powerful force in American official thinking on commercial policy questions. The dangers can be amply illustrated by reference to the favoritism and the lobbying activity that accompany the fixing of the United States sugar import quotas. It is, however, both insulting and defeatist to regard the Congress merely as an irresponsible collection of narrow self-seeking politicians who cannot be trusted to legislate in the public interest. Congress in the past has been inspired to heights of true statesmanship—and not always in reluctant submission to the *force majeure* of able Presidential leadership—and it has shown itself capable of great generosity toward the less-developed countries. There is no real justification for assuming that it could not be induced to accept a preferential system that would genuinely help the less-developed countries.

TRADE PREFERENCES AND DEVELOPMENT

The crucial question is how far trade preferences could serve to promote economic development, or, more concretely and manageably, to promote the industrial exports of the less-developed countries. The most careful statement available of the view that preferences would do relatively little in this respect has been provided by Professor Gardner Patterson, in the article referred to earlier.

Patterson starts from the estimate that the average *ad valorem* tariff rate on manufactured goods in the advanced industrial countries is now about 15 per cent, and he assumes that the Kennedy Round of negotiations will be successful eventually in reducing such tariffs by about 35 per cent, to an average of 10 per cent. He then remarks that the advanced countries would be reluctant to give preferences resulting in "zero duties," and assumes a 50 per cent preference, yielding a preference margin of 5 per cent. Finally, he concludes that the industries in which a preference margin of 5 to 7 per cent would enable less-developed countries to take markets away from domestic and developed-country competitors, excluding those cases where a non-discriminatory tariff reduction would do as well, constitute a very short list indeed.

Even on its own terms, this argument leaves something to be desired as an assessment of the potentialities of preferences. First, as intervening events have shown, it is premature to take credit for a successful conclusion of the Kennedy Round. Second, it is invalid to use the assumption that only limited preferences will be given, to prove that preferences would have little economic effect. Third, it is not legitimate to exclude commodities for which non-discriminatory tariff reductions would do as well, since there is no reason to expect that such reductions will, in fact, take place.

EFFECTIVE TARIFF RATES

The fundamental objections to this analysis, however, relate to the use of nominal tariff rates to assess the barriers to trade inherent in existing tariff schedules. Tariff averages conceal the fact that tariff rates tend to be significantly higher than average on the consumer goods in which the developing countries have an actual or potential exporting capacity. Of much greater importance, the protective effects of tariff schedules on domestic production cannot be evaluated by reference to the duty rate on commodities. They must be measured by the effective rates of protection of the value added in the production processes that turn out the goods.

Imported goods are used in a modern industrial economy both as raw materials for domestic production (inputs) and as substitutes for home-produced goods. Tariffs on imported substitutes provide protection to domestic producers, but tariffs on imported inputs constitute a tax on domestic producers. To arrive at the net protective effect, it is necessary to calculate the net subsidy (or possibly tax) on value added in an industry provided by the entire tariff schedule. When this is done, it turns out that effective protection rates on manufactures are typically one and one-half times to twice as high as the nominal tariff rates, and that they rise progressively with the stage of production or degree of fabrication of the product.[5]

This fundamental point is illustrated by the data in Table 7.1, which draws on a recent empirical study by Professor Bela Balassa. This demonstrates fully that the order of magnitude of the barriers that less-developed countries have to face in competing with producers in developed countries is not the 15 per cent average cited by Patterson, but rather something in the neighborhood of 25 to 50 per cent, and in particular cases even higher. It is in this context that the stimulus to industrial exports that might be provided by preferences needs to be evaluated.

As is well known, preferences have two sorts of effect on trade. They create trade by enabling the preference-receiving producers to compete more effectively with domestic producers, and they divert trade from non-preferred to preferred suppliers. In the context of the effective protection concept, the trade-creating incentive might be substantially greater than the calculated effective protection rates would suggest. For the preference might reduce the subsidy to domestic production given by the tariff on the finished good, without reducing the taxation of domestic production implicit in the tariffs levied on other goods used as inputs in the production process. The potential importance of this point is illustrated by Table 7.2, which presents the implicit rates of taxation by national tariff schedules of domestic value added for the industries of Table 7.1, or the extent to which domestic value added would have to cost less than foreign value added for the industry to be able to compete if no tariff were levied on its product.

With respect to trade diversion, the calculated effective protection rates are irrelevant, since foreign producers do not pay domestic tariffs on their raw materials. Here the relevant consideration indicated by the effective protection concept is that the incentive to trade diversion is measured not by the extent to which it allows the price of the preferred producer's product to be higher than his rival's, but by the extent to which it allows

TABLE 7.1.—NOMINAL AND EFFECTIVE TARIFF RATES ON MANUFACTURES OF EXPORT INTEREST TO DEVELOPING COUNTRIES
(In per cent)

Class	Products	United States Nominal	United States Effective	U. K. Nominal	U. K. Effective	E. E. C. Nominal	E. E. C. Effective	Sweden Nominal	Sweden Effective	Japan Nominal	Japan Effective
1. Manufactures where main inputs are natural raw materials	Thread and yarn	11.7	31.8	10.5	27.9	2.9	3.6	2.2	4.3	2.7	1.4
	Wood products including furniture	12.8	26.4	14.8	25.5	15.1	28.6	6.8	14.5	19.5	33.9
	Leather	9.6	25.7	14.9	34.3	7.3	18.3	7.0	21.7	19.9	59.0
	Synthetic materials	18.6	33.5	12.7	17.1	12.0	17.6	7.2	12.9	19.1	32.1
	Other chemical material	12.3	26.6	19.4	39.2	11.3	20.5	4.5	9.7	12.2	22.6
	CLASS AVERAGE	8.8	17.6	11.1	23.1	7.6	12.0	3.0	5.3	11.4	23.8
2. Intermediate goods at high levels of fabrication	Textile fabrics	24.1	50.6	20.7	42.2	17.6	44.4	12.7	33.4	19.7	48.8
	Rubber goods	9.3	16.1	20.2	43.9	15.1	33.6	10.8	26.1	12.9	23.6
	Plastic articles	21.0	27.0	17.9	30.1	20.6	30.0	15.0	25.5	24.9	35.5
	Miscellaneous chemical products	12.6	15.6	15.4	16.7	11.6	13.1	2.5	0.0	16.8	22.9
	Ingots and other primary steel forms	10.6	106.7	11.1	98.9	6.4	28.9	3.8	40.0	13.0	58.9
	Metal manufactures	14.4	28.5	19.0	35.9	14.0	25.6	8.4	16.2	18.1	27.7
	CLASS AVERAGE	15.2	28.6	17.2	34.3	13.3	28.3	8.5	20.8	16.6	34.5
3. Consumer goods	Hosiery	25.6	48.7	25.4	49.7	18.6	41.3	17.6	42.4	26.0	60.8
	Clothing	25.1	35.9	25.5	40.5	18.5	25.1	14.0	21.1	25.2	42.4
	Other textile articles	19.0	22.7	24.5	42.4	22.0	38.8	13.0	21.2	14.8	13.0
	Shoes	16.6	25.3	24.0	36.2	19.9	33.0	14.0	22.8	29.5	45.1
	Leather goods other than shoes	15.5	24.5	18.7	26.4	14.7	24.3	12.2	20.7	23.6	33.6
	Bicycles and motorcycles	14.4	26.1	22.4	39.2	20.9	39.7	17.1	35.8	25.0	45.0
	Precision instruments	21.4	32.2	25.7	44.2	13.5	24.2	6.6	9.1[a]	23.2	38.5
	Sports goods, toys, jewelry, et cetera	25.0	41.8	22.3	35.6	17.9	26.6	10.6	16.6	21.6	31.2
	CLASS AVERAGE	17.5	25.9	23.8	40.4	17.8	30.9	12.4	23.9	27.5	50.5
4. Investment goods	Non-electrical machinery	11.0	16.1	16.1	21.2	10.3	12.2	8.8	11.6	16.8	21.4
	Electrical machinery	12.2	18.1	19.7	30.0	14.5	21.5	10.7	17.7	18.1	25.3
	CLASS AVERAGE	10.3	13.9	17.0	23.0	11.7	15.0	8.5	12.1	17.1	22.0
	AVERAGE: 34 manufactured goods	11.6	20.0	15.5	27.8	11.9	18.6	6.8	12.5	16.2	29.5

Source: Balassa (1965, Tables 1 and 5).
a. Erroneously given as 14.9 in Professor Balassa's original Table.

TABLE 7.2—IMPLICIT RATES OF TAXATION OF DOMESTIC VALUE ADDED IN MANUFACTURING
(In per cent)

Class	Products	U.S.A.	U.K.	E.E.C.	Sweden	Japan
1. Manufactures where main inputs are natural raw materials	Thread and yarn	10.0	9.6	6.8	3.6	8.2
	Wood products including furniture	2.7	8.1	5.7	1.0	10.4
	Leather	6.3	15.4	6.0	1.6	7.3
	Synthetic materials	15.4	16.3	14.0	6.1	18.2
	Other chemical material	5.8	11.9	9.2	2.1	9.5
2. Intermediate goods at high levels of fabrication	Textile fabrics	24.7	22.5	10.6	6.3	12.8
	Rubber goods	9.7	12.2	8.3	3.9	12.2
	Plastic articles	25.5	14.7	21.5	12.0	26.8
	Miscellaneous chemical products	12.4	17.5	12.7	5.6	14.4
	Ingots and other primary steel forms	11.1	24.4	42.2	2.2	85.5
	Metal manufactures	8.4	12.8	10.3	5.3	18.7
	Hosiery	18.7	17.1	7.7	3.9	7.6
	Clothing	31.9	28.4	24.9	16.7	25.7
	Other textile articles	34.9	31.8	27.9	18.2	31.9
3. Consumer goods	Shoes	10.0	14.9	9.3	7.0	17.7
	Leather goods other than shoes	12.4	18.1	10.7	8.4	22.6
	Bicycles and motorcycles	11.8	19.8	15.3	9.2	20.8
	Precision instruments	6.7	2.5	0.4	2.9	3.7
	Sports goods, toys, jewelry, et cetera	8.2	9.0	9.2	4.6	12.0
4. Investment goods	Non-electrical machinery	6.4	11.7	8.8	6.4	12.9
	Electrical machinery	4.9	7.2	5.9	2.5	8.9

Source: Computed from Table 7.1 with the help of value-added coefficients kindly supplied by Professor Balassa.

him to charge more for the value added to those inputs that are equally available in the world market to all competitors. Since value added typically runs somewhat under one-half of sales value, one might guess that the premium on value added given by a preference would be roughly about twice the margin of preference on the commodity produced. Detailed calculations of the effective rates of preference that would be entailed by a 100 per cent preference given to developing countries in the major industrial-country markets for the manufactures listed in Tables 7.1 and 7.2 are presented in Table 7.3. On the assumption employed in constructing the tables—that the value-added coefficients are the same for all countries—the figures in the three tables are related as follows: effective preference rate (Table 7.3) equals effective protection rate (Table 7.1) plus implicit tax rate (Table 7.2).[6]

Moreover, since in the long run, capital, like the raw materials used in production, is freely mobile between countries, preferences should probably be conceived essentially as paying a premium for the use of the preference-receiving nation's labor over the labor of its competitors. On this basis, a small margin of preference on the finished product might amount to a very high premium indeed on labor cost. Concretely, small margins of preference might have a powerful effect in inducing enterprises domiciled in advanced countries to establish production facilities in developing countries in order to circumvent the tariffs levied on their direct exports to other developed countries.

Analysis on effective protection lines, therefore, indicates that, within existing tariff structures, trade preferences for developing countries, even if not at the 100 per cent level, might provide powerful incentives for the expansion of their industrial exports. Would the developing countries, however, be able to respond effectively to such export opportunities? As already mentioned, their price and cost levels are often well above world market levels, and frequently the excess is substantially greater than the tariff-created excess of domestic over world market prices in the developed countries. In such cases, even 100 per cent preferences could not offset the competitive disadvantage. It would appear that preferences would be of no avail unless they were accompanied by drastic reform of the currency-overvaluation and protectionist import-substitution policies that make these countries unable to compete in world markets.

TABLE 7.3.—NOMINAL AND EFFECTIVE PREFERENCE RATES ON MANUFACTURES OF EXPORT INTEREST TO DEVELOPING COUNTRIES CONFERRED BY 100 PER CENT PREFERENCES GRANTED BY DEVELOPED COUNTRIES (*In per cent*)

Class	Products	United States Nominal	United States Effective	U. K. Nominal	U. K. Effective	E. E. C. Nominal	E. E. C. Effective	Sweden Nominal	Sweden Effective	Japan Nominal	Japan Effective
1. Manufactures where main inputs are natural raw materials	Thread and yarn	11.7	41.8	10.5	37.5	2.9	10.4	2.2	7.9	2.7	9.6
	Wood products including furniture	12.8	29.1	14.8	33.6	15.1	34.3	6.8	15.5	19.5	44.3
	Leather	9.6	32.0	14.9	49.7	7.3	24.3	7.0	23.3	19.9	66.3
	Synthetic materials	18.6	48.9	12.7	33.4	12.0	31.6	7.2	19.0	19.1	50.3
	Other chemical material	12.3	32.4	19.4	51.1	11.3	29.7	4.5	11.8	12.2	32.1
2. Intermediate goods at high levels of fabrication	Textile fabrics	24.1	75.3	20.7	64.7	17.6	55.0	12.7	39.7	19.7	61.6
	Rubber goods	9.3	25.8	20.2	56.1	15.1	41.9	10.8	30.0	12.9	35.8
	Plastic articles	21.0	52.5	17.9	44.8	20.6	51.5	15.0	37.5	24.9	62.3
	Miscellaneous chemical products	12.6	28.0	15.4	34.2	11.6	25.8	2.5	5.6	16.8	37.3
	Ingots and other primary steel forms	10.6	117.8	11.1	123.3	6.4	71.1	3.8	42.2	13.0	144.4
	Metal manufactures	14.4	36.9	19.0	48.7	14.0	35.9	8.4	21.5	18.1	46.4
3. Consumer goods	Hosiery	25.6	67.4	25.4	66.8	18.6	49.0	17.6	46.3	26.0	68.4
	Clothing	25.1	67.8	25.5	68.9	18.5	50.0	14.0	37.8	25.2	68.1
	Other textile articles	19.0	57.6	24.5	74.2	22.0	66.7	13.0	39.4	14.8	44.9
	Shoes	16.6	35.3	24.0	51.1	19.9	42.3	14.0	29.8	29.5	62.8
	Leather goods other than shoes	15.5	36.9	18.7	44.5	14.7	35.0	12.2	29.1	23.6	56.2
	Bicycles and motorcycles	14.4	37.9	22.4	59.0	20.9	55.0	17.1	45.0	25.0	65.8
	Precision instruments	21.4	38.9	25.7	46.7	13.5	24.6	6.6	12.0	23.2	42.2
	Sports goods, toys, jewelry, et cetera	25.0	50.0	22.3	44.6	17.9	35.8	10.6	21.2	21.6	43.2
4. Investment goods	Non-electrical machinery	11.0	22.5	16.1	32.9	10.3	21.0	8.8	18.0	16.8	34.3
	Electrical machinery	12.2	23.0	19.7	37.2	14.5	27.4	10.7	20.2	18.1	34.2

Source: Computed from Table 7.1 with use of value-added coefficients kindly supplied by Professor Balassa.

TRADE PREFERENCES AND
TRADE LIBERALIZATION

Preferential trading arrangements may be designed for either of two contrasting purposes: to extend the area of protection, or to extend the area of free competition. The spirit of the demand for trade preferences voiced at the first UNCTAD conference was definitely protectionist, and so, in the main, has been the response of those in the developed countries who favor the proposal. Preferential arrangements for less-developed countries could be devised, however, that would be trade-liberalizing in spirit. Such arrangements would seek to maximize trade creation and to minimize trade diversion. This would require concentrating the preferences on products in which the developed countries have a visible comparative disadvantage and the less-developed countries have an established or potential comparative advantage. Broadly speaking, it would mean concentrating on products demanding only unskilled or semi-skilled labor and relatively little capital, and which employ a relatively simple technology. The objective would be a "new international division of labor," to be achieved by a planned transfer of such industries from the developed countries to the less-developed countries.

The process would be politically unpopular on both sides. The developed countries would have to devise policies for the planned contraction or extermination of established protected industries. The less-developed countries would have to give up their aspirations for industrial self-sufficiency. However, it would contribute both to increased efficiency in the utilization of the world's human and material resources and to the economic development of the less-developed world. There would be no need to rely on the infant-industry argument; the preferences could be installed as a permanent feature of world trading relationships (subject to reduction by future non-discriminatory trade liberalization), thus avoiding the complexities of administering temporary preferences.

NOTES

1. This chapter first appeared as an article in *Lloyds Bank Review*, No. 80, April, 1966, pp. 1-18, and is reprinted here, with only minor editorial changes, by permission of the author and the editor of *Lloyds Bank Review*.

2. The academic reasoning behind the official American position has been presented with admirable clarity and balance by Professor Gardner Patterson (1965).

3. Pincus (1965, Ch. 5) estimates that conventional measures of aid overstate its real cost to the donors by 70 to 100 per cent.

4. This point is implicitly accepted in the specially favorable treatment accorded to the protectionist policies of the less-developed contracting parties to GATT.

5. A hypothetical example may help to show how this conclusion is reached. Suppose a commodity has a world price of $1.00, of which $0.60 represents raw materials and $0.40 the value added by foreign producers. Assume imports of the commodity are subject to a tariff of 15 per cent, while domestic producers have to pay a tariff of 5 per cent on their raw materials. The domestic producer can thus incur a maximum expenditure of $1.15 to produce the commodity. How much more can he spend on value added than the foreigner? This is the effective rate of protection.

	Foreign Product	Domestic Product
	$	$
Domestic market price	1.15	1.15
Price to producer	1.00	1.15
Cost of materials	0.60	0.63
Price chargeable for value added	0.40	0.52

The excess of domestic over foreign value added is $0.12, which, as a percentage of foreign value added is 30 per cent. This is the *effective protection rate*, equal to the difference between the gross subsidy on value added provided by the tariff on the final product ($.15/.40 = 37\frac{1}{2}$ per cent) and the *implicit tax on value added* as a result of the tariff on raw material ($.03/.40 = 7\frac{1}{2}$ per cent).

6. In terms of the example given in footnote 5, if the foreigner were allowed free entry, the domestic producer would have a negative protection of *minus* $7\frac{1}{2}$ per cent. If one foreigner were allowed free entry, but another not, the former would have an *effective preference rate* over the latter of $37\frac{1}{2}$ per cent.

LITERATURE CITED

BALASSA, BELA. 1965. Tariff protection in industrial countries: an evaluation. J. Political Econ. LXXIII(6): 573-594.

PATTERSON, GARDNER. 1965. Would tariff preferences help economic development? Lloyds Bank Review. No. 76: 18-30.

PINCUS, JOHN, 1965. Economic aid and international cost sharing. Johns Hopkins Press. Baltimore, Md.

8

A Dynamic Linear Programming
Model for Development Planning

Max R. Langham

Hope for economic development at the area or regional level
rests on the intra-area (intra- and inter-farm) reorganization
of resources with some minimal assistance from inter-area
resource shifts. Development policies, whether for an underdeveloped country or for a low-income area of a developed country,
generally recognize this need for resource adjustment. The necessary
kinds and amounts of intra- and inter-area resource adjustments
are less well-recognized by policy.

Since development does deal with resource allocation over time,
dynamic linear programming offers an approach to a quantitative
determination of the necessary resource adjustments for the development of agricultural areas.

This chapter conceptualizes the development process at the
farm level—a very disaggregative approach. There are, to my
knowledge, no applications of dynamic linear programming to
problems at the national level. National policies are of prime
importance in the overall development process since they establish
the institutional framework within which development at the farm
level must take place. Models such as the one in this chapter can
contribute to national policy-making by providing a means of
comparing alternate policies. Other studies using a dynamic linear

programming approach at the farm or regional level have recently been presented by Luan and Baker (1966) and Dean and De Benedictis (1964). Coffey (1966) developed static linear programming models for each of three periods (1963-64, 1980, and 2000) to determine the feasibilty of transforming Peru's traditional agriculture.

In this chapter the development problem is formulated as a single linear programming problem in which production periods are linked and a single objective function is maximized. The method, therefore, is dynamic in the Hicksian sense in that inputs and outputs are dated. An alternative formulation, recursive programming, has been developed by Day (1963). By using Day's approach, an infinite sequence of linear programming problems is solved, in which adjustment from one time period to the next is constrained within certain defined limits by flexibility constraints.

The method proposed in this chapter is also non-stochastic in that it assumes the economic development process is one that changes over time in a certainty manner. In contrast, a stochastic model is one whose changes over time are subject to random fluctuations.

THE MODEL

Some data from British Honduras have been used to provide an empirical illustration of the model.[1]* The model covers three production periods and is presented in simplified form in Table 8.1. In this table, only one production alternative (corn), one consumption requirement (again corn), and one labor restriction is presented during the first period. In addition, the alternative to fertilized corn is presented in the second and third periods.

The data were collected from Maya Indians following a traditional agriculture on the San Antonio reservation.[2]

Alternatives for Use of Resources.—Production alternatives in traditional agriculture include corn, corn and beans (double cropped), rice, and hogs. The rice may be harvested by hand or with a government machine for a cost of $3.60 per acre.[3] Each enterprise provides an input to its respective balance equation. This input, when transferred for sale by the appropriate transfer activity, adds capital for the subsequent production period.

*Notes for this chapter begin on page 153.

TABLE 8.1.—A SIMPLIFIED PRESENTATION OF THE DYNAMIC LINEAR PROGRAMMING MODEL FOR DEVELOPMENT PLANNING, BRITISH HONDURAS, 1965.

Resource or restraint	Unit	Resource level	Type of restraint	Year 1				
				Corn prod. traditional (acre)	Corn consumption (cwt.)	Labor hire (man-day)	Capital borrowing (dollar)	Capital transfer to year 2 (dollars)
Year 1								
Capital	dollars	200	≥	.40		2.00	−1	1
Feb.–Mar. labor	man-days	67.6	≥	9.0		−1		
Corn consumption	pounds	2350	≥	.0426	100			
Capital borrowing	dollars	250	≤				1	
Year 2								
Capital	dollars	0	≥				1.12	−1
Feb.–Mar. labor	man-days	67.6	≥					
Corn consumption	pounds	0	≥		−100			
Capital borrowing	dollars	250	≤					
Fertilizer	cwt.	0	=					
Year 3								
Capital	dollars	0	≥					
Feb.–Mar. labor	man-days	67.6	≥					
Corn consumption	pounds	0	≥		−100			
Capital borrowing	dollars	250	≤					
Fertilizer	cwt.	0	=					
Corn balance, yr. 1	pounds	0	=	−1,100	100			
Corn balance, yr. 2	pounds	0	=					
Corn balance, yr. 3	pounds	0	=					
Corn selling	cwt.	0	=	−.40		−2.00	−1	
Profit	dollars	0	=					

(Continued)

Table 8.1 (Continued)

Resource or restraint	Unit	Resource level	Type of restraint	Year 2						
				Corn prod. trad. (acre)	Corn prod. fertilized (acre)	Corn consumption (cwt.)	Labor hire (man-day)	Capital borrowing (dollar)	Capital transfer to year 3 (dollar)	Fertilizer purchase (cwt.)
Year 1										
Capital	dollars	200	≥							
Feb.-Mar. labor	man-days	67.6	≥							
Corn consumption	pounds	2350	≥							
Capital borrowing	dollars	250	≤							
Year 2										
Capital	dollars	0	≥	.40	.40	.0426	2.00	−1	1	10.25
Feb.-Mar. labor	man-days	67.6	≥	9.0	9.0		−1			
Corn consumption	pounds	0	≥			100				
Capital borrowing	dollars	250	≤					1		
Fertilizer	cwt.	0	=		1.5					−1
Year 3										
Capital	dollars	0	≥					1.12	−1	
Feb.-Mar. labor	man-days	67.6	≥							
Corn consumption	pounds	0	≥							
Capital borrowing	dollars	250	≤							
Fertilizer	cwt.	0	=							
Corn balance, yr. 1	pounds	0	=	−1,100						
Corn balance, yr. 2	pounds	0	=		−2,000					
Corn balance, yr. 3	pounds	0	=			100				
Corn selling	cwt.	0	=							
Profit	dollars	0	=	−.357	−.357		−1.79	−.893		−9.15

Table 8.1 (Continued)

Resource or restraint	Unit	Resource level	Type of restraint	Year 3					
				Corn prod. trad. (acre)	Corn prod. fertilized (acre)	Corn consumption (cwt.)	Labor hire (man-day)	Capital borrowing (dollar)	Fertilizer purchase (cwt.)
Year 1									
Capital	dollars	200	≥						
Feb.-Mar. labor	man-days	67.6	≥						
Corn consumption	pounds	2350	≥						
Capital borrowing	dollars	250	≥						
Year 2									
Capital	dollars	0	≥						
Feb.-Mar. labor	man-days	67.6	≥						
Corn consumption	pounds	0	≥						
Capital borrowing	dollars	250	≥						
Fertilizer	cwt.	0	=						
Year 3									
Capital	dollars	0	≥	.40	.40	.0426	2.00	−1	10.25
Feb.-Mar. labor	man-days	67.6	≥	9.0	9.0		−1		
Corn consumption	pounds	0	≥			100			
Capital borrowing	dollars	250	≥					1	
Fertilizer	cwt.	0	=		1.5				−1
Corn balance, yr. 1	pounds	0	=	−1,100					
Corn balance, yr. 2	pounds	0	=		−2,000				
Corn balance, yr. 3	pounds	0	=			100			
Corn selling	cwt.	0	=						
Profit	dollars	0	=	−.319	−.319		−1.59	−.797	−8.17

(Continued)

Table 8.1 (Continued)

Resource or restraint	Unit	Resource level	Type of restraint	Corn Transfer			Corn selling (cwt.)
				Year 1 (cwt.)	Year 2 (cwt.)	Year 3 (cwt.)	
Year 1							
Capital	dollars	200	≤				
Feb.-Mar. labor	man-days	67.6	≤				
Corn consumption	pounds	2350	≥				
Capital borrowing	dollars	250	≤				
Year 2							
Capital	dollars	0	≤	−1.62			
Feb.-Mar. labor	man-days	67.6	≤				
Corn consumption	pounds	0	≥				
Capital borrowing	dollars	250	≤				
Fertilizer	cwt.	0	=				
Year 3							
Capital	dollars	0	≤				
Feb.-Mar. labor	man-days	67.6	≤		−1.62		
Corn consumption	pounds	0	≥				
Capital borrowing	dollars	250	≤				
Fertilizer	cwt.	0	=				
Corn balance, yr. 1	pounds	0	=	100			
Corn balance, yr. 2	pounds	0	=		100		
Corn balance, yr. 3	pounds	0	=			100	
Corn selling	cwt.	0	=	−89.3	−79.7	−71.2	100
Profit	dollars	0	=				1.62

An improvement in technology was permitted during the second and third production periods. The crops could be fertilized at a rate of 150 pounds (18-46-0)[4] per acre at a cost of $10.25 per hundred pounds.[5] One man-day of effort in the second labor period was required to learn about fertilization.

Corn, beans, and rice yield 1,100, 600, and 1,200 pounds per acre, respectively, when unfertilized and 2,000, 845, and 2,180 pounds when fertilized.

Conceptually, one would like to have adequate data to permit the inclusion of more opportunities to adopt improved technologies. With such data, the planning horizon in the model could be extended. One would, of course, need to be realistic in making time requirements to adopt the technology consistent with the agricultural educational program carried on in the country.

The only livestock alternative included in the model is hog production. Only labor to haul corn from the *milpa* (the name given the plot of land farmed by the *milpero*) to the house is required to produce hogs. It is assumed that the women and children do the other work. It is assumed that a sow has one litter of four pigs. Pigs are marketed at an age at which they weigh 120 pounds.

Most Indian families own a few chickens. These are kept mainly for family consumption and are not included in the model.

Objective in the Use of Resources.—The objective of the model is to maximize the present value of net returns over the three-year planning horizon. Net returns as used in the model means returns to labor and capital above all production and living expenses. Returns, therefore, are actually accumulations of liquid capital assets.

It was assumed that expenses were paid at the first of each production period with interest on borrowed money due at the end of each production period. It was further assumed that consumption was from production and that production for a given period was forthcoming at the end of the period.

Since the objective was to maximize present value of net returns, production at the end of year one was discounted one period, year two, two periods, and year three, three periods. An effective interest rate of 12 per cent was used in discounting future production. Quantities produced, rather than prices, were discounted to facilitate variable price programming.

Assumed base prices were $3.00, $6.03, $13.70, and $17.00 per hundred pounds for corn, rice, beans, and hogs, respectively. These prices were based on average prices paid by the Marketing Board in Punta Gorda in 1964. Charges for bags and transportation to Punta Gorda were $1.38, $.38, and $.38 per hundred pounds for corn, rice, and beans, respectively, and $.40 per head for hogs. The additional one dollar marketing charge for corn was a labor charge for backing the corn from the *milpero* to San Antonio.

Restraints on Attainment of Objective.—Land on the reservation is non-restrictive, and an Indian can farm as much as his labor and capital resources will permit.

A capital supply of $200 is available, and an additional $250 may be borrowed. Borrowed money must be repaid by the end of the planning period. Capital not used in one period may be transferred to a subsequent production period.

A labor supply of 1.3 men per family was assumed. Each man works about twenty-six days per month. Total annual labor requirements for production were expressed in man-day units and distributed over six two-month periods. Additional labor could be hired in each two-month period at a cost of $2.00 per day.

Four household consumption requirements were specified. These were 1.71 pigs, 2,350 pounds of corn [1.31 pounds (Steggerda, 1941, 123) per person per day for a family of 4.9 persons], 60 pounds of beans, 530 pounds of rice, and $150 cash. The consumption restraints could be set up on the basis of programmed satisfactory minimum diets. However, the requirements here were based on estimated actual consumption of the food items. The money requirement was for purchased food items and other needs not furnished by household labor. One-fourth man-day of labor was required to haul 100 pounds of corn for consumption from the *milpa* to the house.

Consumption in year one sets the consumption levels in subsequent production periods. In the model, consumption requirements were assumed to be static. This assumption could be relaxed by changing the magnitude of coefficients at the intersections of rows representing consumption requirements in subsequent years and the columns representing consumption in year one.

Balance equations for the four farm products were introduced to allow for variable price programming of these commodities and to permit variable resource programming of the consumption requirements. In addition, the balance equations and commodity transfer activities permit variable resource programming of capital.

Variable resource programming on the capital restriction in year one permits the determination of the firm's demand for capital in each production period. Similarly, parametric programming on the price of a commodity permits the determination of supply function for the commodity in each production period.

Household-Firm Interrelationships.—The model provides a method of looking at the interrelationships between the households and the firm. In an underdeveloped country one could determine the effect of household consumption behavior on firm growth.

For low-income areas of developed nations, household consumption propensities may outweigh opportunities for capital in agricultural production. If so, agricultural development may be a poor choice of development policy. Encouraging out-migration of the population to a more developed area may offer the best policy alternative. The model will at least show the sacrifices which the household must make in order to permit development of the productive capacity of the farm firm.

The Results

Cash living costs above basic home-produced foods were set at what was considered a minimum level of $150 per family (4.9 persons) per year. This requirement was varied upward to determine the effect of family living expenses on discounted net returns (Fig. 8.1) and hence, the firm's ability to grow. Net returns were $1,250 for the three-year period with cash living cost of $150. A living cost of $334 per year put the firm in a static position with respect to growth, and living expenses above $372 made the situation completely impossible for the firm.

Tables 8.2, 8.3, and 8.4 provide information from the solution when annual family living expenses were at $334 per year and the firm was in a static condition with respect to growth.

Most of the family labor was utilized with some outside labor hired during the critical first period. Acreages tilled ranged from 11.3 in the first year to 8.5 during the second. Rice was the only cash crop.

Since labor hiring was permitted, capital was the only effective restraint. The results indicate very high marginal value productivities for capital, and the necessary additions to prices in Table 8.3 indicate a stable solution.

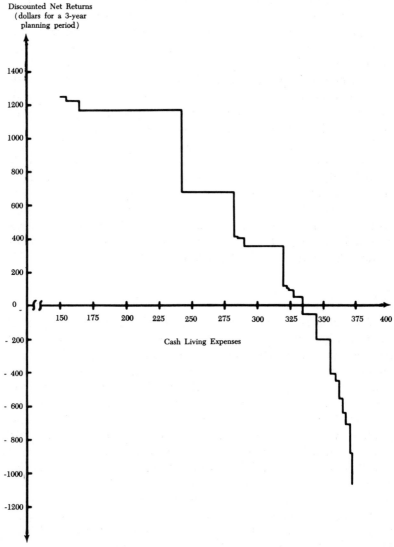

FIGURE 8.1. Discounted net returns as a function of annual cash living expenses of the family—labor hiring an alternative.

Tables 8.5, 8.6, and 8.7 present information contained in the solution of the model when annual family living expenses were held at $150 and labor hiring was not permitted. Fewer acres were tilled under this situation, and net returns were about one-

TABLE 8.2.—OPTIMUM SOLUTION WITH ANNUAL CASH LIVING EXPENSES OF $334[a] PER FAMILY, LABOR HIRING AN ALTERNATIVE

Activity	Level of activity		
	Year 1	Year 2	Year 3
Real			
Corn (acres)	3.0		
Corn, fertilized (acres)	b	1.6	1.6
Corn and beans (acres)	.1		
Corn and beans, fertilized (acres)	b	.1	.1
Rice (acres)	3.0		
Rice, custom harvested (acres)	5.2		
Rice, fertilized (acres)	b	5.7	5.3
Rice, fertilized and custom harvested (acres)	b	1.1	1.9
Hogs (litters)	.4	.4	.4
ACRES TILLED	11.3	8.5	8.9
Disposal			
February-March labor (days)	−36[c]	−10[c]	−15[c]
April-May labor (days)	− 4[c]	4	0
June-July labor (days)	2	16	12
August-September labor (days)	6	12	10
October-November labor (days)	0	0	0
December-January labor (days)	38	15	18
Borrowing capacity (dollars)	0	0	250
Rice selling (cwt.)	94	142	153

a. Present value of net returns were zero when annual cash family living costs were $334.
b. This activity was not an alternative in Year 1.
c. Negative figures represent the amount of labor hired.

TABLE 8.3.—NECESSARY ADDITIONS TO PRICE TO MAKE CROPS NOT PRODUCED ENTER THE SOLUTION, ANNUAL FAMILY CASH LIVING EXPENSES OF $334, LABOR HIRING AN ALTERNATIVE

Crop	Unit	Dollars per unit	
		Year 2	Year 3
Corn	acre	8.27	7.30
Corn and beans	acre	81.55	36.41
Rice	acre	13.59	12.28
Rice, custom harvested	acre	13.59	12.28

TABLE 8.4.—Marginal value productivities of scarce resources, annual cash family living expenses of $334, labor hiring an alternative

Resource	Unit	Value per unit in dollars		
		Year 1	Year 2	Year 3
February-March labor	day	16.58	9.49	3.12
April-May labor	day	16.58	0	3.12
October-November labor	day	5.43	3.11	1.02
Capital	dollar	7.29	3.85	.77
Capital borrowing	dollar	1.98	2.10	0

half of what they were when labor hiring was permitted. Rice was the only cash crop in year one and rice and beans were cash crops in years two and three. First-period labor was the most scarce resource (Table 8.7). The marginal value productivity of capital is net since the model replaces each dollar expended.

The necessary additions to price presented in Table 8.6 indicate that the solution was quite stable.

Tables 8.8, 8.9, and 8.10 present information contained in the

TABLE 8.5.—Optimum solution with annual cash living expenses of $150 per family, labor hiring not an alternative[a]

Activity	Level of activity		
	Year 1	Year 2	Year 3
Real			
Corn (acres)	3.0		
Corn, fertilized (acres)	b	.8	
Corn and beans (acres)	.1		
Corn and beans, fertilized (acres)	b	.9	1.7
Rice (acres)	4.2		
Rice, fertilized (acres)	b	5.1	4.6
Hogs (litters)	.4	.4	.4
Acres tilled	7.3	6.8	6.3
Disposal			
April-May labor (days)	23	12	11
June-July labor (days)	30	27	30
August-September labor (days)	28	23	27
October-November labor (days)	8	3	2
December-January labor (days)	27	12	10
Capital (dollars)	0	0	376
Borrowing capacity (dollars)	250	250	250
Bean selling (cwt.)	0	7	14
Rice selling (cwt.)	45	106	96

a. Present value of returns to labor and capital, $618.27.
b. The activity was not an alternative in Year 1.

solution of the model when annual living expenses were held at $150 and labor hiring was again permitted in each period. The solution was quite similar to the one just discussed except more acres were tilled. Considerable labor was hired in the first period.

TABLE 8.6.—NECESSARY ADDITIONS TO PRICE TO MAKE CROPS NOT PRODUCED ENTER THE SOLUTION, ANNUAL CASH FAMILY LIVING EXPENSES OF $150, LABOR HIRING NOT AN ALTERNATIVE

		Dollars per unit		
Crop	Unit	Year 1	Year 2	Year 3
Corn	acre		27.14	29.42
Corn, fertilized	acre	a		4.62
Corn and beans	acre		53.14	48.04
Rice	acre		27.53	27.17
Rice, custom harvested	acre	4.27	31.42	30.04
Rice, fertilized and custom harvested	acre	a	3.89	2.87

a. This activity was not an alternative in Year 1.

TABLE 8.7.—MARGINAL VALUE PRODUCTIVITIES OF SCARCE RESOURCES, ANNUAL CASH FAMILY LIVING EXPENSES OF $150, LABOR HIRING NOT AN ALTERNATIVE

		Value per unit in dollars		
Resource	Unit	Year 1	Year 2	Year 3
February-March labor	day	7.97	8.91	8.27
Capital	dollar	.19	.19	

Labor in the form of custom harvesting was also purchased in the October-November period.

Table 8.9 indicates that the solution was quite stable, and the marginal value productivities in Table 8.10 show, as must be the case when labor hiring is permitted, that capital was the most scarce resource.

The capital supply at the beginning of the planning period was varied from $200 to $573—the value at which the solution became unbounded. The marginal value productivities of capital at each capital level trace out a stepped demand function for capital in each period (Fig. 8.2). Regardless of the level of capital in period one, the availability of capital during the third year had reached an adequate level to make the demand for capital perfectly elastic at an interest rate of 21 per cent. Higher living expenses or the consideration of smaller capital supplies would have given all three functions a stepped structure. Since land was not restrictive and labor could be hired, capital was the only effective restraint. The perfectly elastic demand in period three indicates that capital had reached an unbounded level.

One would expect that the firm's ability to use capital would

TABLE 8.8—OPTIMUM SOLUTION WITH ANNUAL CASH LIVING EXPENSES OF $150 PER FAMILY, LABOR HIRING AN ALTERNATIVE[a]

Activity	Level of activity		
	Year 1	Year 2	Year 3
Real			
Corn (acres)	3.0		
Corn, fertilized (acres)	b	1.5	
Corn and beans (acres)	.1		
Corn and beans, fertilized (acres)	b	.2	1.7
Rice (acres)	2.8		
Rice, custom harvested (acres)	5.8		
Rice, fertilized (acres)	b	3.9	
Rice, fertilized and custom harvested (acres)	b	5.4	16.2
Hogs (litters)	.4	.4	.4
ACRES TILLED	11.7	11.0	17.9
Disposal			
February-March labor (days)	−39[c]	−34[c]	−104[c]
April-May labor (days)	− 7[c]	−17[c]	− 79[c]
June-July labor (days)	0	− 2[c]	− 51[c]
August-September labor (days)	4	0	− 34[c]
October-November labor (days)	0	0	− 13[c]
December-January labor (days)	40	30	52
Borrowing capacity (dollars)	172	250	250
Bean selling (cwt.)		1	14
Rice selling (cwt.)	98	198	348

a. Present value of returns to labor and capital was $1250.96.
b. This activity was not an alternative in Year 1.
c. Negative figure represents the amount of labor hired.

TABLE 8.9.—NECESSARY ADDITIONS TO PRICE TO MAKE CROPS NOT PRODUCED ENTER THE SOLUTION, ANNUAL CASH LIVING EXPENSES OF $150 PER FAMILY, LABOR HIRING AN ALTERNATIVE

Crop	Unit	Dollars per unit	
		Year 2	Year 3
Corn	acre	11.51	15.00
Corn, fertilized	acre		5.70
Corn and beans	acre	44.50	32.53
Rice	acre	25.21	33.36
Rice, custom harvested	acre	25.21	21.86
Rice, fertilized	acre		11.49

grow with the development process. This result was indicated by the increased demand for capital in year two.

Net returns as a function of capital supply at the beginning of the production period is presented in Figure 8.3.

Corn appears to have little potential as a cash crop (Fig. 8.4). A

TABLE 8.10.—MARGINAL VALUE PRODUCTIVITIES OF SCARCE RESOURCES, ANNUAL CASH LIVING EXPENSES OF $150 PER FAMILY, LABOR HIRING AN ALTERNATIVE

Resource	Unit	Value per unit in dollars		
		Year 1	Year 2	Year 3
February-March labor	day	5.97	3.55	2.02
April-May labor	day	5.97	3.55	2.02
June-July labor	day	.62	3.55	2.02
August-September labor	day		.04	2.02
October-November labor	day	1.95	1.15	2.02
Capital	dollars	1.98	.88	.21

price of seven dollars per hundred was required to make much corn available for market. This price was more than twice as high as that in 1964. Figure 8.4 indicates the type of information on firm supply response that the model provides during each year of the planning period.

A CRITIQUE OF THE MODEL

At the farm level, a development program may be broken down into two phases—an extensive phase in which the major objective is to assist families to obtain enough resources to earn a specified minimum level of living, and an intensive phase to provide for the improvement of individual holdings at some specified rate of growth greater than or equal to zero.

Initially, the program would be concerned with the extensive development of agriculture. During this phase the rate of growth of individual holdings would probably be held near the minimum in order to permit development resources to be used to provide all farm families with the minimum resources required for a specified minimum level of living.

As available land became occupied, development resources would be shifted to intensive development. This phase would be marked by such factors as more generous production credit, more educational services to management, and the adoption of more improved practices of production.

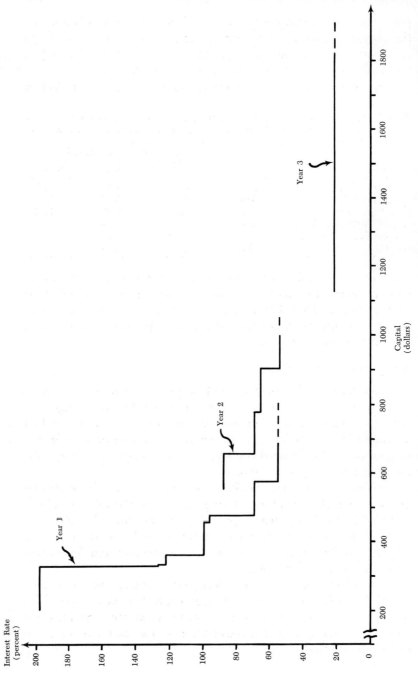

FIGURE 8.2. Firm's demand for capital during each year of the planning period—annual family living expenses of $150 and labor hiring as an alternative.

The approach discussed in this chapter does not have any particular advantage over a general linear programming model in establishing policy bench marks for the extensive phase of de-

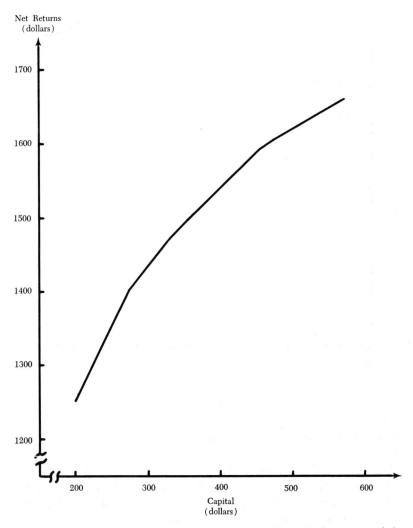

FIGURE 8.3. Relationship between the capital supply at the beginning of the planning period and discounted net returns to capital and labor for the three-year period—annual family living expenses of $150 and labor hiring as an alternative.

velopment. The general linear programming model could be used to do this by estimating minimum resource requirements for specified levels of income. However, the model used does facilitate computing bench mark estimates in the intensive phase. Credit,

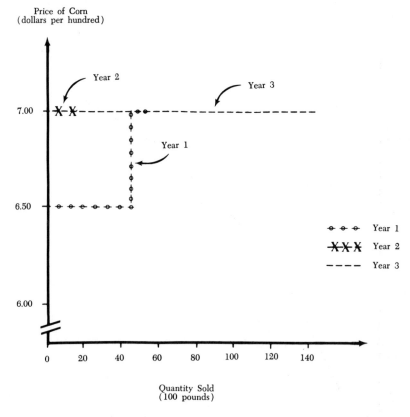

FIGURE 8.4. Firm's supply functions for corn during each year of the planning period—annual cash family living expenses of $334 and labor hiring as an alternative.

educational policy, and household decisions determine whether the farm is to grow and, if so, the rate at which it will grow.

The method has the following operational advantages in aiding the formulation of development programs:

1. It provides a normative solution. This type of solution appears desirable since policy needs bench marks to "shoot for" and from which to measure progress.

2. The method is dynamic and provides a path, if a path exists, for firm development.

3. The method shows, in part, the internal and external sacrifices required to reach a specified level of development. Internal sacrifices relate to those that must be made within the farm household whereas external sacrifices relate to those arising from redistribution of external resources. Knowledge of these sacrifices is essential to determine whether intra-area development is feasible and, if so, what rate of development can be expected.

4. The method determines the amount of labor resources which may be shifted from the farm to the non-farm sectors of the economy. This information will provide some basis for determining development needs in the non-farm sectors of the economy.

5. The method can provide estimates of "normative" firm supply functions for commodities over time. Such information in underdeveloped countries would be helpful in planning import and export requirements.

6. The method can provide estimates of "normative" firm demand functions for "key inputs" over time. This information would aid in the estimation of farm input subsidies (external sacrifices in [3] above) required for development.

The method presented here has three notable shortcomings. It does not simultaneously consider the interdependencies of the farm and non-farm sectors of the economy in the development process. It does not explicitly consider risk of various alternatives faced by the farm family. In underdeveloped countries where the risk of starvation may be very real, this limitation may be quite serious and may lead to frustrating (to the developers) gaps between policy norms and actual development progress. The method does not face the aggregation problem; i.e., it ignores the possibility that what is best for a given farm may not be best for the country.

In addition to the above shortcomings, data requirements for the model are quite demanding, especially in underdeveloped countries where data gaps are serious.

Because of lack of data of suitable quantity and quality, there has been some reluctance to apply methods that have rather strong data requirements to problems in underdeveloped areas. However, even with poor data it is still necessary to make the best decisions possible. A formal approach probably helps in this regard. Admittedly, much of the help may come indirectly from the insight into the problem provided by conceptualizing the formal framework. In addition, the formal approach points to the types of data needed for better decisions, and knowledge of the types of data needed is an important piece of information for a developing economy.

A somewhat different case for using a formal approach to a development problem has been advanced by Clayton (1963, 61): "It may perhaps be objected that the application of this technique is irrelevant to traditional peasant societies where the profit motive does not greatly influence farming decisions. But this is to misconceive the role and purpose of the technique. The results of linear programming have the same function as any other scientifically-based recommendations. They are, in short, extension or advisory tools. And just as it is wrong to condemn a policy recommending the adoption of ley husbandry principles (where this is technically desirable) because the peasant is ignorant of the need for fertility maintenance, so it is wrong to condemn a policy which fosters maximum-profit farm systems when economic motivation is lacking. In both cases, it is essential to know the right direction to take even though it is difficult to achieve."

Another conceptual advantage over the classical approach is that linear programming does not necessarily assume away the technical maximization problem, but is capable of making it a part of the solution. The classical concept of the production function assumes that a technical maximization problem has been solved.[6] On this same issue, Dorfman, Samuelson, and Solow (1958, 203) have stated: "Perhaps economists would not have gotten into the habit of making this assumption so glibly if they had realized what, and how much, they were assuming." This assumption that a particular firm is operating on a classical economist's production function is even more discomforting in an underdeveloped area than in a developed economy.

A final feature of the linear programming approach which makes it relevant for problems in underdeveloped areas is that it will easily accommodate restrictions on the profit maximizing motive. Admittedly, the approach must optimize (maximize or minimize) some function, however, the researcher has a great deal of flexibility in placing restraints on the maximizing or minimizing process.

NOTES

1. The author is indebted to Mr. John Gerald Feaster for the data, which were collected through personal interviews for the purpose of determining important identifying characteristics of innovators in a peasant agriculture. The author is responsible for all assumptions required in adapting the data for the purpose of this study.

2. Slash and burn is the typical cultivating system used by the *milperos*— a name given to native farmers in much of Latin America. Descriptions of the people and the type of agriculture followed are available in Feaster (1966) and Wright *et al.* (1959).

3. All prices and costs are in Honduran dollars. The Honduran dollar is worth .70 in United States currency.

4. Eighteen per cent nitrogen by weight, 46 per cent available phosphoric acid, and zero per cent potash.

5. There has been very little research done on the fertilization of food crops with traditional cultivating methods. An 82 per cent increased yield response was assumed for corn and rice. No fertilizer was applied to the beans. A response of 42 per cent was assumed for beans as a consequence of the utilization of residual fertilizer from the corn. The 82 per cent increase was based on yields obtained in a corn fertilizer trial reported in Govt. of Honduras, Agr. Dept. (1962, 20).

6. According to Carlson (1956, 14-15): "If we denote the quantity of output by x, and the quantities of the variable productive services, n in number, by v_1 . . ., v_n, we write:

$$(I) \quad x = \varphi \ (v_1, \ . \ . \ ., v_n).$$

This in [*sic*] our *production function*. The production function, it must be remembered, is defined in relation to a given plant; that is certain fixed services. A given amount of output may frequently be produced from a number of different service combinations. It may also be true that the same combination of productive services gives varied amounts of output, depending upon how efficiently the productive services are organized. The output of an automobile factory, for instance, may vary for different organizations of the same workers and tools on the assembly line. If we want the production function to give only one value for the output from a given service combination, the function must be so defined that it expresses the *maximum product* obtainable from the combination at the existing state of technical knowledge. Therefore, the purely *technical* maximization problem may be said to be solved by the very definition of our production function."

LITERATURE CITED

CARLSON, SUNE. 1956. A study of the pure theory of production. Kelley and Millman, N.Y.

CLAYTON, E. S. 1963. Economic planning in peasant agriculture. Dept. of Agr. Econ., Wye College, Univ. of London, near Ashford, Kent.

COFFEY, JOSEPH D. 1966. Prospects of transforming Peru's traditional agriculture, Ph.D. Dissertation. Dept. Econ., North Carolina State University, Raleigh.

DAY, RICHARD H. 1963. Recursive programming and production response. North Holland Publishing Company, Amsterdam.

DEAN, GERALD W., and DE BENEDICTIS, MICHELE. 1964. A model of economic development for peasant farms in Southern Italy. J. Farm Econ. 46(2): 295-312.

DORFMAN, ROBERT, SAMUELSON, PAUL A., and SOLOW, ROBERT M. 1958. Linear programming and economic analysis. McGraw-Hill Book Company, N.Y.

FEASTER, JOHN GERALD. 1966. Farm managerial decision making of shifting cultivators in a tropical area. Master's Thesis. Dept. Agr. Econ., Univ. Florida, Gainesville.

GOVT. OF BRITISH HONDURAS, AGR. DEPT. 1962. Annual report of the agricultural department for the year 1962. British Honduras Printing Dept., Belize.

LUAN, CHAU TAM, and BAKER, C. B. 1966. Economic planning in South Vietnam. Illinois Agr. Econ. 6: 1-10.

STEGGERDA, M. 1941. Maya indians of Yucatan. Carnegie Institute of Washington, Washington, D.C.

WRIGHT, A. C. S., ROMMNEY, D. H., ARBUCKLE, R. H., and VIAL, V. E. 1959. Land in British Honduras, report of the British Honduras land use survey team. Her Majesty's Stationary Office. London.

9

Strategy for Increasing Rice Production in Southeast Asia

Vernon W. Ruttan

A basic premise of the technical assistance and agricultural development programs of the late 1940's and early 1950's was that activity centered around the following types of actions should result in rapid growth in agricultural productivity and output: (1) the diffusion of practices employed by the best farmers, (2) the transfer of known agricultural technologies from the high productivity to the low productivity countries, (3) the development of more effective rural credit and marketing institutions, and (4) capital investment in mechanization, land development, and transportation.[1]* These expectations have failed to materialize. The rate of growth of crop output has, in most developing countries, failed to equal the rate of growth of demand. Furthermore, a relatively large share of the production increases that have occurred, even in densely populated countries, have been based on expansion of area planted rather than on yield increases (USDA, 1965).

A consensus, which appears to be emerging, is that intensive investment in research and development designed to produce improvements in the quality of agricultural inputs represents an important missing link in the agricultural development process. This position has been argued most vigorously by Schultz (1964a,

*Notes for this chapter begin on page 180.

1964b). There is increasing recognition that the traditional practices employed by the more successful farmers in each area do not
have a sufficiently high payoff for their diffusion to be relied on
to narrow significantly the frequency distribution which describes
the results obtained by all farmers in a general area or to provide
a basis for rapid growth in aggregate output. There is growing
agreement that much of agricultural research and development
is highly location specific, i.e., it must be performed where the
biological and economic environment approximates that where the
innovation is to be employed.

There is danger that these insights may be contributing to a
new set of oversimplifications regarding the requisites for rapid
agricultural development. Kellogg (1964) also has stressed this
point. The evidence presented in this paper emphasizes the essential complementarity between: (1) investment in research and
development, and (2) investment in infrastructure development.
Infrastructure investment refers to investments by public or semi-
public (local, regional, or national) agencies designed to provide
inputs or services that cannot be provided effectively by individual
farmers. The investments classified under this heading will depend
on both the physical environment and the organization of the
agricultural sector. For example, it may be necessary to organize
public programs of insect and rat control in an area characterized
by small farms, whereas the same activities might be effectively
conducted by the private sector in an area characterized by large
farms. The development of gravity irrigation systems is typically
organized by public or semi-public agencies to provide irrigation
water to larger river basins, but may be developed by the private
sector in small watersheds.

SOURCES OF OUTPUT GROWTH

A hierarchical format such as that of Figure 9.1 represents a
useful framework in which to analyze the factors that affect the
growth of agricultural output. The solid lines indicate the dominant
relationships, and the dotted lines indicate a few of the more
important patterns of interaction. On the right are those activities
which we classify as research and education. Much of the biological
research at the International Rice Research Institute,[2] for example,
would be categorized under the headings at the right-hand side

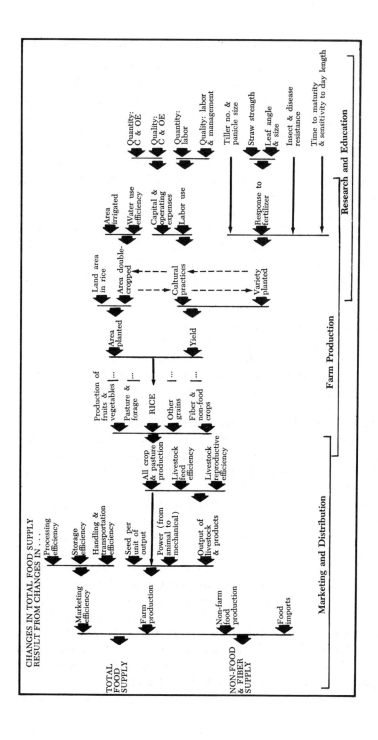

FIGURE 9.1. Sources of output growth.

of Figure 9.1. Those activities classified under the heading of farm production occupy an intermediate position in the hierarchy.

Each solid arrow can be regarded as an input-output linkage. These linkages typically involve the transfer of both information and materials. The magnitude and rate of transmission of information and materials across these linkages reflects explicit decisions of research scientists, research administrators, extension workers, farmers, employees and managers of marketing agencies, consumers, and others. The actions taken as a result of these decisions involve the interaction of the skills and motivations which characterize the persons directly involved as well as the institutional matrix in which these individuals operate. These institutions include research institutes and departments, extension organizations, rural communities, factor and product markets, and others.

The effectiveness of any linkage requires: (1) the development of functional institutional arrangements, and (2) the allocation of resources of manpower and capital to the particular activity involved. Knowledge of the parameters of the technical and behavioral relationships which describe each would be extremely useful in designing a national strategy to achieve increases in agricultural output. We are not, in this chapter, able to provide such quantitative knowledge for the entire hierarchy of input-output linkages presented in Figure 9.1. It is possible, however, to summarize many factors which contribute to changes in rice production in terms of changes in area planted, and changes in yield or production per unit of land.

Most countries in Southeast Asia have been, and continue to be more dependent on *increased area* than on *increased yield* as a source of growth in rice production (Table 9.1). This dependency on area is in contrast to the countries of Northeast Asia and South Asia where increases *in yield* have typically been more important than increases *in area* in recent years. However, Taiwan is the only country in the region which achieved its total increase in output during the last decade from yield increases. The Philippines stand at the opposite extreme. Thailand occupies a median position. Changes in yield and changes in area planted have been of approximately equal importance in accounting for increases in rice production in Thailand during the last decade.

The hypothesis that underlies the studies reported in this chap-

TABLE 9.1.—Changes in production, area, and yield of paddy (rough rice) in Asia

Region	Production			Area			Yield			Relative contribution to change in production		
	1951/52 1953/54	1960/61 1962/63	Change	1951/52 1953/54	1960/61 1962/63	Change	1951/52 1953/54	1960/61 1962/63	Change	Change in area	Change in yield	Log. interaction term
	1,000 metric tons		per cent	1,000 hectares		per cent	1,000 metric tons		per cent	per cent		
Southeast Asia[a]												
Burma	5,754	7,900	37.3	3,978	4,789	20.4	1.45	1.65	13.8	58.5	40.8	0.7
Cambodia	1,281	1,493	16.5	1,197	1,395	16.5	1.07	1.07	0.0	100.0	0.0	0.0
Indonesia	10,893	13,024	19.6	6,397	7,160	11.9	1.70	1.82	7.1	63.1	38.2	−1.3
Malaysia	675	911	34.9	339	384	13.1	1.99	2.37	19.1	41.2	58.4	0.4
Philippines	3,176	3,901	22.8	2,650	3,161	19.3	1.20	1.23	2.5	85.8	12.0	2.2
Thailand	6,850	9,100	32.8	5,165	6,068	17.5	1.31	1.50	14.5	56.7	47.7	−4.4
TOTAL	28,629	36,329	26.9	19,726	22,957	16.4	1.45	1.58	9.0	65.0	36.0	−1.0
South Asia (total)	52,280	70,047	31.5	42,247	43,895	8.6	1.24	1.60	29.0	30.3	71.0	−1.3
Northeast Asia (total)	16,596	22,205	33.8	4,983	5,196	4.3	3.33	4.27	28.2	14.4	88.5	−2.9

Source: Venegas (1964).
a. Laos is not included because of incomplete data; Vietnam is not included because of a change in reporting procedure.

ter is that the yield increases of the last decade, and the yield differences among major rice-producing areas within Southeast Asia at the present time, reflect primarily variations in the environmental factors under which rice is grown (soil, season, water, and weather differentials) rather than differences in variety or cultural practices. That is, when one standardizes the data for environmental factors, most of the differences in rice yields among Southeast Asian countries, such as those shown in Table 9.1, disappear. A specific test of this hypothesis, using data from the Philippines and Thailand, is presented.

The first step involves a review of the long-term trends in rice production, area, and yield in the two countries. An attempt is then made to show that most of the yield changes that have occurred and that most of the yield differentials among regions within each country are associated with shifts in the regional distribution of area devoted to rice or to modifications in the environmental factors. Finally, these data are used to demonstrate the important interaction between technological change and conventional capital investment in infrastructure development that must be taken into consideration if the new technology is to have any substantial impact on aggregate yields.

Major emphasis will be placed on factors associated with changes or differences in yield. An attempt is not made in this chapter to analyze the factors associated with the expansion or decline of area planted to rice. Additional work has recently been completed, at the International Rice Research Institute, which relates the response of area devoted to rice and other crops to product and factor price behavior. In general, the results indicate that the area planted to rice tends to be highly responsive to changes in prices of rice in relation to prices of competing crops. These studies typically did not identify any yield response to changes in relative prices (Mangahas, 1965; Mangahas *et al.*, 1966).

TRENDS IN RICE PRODUCTION,
AREA, AND YIELD IN THE
PHILIPPINES AND THAILAND

There are a number of important similarities in the long-term changes in rice production, area, and yield in the Philippines and Thailand (Table 9.2, Figs. 9.2 and 9.3). Both countries have experienced relatively rapid rates of growth in rice production. Both countries have relied primarily on increases in area devoted to rice, rather than on increases in yield, as a dominant source of growth in rice production. In the Philippines, the yield per hectare has remained essentially unchanged at approximately 1.2 metric tons per hectare since the early 1920's. In Thailand, rice yields

TABLE 9.2.—Changes in rice production, area, and yield in Thailand and the Philippines.

Year	Production	Area		Yield per hectare	
		Planted	Harvested	Planted	Harvested
Thailand	1,000 metric tons	1,000 hectares		Metric tons	
Amount					
1907/08-1908/09	2,475	1,479	1,319	1.67	1.88
1920/21-1921/22	4,250	2,521	2,298	1.68	1.85
1946/47-1948/49	4,974	4,404	3,907	1.13	1.27
1962/63-1963/64	9,711	6,625	6,288	1.47	1.54
Annual Rate					
1907/08-1908/09 to 1920/21-1921/22	4.2	4.2	4.4		−0.1
1920/21-1921/22 to 1946/47-1947/48	0.6	2.2	2.1	−1.5	−1.4
1946/47-1947/48 to 1962/63-1963/64	4.3	2.6	3.0	1.7	1.2
1907/08-1908/09 to 1947/48-1962/63	2.5	2.7	2.9	−0.2	−0.4
Philippines					
Amount					
1908/09-1909/10	798	1,174		0.68	
1925/26-1926/27	2,140	1,781		1.20	
1952/53-1953/54	3,163	2,650[a]		1.19[a]	
1962/63-1963/64	3,905		3,124[a]		1.25[a]
Annual Rate					
1908/09-1909/10 to 1925/26-1926/27	6.0	2.5		3.4	
1925/26-1926/27 to 1952/53-1953/54	1.5	1.5[a]		0.0[a]	
1952/53-1953/54 to 1962/63-1963/64	2.1		1.7[a]		0.5[a]
1908/09-1909/10 to 1962/63-1963/64	3.0	1.8[a]		1.1[a]	

Source: Ruttan, Soothipan, and Venegas (1966a and 1966b).

a. In crop year 1953/54, the Philippine area and yield data were shifted from an area-planted to an area-harvested basis.

declined continuously from the early 1920's until the late 1950's.
 In both countries, the trend since the early 1900's can be divided
into three major periods.

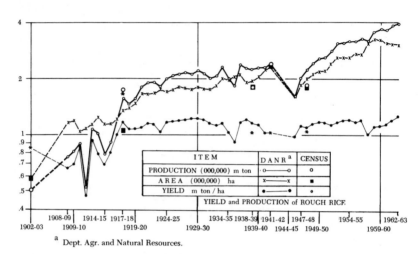

a Dept. Agr. and Natural Resources.

FIGURE 9.2. Long-term trend of rice production, area, and yield in the Philippines (1902/03 to 1962/63).

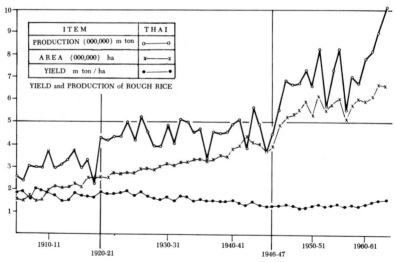

FIGURE 9.3. Long-term trend of rice production, area, and yield in Thailand (1907/08 to 1963/64).

(1) The years prior to the early or mid-1920's were character-ized by rapid growth in rice production in both countries. In Thailand, yields remained essentially unchanged. The increase in production was accounted for almost entirely by increases in the area of rice planted. In the Philippines, increases in both area and yield contributed to the growth in production.

(2) The period from the early 1920's until after World War II was characterized by relative stability in rice production in both countries. Yields declined in Thailand and remained essentially unchanged in the Philippines. The annual increase in area devoted to rice was slower than in the previous period in both countries. During World War II, rice production declined sharply in the Philippines. In Thailand, the decline was less severe and extended over fewer years.

(3) During the third period, since recovery from the effects of World War II, production has again expanded at a more rapid rate in both countries. In contrast to the preceding period, in-creases in yield appear to have emerged as a significant factor in accounting for growth in output, particularly during the last few years.

Since the early years of this century, the national average yield in the Philippines has been lower than in Thailand. In 1908/09 when the national average yield in Thailand was 1.67 metric tons per hectare, the national average yield in the Philippines was 0.68 metric tons per hectare. Higher yields in the Philippines and lower yields in Thailand have narrowed this gap. From 1962/63 to 1963/64, the national average yield in Thailand was 1.54 metric tons per hectare, whereas the national average yield in the Philip-pines was 1.25 metric tons per hectare. Most of the yield increase in the Philippines occurred prior to the early 1920's. Most of the yield decline in Thailand occurred between the early 1920's and the mid-1950's. In both countries, yields have tended to increase in the last few years.

Both the long-term stability in national average yield in the Philippines and the long-term decline in national average yield in Thailand are difficult to explain. It appears that the stability in national average yield in the Philippines reflects the combined ef-fect of expansion in area devoted to low-yielding upland and rain-fed rice and a stable or declining area devoted to rice produc-tion in the higher yielding irrigated areas. In Thailand, it appears that increases in area devoted to rice in the low-yielding provinces of the northeast have more than offset the effect of stable or rising yields in the central and northern provinces. Regional data are not available to determine definitely the factors involved for the entire period since the early 1900's. It is possible, however, to examine the regional changes that have occurred since the early 1950's in each country in greater detail.

EFFECTS OF REGIONAL PRODUCTION PATTERNS IN THE PHILIPPINES AND THAILAND

Philippines.—In the Philippines, rice is produced under many conditions. Each province grows some rice in each season. In each season, some rice is grown under irrigated, rain-fed, and upland conditions. Regional or national average yields differ, depending on season (wet or dry) and water treatment (irrigated, rain-fed, or upland).[3] Thus, the average rice yield in each province or region (Fig. 9.4) and in the Philippines as a whole is determined by: (1) the yield obtained under different production conditions, and (2) the percentage of the total area on which different production practices are employed.

In Ilocos, Cagayan, central Luzon, and eastern Visayas, less than 10 per cent of the total rice area is accounted for by area planted to upland rice (Fig. 9.5). In some regions, such as southern Tagalog and southern and western Mindanao, however, the area in upland rice relative to lowland rice is large. Non-irrigated (i.e., rain-fed) first crop (wet season) areas are most prevalent in almost all regions. Irrigated first crop areas are substantial only in some regions, such as central Luzon, Bicol, and southern and western Mindanao. The area devoted to the lowland second crop (dry season) rice is relatively small in all regions.

The data in Table 9.3 represent an attempt to measure the effect of season and water treatment on regional average yields. The data in column (1) are the actual average yields obtained in 1960/61-1961/62 in each region. The data presented in column (3) are the average yields that would have been reported for the region if the distribution of rice hectarage by season and water treatment in the region had been the same as the national average. The only year for which sufficient data are available to make this calculation is 1960/61-1961/62.

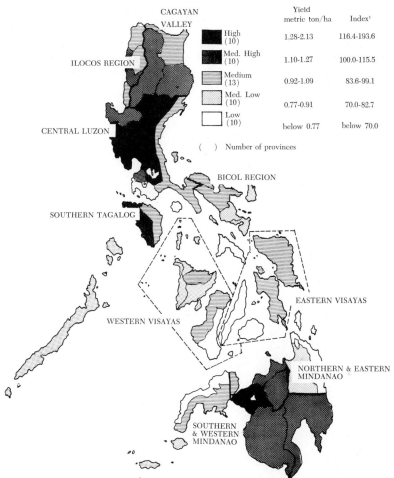

	Yield metric ton/ha	Index[1]
High (10)	1.28-2.13	116.4-193.6
Med. High (10)	1.10-1.27	100.0-115.5
Medium (13)	0.92-1.09	83.6-99.1
Med. Low (10)	0.77-0.91	70.0-82.7
Low (10)	below 0.77	below 70.0

( )   Number of provinces

CAGAYAN VALLEY

ILOCOS REGION

CENTRAL LUZON

BICOL REGION

SOUTHERN TAGALOG

EASTERN VISAYAS

WESTERN VISAYAS

NORTHERN & EASTERN MINDANAO

SOUTHERN & WESTERN MINDANAO

SOURCE: Division of Agricultural Economics, Department of Agriculture and Natural Resources.

[1] Philippine average yield of 1.10 metric ton/ hectare for 1956-57 to 1958-59 equals 100.

FIGURE 9.4. Distribution of rice yields among Philippine provinces (3-year average, 1956/57 to 1958/59).

In central Luzon, for example, the actual average yield in 1960/
61-1961/62 was 1.574 metric tons of rough rice (*palay*) per hectare, or almost 36 per cent above the national average. If the
distribution of area between the wet and the dry season and
among irrigated, rain-fed, and upland areas had been the same as
the national average, the 1960/61 average yields in central Luzon
would have been 1.382 metric tons or only 19 per cent instead of

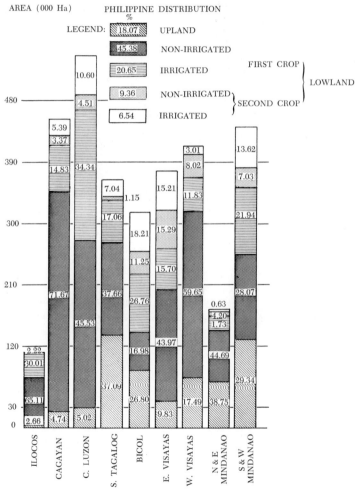

FIGURE 9.5. Regional distribution of rice area, Philippines, 1960/61.

Source: Venegas and Ruttan (1964).

36 per cent above the national average. This means that almost half of the difference between the actual average yield in central Luzon and the average national yield is accounted for by the relatively favorable area distribution with respect to season and water treatment, rather than by actual yield differences under similar environmental conditions. In the Ilocos region, about three-

TABLE 9.3—EFFECT OF DIFFERENCES IN REGIONAL PRODUCTION PATTERNS ON REGIONAL AVERAGE YIELDS

	Actual yield		Standardized yield[a]	
Region	ton/ha. (1)	Index (2)	ton/ha. (3)	Index (4)
Philippines (1960/61-1961/62)	1.159	100.0	1.159	100.0
Ilocos	1.278	110.3	1.201	103.6
Cagayan Valley	1.087	93.8	1.174	101.3
Central Luzon	1.574	135.8	1.382	119.2
Southern Tagalog	1.049	90.5	1.143	98.6
Bicol	1.025	88.4	1.013	87.4
Eastern Visayas	0.891	76.9	0.891	76.9
Western Visayas	1.263	109.0	1.289	111.2
North and east Mindanao	0.847	73.1	0.851	73.4
South and west Mindanao	1.127	97.2	1.176	101.5
Thailand (1961/62-1963/64)	1.514	100.0	1.514	100.0
Central Plain	1.766	116.6	1.394	92.1
Northeast	1.123	74.2	1.409	93.1
North	2.144	141.6	2.125	140.4
South	1.602	105.8	1.770	116.9

Source: Ruttan, Soothipan, and Venegas (1966a and 1966b).

a. In the Philippines, regional yields of rough rice from (1) first crop irrigated, (2) non-irrigated, (3) second crop irrigated, and (4) non-irrigated, and (5) upland areas are weighted by the national average area distribution for the five categories to obtain the standardized yields. In Thailand, the regional yields of rough rice for irrigated and non-irrigated areas are weighted by the national area distribution to obtain the standardized yields.

fifths of the margin of actual yield over the national average yield results primarily from the favorable area distribution.

In the Cagayan Valley, southern and western Mindanao, and southern Tagalog regions, the relatively high proportion of upland area accounts for the below-average yields obtained in these three regions. If the distribution of area among different types of production had been the same as the national average, yields in these three regions would have approximated the national average.

The case of western Visayas is particularly striking because of the close agreement between the actual and standardized yields. This implies that the higher than average yields are primarily the result of higher real yields rather than hectarage distribution. However, in Bicol, eastern Visayas, and northern and eastern Mindanao, low yields cannot be attributed to area distribution. Yields in these areas are low in spite of a distribution of production which is close to the national average.

The limited proportion of the total area devoted to rice that is irrigated in both the wet and the dry seasons represents a major barrier to increased production and higher average yields in most regions. Even in central Luzon, where yields are relatively high in comparison to other regions, a shift of one hectare from production of one crop of rain-fed rice to production of both a wet and dry season irrigated rice would add almost 1.22 tons to the total production, under 1961 cultural practices. This represents a 168 per cent increase in rice production per hectare per year.[4]

Thailand.—In Thailand the range in yield variation among provinces is similar to that in the Philippines (Fig. 9.6). However, most of the rice is grown under irrigated or rain-fed conditions. The percentage of upland rice is low, and probably not more than 1 per cent in recent years. The second crop or dry season production is also low. It accounts for less than 1 per cent of the total area planted (or harvested). Most of the dry season crop is grown in the north and in the central plain. However, the relative importance of irrigated and rain-fed areas varies sharply among provinces (Fig. 9.7). In central Thailand almost half of the area planted, and in the north more than one-fourth of the area planted, is irrigated.

There are some difficulties in comparing the production, area, and yield of irrigated and non-irrigated land in Thailand. The Rice Department (Ministry of Agriculture) reports only total production, total area planted and harvested, and provincial, regional, and national average yields. It does not report production, area, and yield for irrigated, non-irrigated, and upland rice separately. Since 1958/59, data on production, area, and yield for irrigated land have been reported by the Royal Irrigation Department (Ministry of National Development). The data on production, area, and yield for non-irrigated land utilized in this report were obtained by subtracting the production and area estimates of the Royal Irrigation Department from the total production and area estimates of the Rice Department. Any bias in the Royal Irrigation

Department data would, therefore, result in an opposite bias in the residual estimates of production, area, and yield in non-irrigated areas. In both Thailand and the Philippines, the definition of

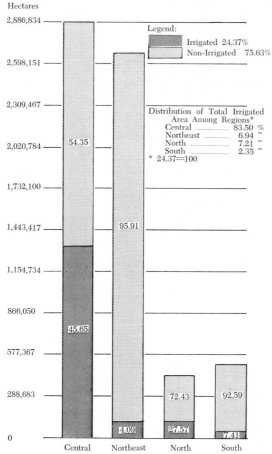

Hectares

Legend:

Irrigated 24.37%
Non-Irrigated 75.63%

Distribution of Total Irrigated
Area Among Regions*
Central .... 83.50 %
Northeast .... 6.94 "
North .... 7.21 "
South .... 2.35 "
* 24.37=100

FIGURE 9.6. Regional distribution of rice area, Thailand (3-year average, 1961/62 to 1963/64).

irrigated land is rather imprecise. In most cases irrigation water is supplied by diversion dams in streams and is available only during the wet season. Thus, in the Philippines the area of the second (dry season) crop that is irrigated may represent a better estimate of the area that is adequately irrigated than the area of the first (wet) season crop that is irrigated (Fig. 9.5). In Thailand,

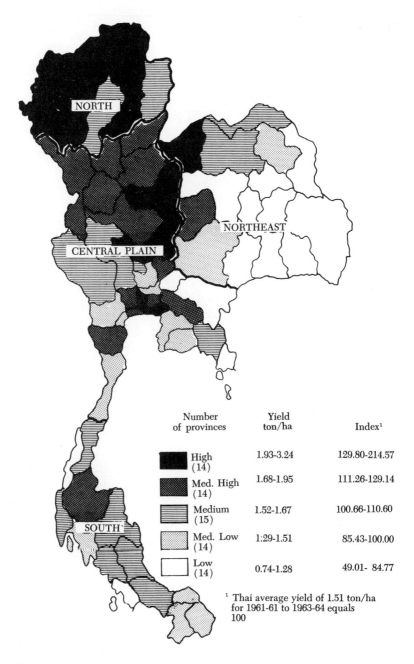

	Number of provinces	Yield ton/ha	Index[1]
High (14)		1.93-3.24	129.80-214.57
Med. High (14)		1.68-1.95	111.26-129.14
Medium (15)		1.52-1.67	100.66-110.60
Med. Low (14)		1:29-1.51	85.43-100.00
Low (14)		0.74-1.28	49.01- 84.77

[1] Thai average yield of 1.51 ton/ha for 1961-61 to 1963-64 equals 100

FIGURE 9.7. Distribution of rice yields among Thai provinces (3-year average, 1961/62 to 1963/64).

substantial areas classified as irrigated are subject to serious flooding and have inadequate drainage.

The yields reported by the Royal Irrigation Department for irrigated areas are substantially higher than the yields estimated for non-irrigated areas by the residual method (Fig. 9.8). Both the irrigated and non-irrigated areas have experienced yield increases since 1958/59. The most dramatic increase occurred on irrigated land in the northeast. Irrigated land represents such a small proportion of the total increases in the northeast that the rise in yield on such land had a relatively minor impact on the average yield for the entire region. In the central plain, the estimated yield on non-irrigated land has risen more rapidly than on irrigated land.

Differences in the proportion of areas irrigated in each region have a substantial impact on the regional average yield. In those regions in which only a small share of the land is irrigated, the average yield is close to the yield on non-irrigated land.

The data for Thailand in Table 9.3 attempt to measure the effect of different regional production patterns on regional yields. The data presented in column (4) are estimates of the average yields that would have been reported for the region if the distribution of hectarage between irrigated and non-irrigated areas in the region had been the same as the national average. In the central plain, for example, the actual average yield in 1961/62 to 1963/64 was 1.766 metric tons of rough rice per hectare, or almost 17 per cent above the national average. If the distribution of area between irrigated and rain-fed culture had been the same as the national average, the 1961/63 average yield in the central plain would have been 1.394 metric tons or 8 per cent below the national average.

The northern region is particularly striking because of the close agreement between the actual and standardized yield. This implies that the higher than average yields are primarily the result of higher rice yields under comparable conditions of water use rather than of a favorable distribution of irrigated area.

Effects of Weather on Yield in Thailand

In Thailand, natural disasters, typically excess flooding in the central plain and both excess flooding and extreme dry weather in the northeast, frequently result in sharp reductions in the

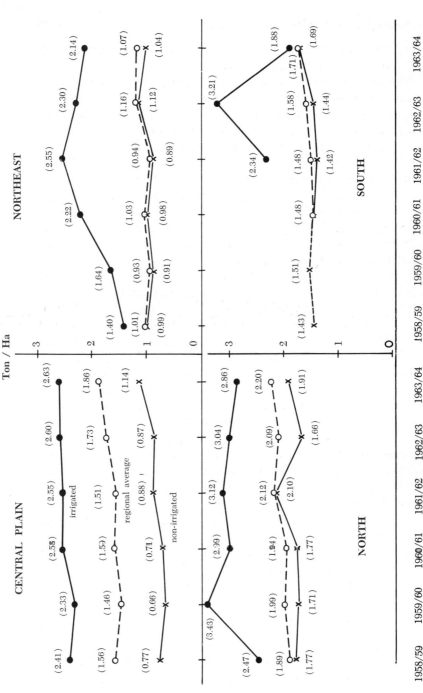

FIGURE 9.8. Regional average yield per hectare harvested in irrigated and non-irrigated areas, Thailand, 1958/59 to 1963/64.

percentage of the area planted that can be harvested. Partial damage in other areas also results in reductions in the yield on land that is harvested in years of severe flooding or drouth.

Data on the relationship between yield per hectare harvested and percentage of planted area reported damaged between 1947/ 48 and 1963/64 are presented in Figure 9.9. A relatively high percentage of the variation in yield from year to year can be explained by variations in the percentage of damaged areas in the northeast and the central plain. In addition, most of the upward trend in yield in these two regions in recent years appears to be the result of a sequence of years in which the damaged area has declined continuously. If damage again rises to the 12 to 17 per cent range as it did in 1958/59 and 1959/60, the average yield in the central plain could again drop to around 1.5 metric tons per hectare. In the northeast, damage in the 9 to 12 per cent range of 1957/58 and 1959/60 could again result in yields of around 1.0 metric tons per hectare.[5]

We have not yet been able to analyze systematically the effects of weather on yields in the Philippines. In certain years, 1958/59, for example, the impact of weather has been relatively severe. However, we have not noted any systematic trend such as that indicated by the decline in area damaged during 1959/60 to 1963/64 in Thailand.

Some Regional Comparisons Between
the Philippines and Thailand

In addition to the comparisons which have been presented among regions within each country, it is interesting to compare yields between regions in the Philippines and Thailand. Clearly, national average yields per hectare harvested are lower in the Philippines than in Thailand, and the difference is greater today than it was a decade ago (Table 9.4).

A comparison of yields in central Thailand and the central Luzon area of the Philippines, the two regions which account for a relatively high percentage of the rice entering the commercial market in the two countries, reveals a rather different pattern than does a comparison of national average yields of the two countries. Average yields in the two regions are almost identical and have risen at approximately the same rate over the last decade.

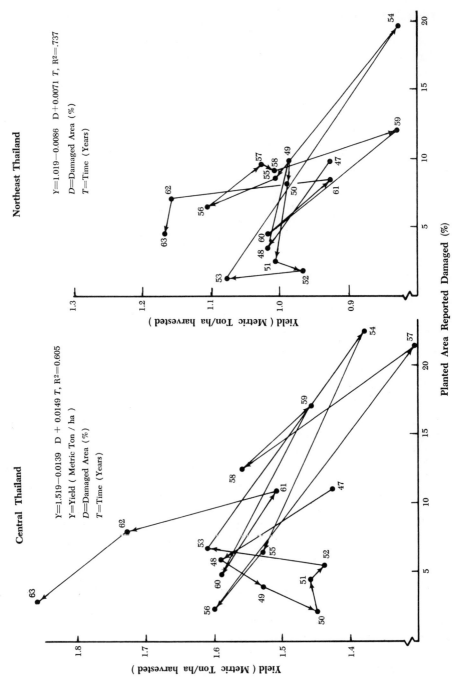

FIGURE 9.9 Relationship between yield per hectare harvested and percentage of planted area reported damaged, Thailand,

TABLE 9.4.—COMPARISON OF YIELD OF ROUGH RICE IN THE PHILIPPINES AND THAILAND, 1953/54 TO 1963/64, IN METRIC TONS OF ROUGH RICE PER HECTARE HARVESTED

Year	National average yields			Major commercial regional yields			Regions with rapid expansion				
	Thailand	Philippines	Ratio (2)/(1)	Central Thailand	Central Luzon	Ratio (5)/(4)	Northeast Thailand	Southern and Western Mindanao	Ratio (8)/(7)	Cagayan Valley	Ratio (10)/(7)
	(1)	(2)	(3)	(4)	(5)	(6)	(7)	(8)	(9)	(10)	(11)
1953/54	1.39	1.20	0.86	1.61	1.33	0.83	1.08	2.04	1.89	1.59	1.47
1954/55	1.26	1.21	0.96	1.38	1.50	1.09	0.93	1.47	1.38	1.31	1.41
1955/56	1.36	1.19	0.88	1.53	1.61	1.05	1.01	1.35	1.34	1.25	1.24
1956/57	1.44	1.21	0.84	1.60	1.61	1.01	1.13	1.36	1.20	1.25	1.11
1957/58	1.30	1.02	0.78	1.30	1.41	1.08	1.03	1.04	1.01	1.08	1.05
1958/59	1.36	1.11	0.82	1.56	1.51	0.97	1.01	1.04	1.03	1.28	1.27
1959/60	1.29	1.13	0.88	1.46	1.39	0.95	0.93	1.03	1.11	1.38	1.48
1960/61	1.39	1.16	0.83	1.59	1.57	0.99	1.03	1.13	1.10	1.09	1.06
1961/62	1.44	1.23	0.85	1.51	1.80	1.19	0.94	1.14	1.21	1.21	1.29
1962/63	1.49	1.25	0.84	1.73	1.82	1.05	1.16	1.26	1.09	1.28	1.10
1963/64	1.59	1.24	0.78	1.86	1.86	1.00	1.17	1.26	1.08	1.13	0.97

Source: Ruttan, Soothipan, and Venegas (1966a and 1966b).

It is also possible to compare yields in the regions where area harvested has been expanding most rapidly. Most of the expansion in rice area in Thailand has been in the northeast. The Philippines has experienced a rapid expansion in area in southern and western Mindanao, particularly since 1956/57. In the early 1950's, rice yields in southern and western Mindanao were substantially higher than in northern Thailand. With the rapid expansion in area in southern and western Mindanao, yields have declined and are now only slightly higher than in northeast Thailand. The process of area expansion apparently occurs primarily through the addition of upland and rain-fed rice areas. Rice yields under this type of cultivation are low, and apparently are not very different in northeast Thailand and southern and western Mindanao in spite of rather substantial differences in soil and climate. Thus, standardization for environmental factors results in convergence of yields, not only within each country, but among comparable regions between the two countries.

CONCLUSIONS

Despite numerous deficiencies, the data examined in this paper are consistent with the hypothesis that both the yield increases of the last decade and the yield differences among major rice-producing regions in the Philippines and Thailand primarily reflect variations in the environmental factors under which rice is grown rather than differences from variety planted or cultural practices. *After the effects of the environmental factors are taken into account, there is little yield increase or yield differential left to be explained by such factors as new varieties, better cultural practices, more intensive use of technical inputs such as fertilizer and insecticides, or economic and social differences among regions and between Thailand and the Philippines.*

This conclusion would not have much significance if there had been no changes in varieties, cultural practices, or the use of technical inputs. Fertilizer is not widely used on rice in Southeast Asia. A major obstacle to higher levels of fertilizer use is the limited response to higher levels of nitrogen, particularly during the wet season when most rice is grown (von Uexkuell, 1964). However, there have been significant changes in technology over the last decade and a half both in the Philippines and in Thailand.

Most of the varieties being recommended by the Bureau of Plant Industry in the Philippines were not available to farmers until after 1950. In the Philippines, straight row planting and use of the mechanical weeder have resulted in better weed control practices in extensive areas. Increasingly effective insecticides have been introduced in both countries. Prices paid to farmers for rough rice have been substantially higher in the Philippines than in Thailand.

It seems apparent that the innovations that have been introduced during the last several decades have not yet had any measurable impact on national average yields. There is some indication, however, that they may have induced limited yield increases in regions such as central Luzon where irrigation development is most adequate (Table 9.4). It is also possible that the new varieties and practices may have partly offset yield decreasing forces.

The data presented in this chapter, coupled with recent experimental data, do permit us to go beyond the conclusions drawn from the historical record to some inferences concerning the strategy of achieving increases in rice production in the Philippines and Thailand (Fig. 9.1).

A prerequisite for the development of an effective national rice production strategy is a clear understanding of the basis for the differences: (1) between national or regional average yields and the yields being achieved in those provinces, villages, and farms with the highest yields, (2) between the yields obtained in the best provinces, villages, and farms and the yields obtained with the same varieties under experimental conditions, and (3) between yields obtained under experimental conditions with the best available varieties and the potential yields that can be achieved by changing the plant type to increase the response of the plant to sunlight, technical inputs, and management.[6]

Let us review these differences. Both in the Philippines and in Thailand, most of the lowland rice is grown during the rainy season without irrigation. Under this rain-fed system of cultivation, village or provincial average yields rarely exceed 1.5 metric tons per hectare. However, in fully irrigated areas in both countries, such as Chiengmai in Thailand and Laguna in the Philippines, it is not uncommon for average yields to exceed 3.0 metric tons in the wet season and 3.5 metric tons in the dry season over fairly extensive areas. On individual farms, such as those participating in contests or those under experimental conditions, the yields of the same varieties frequently fall in ranges of 4.0 to 4.5 metric tons in the wet season and 5.0 to 6.0 metric tons in the dry season (IRRI, 1965, 50-52, 88-91). Even higher yields are frequently obtained by the winners of rice yield contests (Chandler, 1962). New varieties, now being developed, appear to have yield potentials within ranges of at least 6.0 metric tons during the wet season and 8.0 metric tons during the dry season.

A major implication of this analysis is that the factors which permit a province or region to increase its yields from 1.5 metric tons per hectare in the wet season to the levels currently being achieved in the higher yielding localities in the Philippines and Thailand, such as the irrigated areas in Chiengmai and Laguna, are primarily outside the control of the individual farmers in the major rice-producing regions such as central Luzon or central Thailand. The modifications in the environment necessary to achieve effective water control (irrigation and drainage) during both the wet and the dry seasons, and local environmental control over the other factors such as rats and other pests, will have to come primarily from public or semi-public agencies capable of organizing resources in a manner not available to the individual tenant or farm owner.

A second major implication is that the same limitation on environmental control which prevents farmers from achieving the yield potentials inherent in existing varieties will represent an equally severe limitation on achievement of the yield potentials inherent in the new varieties that will be introduced in the future. They are being designed to be even more sensitive to effective environmental control, technical inputs, and management than are existing varieties. Thus, the same public investment and institutional innovations required to narrow the gap between typical and potential yields under present circumstances will represent a necessary condition if introduction of the new varieties is to be reflected in higher aggregate yields.

These inferences raise a major issue in the strategy of innovation. Failure to make adequate public investment in irrigation and to develop adequate public programs of disease and pest control will clearly hamper the returns from investment in research and development on varietal improvement and on the cultural practices associated with the use of other technical inputs. On the other hand, failure to make adequate investment in research and development will limit the public and private return that can be realized from more adequate investment in irrigation and more effective programs of disease and pest control.

Let us now turn to the problem of organizing to achieve the complementary investments in research and development required to accomplish rapid productivity gains in rice production in Southeast Asia, and to investment in other infrastructure needed to achieve the potential productivity gains inherent in the results of the research. The steps that must be taken to organize research programs to produce the biological, chemical, and engineering technology necessary to obtain feasible increases in yield potentials are becoming better understood. It is increasingly recognized that there is essentially no improved rice production technology from the United States and Japan that can be immediately transferred to Southeast Asia. The ecology of the monsoon tropics and the factor and product price relationships which characterize current development levels rule out the direct transfer of existing rice production technology on the basis of technological and/or economic considerations. What can be transferred is the propensity and the capacity to focus scientific manpower and other resources on technical problems of economic significance, and the skill that comes from having solved similar problems although it was done in a different environment. When the plant breeder at the USDA station in Beaumont, Texas, who developed most of the rice varieties now grown in the United States, came to the International Rice Research Institute he did not bring along little bags of seed to be distributed to Southeast Asia experiment stations and farms. What he did bring was skill in breeding for fertilizer response, disease resistance, grain quality, and other elements, and skill in using the local ecological information supplied by soil chemists, physiologists, entomologists, cereal chemists, agronomists, geneticists, and others that enabled him to select and achieve appropriate breeding objectives and breeding strategy.

The magnitude of the investment that will be required to realize the production potential inherent in the new technology that is being created is less completely realized. There will have to be massive investment in the industries that produce the inputs of fertilizer and insecticides. It will also be necessary to invest heavily in irrigation if the investment devoted to development of new varieties and production of the technical inputs is to achieve a reasonably high return. There will have to be substantial increases in manpower trained to the management tasks related to the direct investment and the educational tasks associated with rapid achievement of the production potentials.

Recognition of the complementarity between these types of infrastructure investments and the investments in infrastructure of research and development to create new production potentials raises a serious question regarding the assumption that placing primary emphasis on research and development alone could provide a relatively inexpensive route to rapid growth of agricultural production during the early stages of agricultural development. Johnston and Tolley (1965, 369) indicate that, "initial emphasis should be placed on innovations that do not require large increases in the use of purchased inputs. This means emphasis upon the development and introduction of innovations such as high yielding varieties, improved crop rotation, optimum spacing and time of planting, and a better seasonal distribution of the work load." This advice does not appear relevant in the tropical rice-producing regions of South and Southeast Asia. Without massive investment in irrigation, these innovations will not result in higher productivity.

Clearly, the investment requirements for growth of the agricultural input sectors and for infrastructure development in the rice-producing countries of South and Southeast Asia will be very high over the next several decades. Furthermore, these investments will be competitive with other development goals. In some countries, India for example, this strategy may require a net flow of capital from the industrial to the agricultural sector, thus reversing the classical pattern assumed in most development literature. Unfortunately, investment in research and development has not opened up a new low-cost route to the rapid growth of agricultural output in the rice-producing areas of South and Southeast Asia.

NOTES

1. This chapter draws from material previously published in Ruttan *et al.* (1966a) and Ruttan *et al.* (1966b).

2. For a detailed discussion of the research program of the International Rice Research Institute, see IRRI (1965).

3. Yield is measured in terms of kilograms of palay or paddy (i.e., rough rice) per hectare per season. Thus, if both a wet and dry season crop

is grown on the same hectare it is counted as two hectares, and the average yield is the total production for both seasons divided by two.

	cavan/ha.	*ton/ha.*
4. Wet season irrigated	44.7	1.97
Dry season irrigated	41.1	1.81
Total irrigated	85.8	3.78
Wet season rain-fed	32.1	1.41
Increase from irrigation	53.7	2.37

One cavan of rough rice (palay) weighs 44.0 kilograms; 22.727 cavans of rough rice equals one metric ton. This is clearly a conservative estimate of the increase in output that would accompany irrigation. The dry season yield reflects a situation where there is inadequate water throughout that period. Experimental evidence from the IRRI and elsewhere indicates that with adequate irrigation the dry season yield should exceed the wet season yield by 25 to 50 per cent.

5. As long as the parameters for damaged area (D) in the equation presented in Figure 9.9 hold true, a decline in the area damaged by 10 percentage points, say from 15 to 5 per cent, would result in a rise in yield of 139 kg (0.139 metric ton)/ha. in the central plain and 86 kg (0.086 metric ton) in the northeast. In contrast, the parameter for time or trend, T, indicates an average rise in yield of only 14.9 kg (.0149 ton)/ha. per year in the central plain and 7.1 kg (.0071 ton) per year in the northeast. The effect is to produce a rather substantial increase in average yield (which could be sharply reversed by one or two bad years) during a period when the damage is declining.

6. Most of the biological work at the IRRI is concerned with the third gap. Recently, however, the Communications Department has instituted a program to explore the second gap, particularly with respect to insecticides. For data on the effect of environmental factors and cultural practices, see Tanaka *et. al.* (1964).

LITERATURE CITED

CHANDLER, R. F. 1962. Maximum yield potentialities for rice. The Philippine Agriculturist 46: 167-174.

IRRI. 1965. Annual report: 1964. International Rice Research Institute. Los Banos, Laguna, Philippines.

JOHNSTON, B. F., and TOLLEY, G. S. 1965. Strategy for agricultural development. J. Farm Econ. 47(2): 365-379.

KELLOGG, C. E. 1964. Interactions and agricultural research in emerging nations, p. 81-94. *In* A. H. Moseman [ed.], Agricultural sciences for the developing nations. Am. Assoc. Adv. Sci. Washington, D.C.

MANGAHAS, MAHAR. 1965. The methodology of estimating the response of Philippine rice farmers to price. Philippine Statistician 14(3): 174-200.

MANGAHAS, MAHAR, RECTO, AIDA, and RUTTAN, V. W. 1966. Price and market relationships for rice and corn in the Philippines. J. Farm Econ. 48(3): 685-703.

RUTTAN, V. W., SOOTHIPAN, A., and VENEGAS, E. C. 1966a. Changes in rice growing in the Philippines and Thailand. World Crops 18 (March): 18-33.

————. 1966b. Technological and environmental factors in the growth of rice production in the Philippines and Thailand. Rural Econ. Problems 3 (May): 63-107.

SCHULTZ, T. W. 1964a. Transforming traditional agriculture. Yale Univ. Press, New Haven, Conn.

————. 1964b. Economic growth from traditional agriculture, p. 185-205. *In* A. H. Moseman [ed.], Agricultural sciences for the developing nations. Am. Assoc. Adv. Sci. Washington, D.C.

TANAKA, A., NAVASERO, S. A., GARCIA, C. V., PRATO, F. T., and RAMIREZ, E. 1964. Growth habit of the rice plant in the tropics and its effect on nitrogen response. International Rice Research Institute. Tech. Bull. 3. Los Banos, Laguna, Philippines.

USDA. 1965. Changes in agriculture in twenty-six developing nations, 1948 to 1963. ERS, For. Agr. Econ. Rep. No. 27. Washington, D.C.

VENEGAS, E. 1964. The relative influence of acreage and yield in world production of rice. (Revised, Jan.) IRRI-AE Staff Memo. Los Banos, Laguna, Philippines.

VENEGAS, E. C., and RUTTAN, V. W. 1964. An analysis of rice production in the Philippines. Econ. Research J. (Univ. of the East) XI (3): 159-180.

VON UEXKUELL, H. R. 1964. Obstacles to using fertilizers for rice in Southeast Asia. World Crops 16 (March): 70-75.

10

Problems of Policy in Planning
the Indus Basin
Investment in West Pakistan

Arthur Gaitskell

It is sometimes tempting to wonder whether the emphasis on
economic development is simply a craze of our age. In the
underdeveloped world, before World War II, emphasis was
placed on political development; economic life was largely left
to the vagaries of external private enterprise profit. Since World
War II concern for economic growth seems to have developed into something approaching the nature of a moral crusade.

The Indus Basin region gives us two clues to this curious
phenomenon. With a population of 50 million people, it illustrates
how population pressure combined with poverty and the risk of
hunger give rise to a general anxiety complex which is perhaps
the most critical reason for the switch in emphasis to economic
growth. And, situated next door to China, it raises the particular
anxiety of a competing ideological solution to that growth. Between
them, these two aspects of life probably form the major cause of
our interest in developing countries today. By contrast, the old
aspect of external private enterprise profit is a far more faltering
stimulus than it used to be.

There are other reasons why the problems of investment in the
Indus Basin are interesting. It is commonplace today to realize
that the backwardness of the rural sector, where most of the
world's population live, is turning out to be an enormous drag

on growth. In many developing countries "getting agriculture moving" is, however, proving bafflingly difficult. There are, of course, many reasons for this, but the one most beyond human control is the uncertainty of the weather. In this respect the Indus Basin has a unique advantage—ample water. It is, in fact, the largest irrigated area in the world. The disastrous famines which are presently occurring in India as a result of the failure of the monsoon underline how important this advantage can be.

Finally, the actual story of the Indus Basin region is full of illustrations of the kind of problems one faces in development, of the extent to which planning is essential, feasible, or desirable in order to promote growth, of the mistakes one makes, and of the puzzles which elude any easy solution in spite of econometrics and computers.

It is impossible, of course, to tell the whole story in a single chapter. One can only pick out some of the technical, human, and institutional facets and illustrate how their interaction poses problems for decision in development, many of which are also relevant in other parts of the world.

TECHNICAL ASPECTS OF THE INDUS BASIN

THE PHYSICAL NATURE OF THE REGION

Geographically and climatically West Pakistan is a continuation of the Middle East rather than a beginning of Asia, forming in this respect a complete contrast with East Pakistan. Its most striking physical characteristic is its dry desert nature. This is curious because the northern and eastern boundaries of the Indus Basin comprise some of the highest mountain ranges in the world— the Himalayas and their adjacent satellite formation. Agriculturally, the most usable part of the Basin is an enormous plain, stretching with a very gentle slope northeast to southwest from the foothills of the Himalayas to the sea, a distance of nearly 1,000 miles. Yet the rainfall isohyets on this plain are astonishingly low and fall in gradation from north to south, from an average of 25 inches in the Potwar Uplands immediately below the foothills, to 16 inches at Lahore, to 12 inches at Lyallpur, to 6 inches at Multan, and to a mere 4 inches in all the lower part of the Basin. The western boundary also consists of mountain ranges and the high plateaus of Baluchistan and Wazaristan, but is even drier, and this dry atmosphere spills over into actual desert in parts of the Basin in Thal, Cholistan, the Sind, and on into Rajasthan over the Indian border. The rainy season is a very short one and is extremely erratic so that averages are no guide to certainty, and reality may be either drought or sudden flood.

The saving grace of the region for humanity is the great Indus River and its tributaries. The Indus itself rises behind the Himalayas in Tibet and Ladakh and flows in a great curve to the north of and along the western side of the great plain. Some of its tributaries come in from the western mountains as the Swat and Kabul rivers, but the critical tributaries are four great rivers which actually traverse the plain from east to west—the Jhelum, Chenab, Ravi, and Sutlej.[1]* These rivers all rise in the Himalayan mountains and unite in sequence until, as a single stream, they join the Indus some 400 miles before it reaches the sea. All these great rivers give their maximum discharge in the summer or Kharif season of the year when the snow melts and the rain falls in the high mountains; they drop to a much lower discharge in the winter. The actual discharges are unpredictable and vary phenomenally from year to year and from river to river.

These physical characteristics of the region determined the original pattern of human habitation in three main divisions: (1) seasonal rain cultivation where the rainfall was sufficient, that is, mainly in the Potwar Uplands below the foothills; (2) seasonal cultivation alongside the rivers by diversion of the flood waters for irrigation; and (3) for the rest of the land (the so-called "doabs" between the rivers) merely sparse seasonal grazing for cattle, sheep, goats, and camels.

IRRIGATION IN BRITISH INDIA

Until the creation of Pakistan as a separate country in 1947, the Indus Basin region formed part of undivided British India. From the latter part of the nineteenth century the British administration sought to improve the natural physical conditions by embarking on an increasingly vast program of irrigation projects. These projects were designed to make more and better use of surface river water instead of letting most of it flow unused to the sea. They originated in a series of barrages on the main rivers so that by raising the level the water could be diverted through a huge network of canals

*Notes for this chapter begin on page 213.

to all that area, the "doabs," which had hitherto been hardly used except for grazing. In such areas the canals were called perennial, that is to say whatever water was available in the river throughout the year was diverted to them. The projects also sought to improve the original flood diversion channels adjacent to the rivers, but the canals in this case were called non-perennial because only the flood waters were allocated to them. It was assumed that cultivators adjacent to the rivers could dig wells and tap seepage water during the winter, whereas those in the "doabs" could not.

There can be no question that these irrigation projects, pursued over a long period and covering 26 million acres, completely transformed the region. Settlement in a largely empty land gradually built up a very big population with villages, townships, road and rail communications, trade, and agricultural production. By 1940, the Indus Basin region had become the major granary for undivided India, producing large quantities of cotton, wheat, rice, sugar, and oilseeds. There were, however, certain characteristics about the whole process which have left a legacy of problems in the different circumstances of our day. In the first place, the irrigation system itself was purely one of gravity and diversion. There were no storage dams. This meant that the water available to any farmer was dependent on the varying discharges of the rivers. Obviously, some water was better than no water, but there could be no certainty that the water would be available in the quantity or on the date which might be desirable.

In the second place, this uncertainty became more important because the principles of distribution of water were dictated more by engineering, financial, and general administrative considerations than by any objective of obtaining maximum yields. Financially, it was held desirable to sell as much government land as possible to cover the cost of the irrigation works. Socially, it was held desirable to spread the benefit as widely as possible. These are obviously laudable objectives, but they led to the assumption that a low water delta would be quite all right. Nor was this assumption necessarily in conflict with agricultural opinion in the days when fertilizer was an expensive rarity and land plentiful so that leaving the land to lie fallow was the cheapest way of restoring fertility after usage.

As a result of these various considerations, the distribution of water throughout the system was planned to give one cusec per

350 acres gross of land. This ration was intended to permit each farmer in the perennial canals to irrigate 25 per cent of his gross area in the Kharif season and 50 per cent in the winter, giving a 75 per cent intensity of cropping during an individual year. In the non-perennial canals it was intended to permit 70 per cent of the gross area to be irrigated in the Kharif with no discharge for winter irrigation at all. In the early days, when families first settled on the land, these ratios may have been adhered to, but as time passed and population increased, farmers tended to spread the water more widely and more thinly over their gross area. The combination of the widespread and the irregular discharge has led to the surprising phenomenon of very low yield per acre in the world's greatest irrigated region just at a period when high yield per acre, and its corollary, higher income per rural family, are becoming top priorities in the struggle for economic growth.

The third weakness in these giant irrigation projects is that they were more engineer-orientated than farmer-orientated. The farmer got the water that the engineer allocated to him, rather than what he might think his crops needed. This lack of attention to the end-use of the water, which today might be regarded as the supreme purpose of having irrigation at all, was further characterized by leaving the farmers themselves to lay out, dig, and repair the channels which led the water to their lands from a canal outlet point. These operations were carried out with very indifferent efficiency. Finally, no serious investment was made to provide an advisory service to teach farmers how to utilize the water most efficiently.

The point in drawing attention to these limitations is not hindsight criticism, for the objectives when these projects were started were somewhat different from what they are today. Agriculture was then regarded more in the nature of a way of life than as an important contribution to growth. The projects were chiefly to provide new openings for family farming, and the farmers were expected to know their own business. The point is rather to indicate that behind the creation of the great granary these inherent technical disabilities do present serious problems in the different circumstances of today. It must be admitted that they also indicate what mistakes to avoid when one is starting new irrigation schemes in our era.

There was finally a fourth technical drawback of a very serious nature. The soil of the great plain contains salts. At the start of the projects, when the groundwater table was 100 feet below ground level, this was of little importance. However, over this long period, what with irrigation, seepage from canals, and rainfall impeded by road, rail, and canal lines running transverse to the natural drainage slope, the water table has been continuously rising. Over quite wide areas it is within 5 feet of the surface, and in certain places it is right over the surface. Apart from the flooding liable to result from this phenomenon, the rise in the water table has brought the salts up with it, and the ensuing salinity has proved toxic to crops. Unfortunately, a spread of salinity has also arisen apart from the rise in the water table. The very pattern of irrigation and land use, with the low irregular water delta and the high proportion of fallow land, has tended to encourage salts to rise to the surface by capillary attraction. As a result of this dual base, the phenomenon of salinity has become increasingly alarming. Seen from the air, the land appears to have been infected by some giant skin disease as patches of farm land all over the region have gradually become unhealthy and unusable. Some 30 per cent of the irrigated region is becoming infected with this salinity disease.

THE PARTITION OF INDIA AND THE INDUS WATERS AGREEMENT

British India was divided in 1947 because the Moslem community, fearing that they would be in an inferior minority position when independence was granted to the country, pressed for partition on a religious basis. Almost the whole of the Indus Basin region fell within the newly created Pakistan so that this great traditional granary was cut off from India.

There was, however, an extremely important exception. Mr. Nehru, the Prime Minister of India, had never wanted partition. He had favored a secular state and an undivided country. At the time of partition the Maharajah of Jammu and Kashmir, who was a Hindu although the vast majority of the population there was Moslem, declared for accession to India. Mr. Nehru accordingly sent in the Indian army to insure the incorporation of Jammu and Kashmir into the Indian Union. This action precipitated what has come to be known as the Kashmir problem, which is beyond the scope of this chapter.

What is pertinent to our story, however, is that the sources of the main tributaries of the Indus are located in Jammu and Kashmir and, in particular, that the headworks of the whole canal system of the two southern rivers, the Ravi and the Sutlej, are located on the Indian side of what came to be the boundary between the two countries. The Indians were therefore in a position to offset some of the loss of their granary by diverting the whole flow of these two rivers to new irrigation areas on their side of the border. This they now proposed to do. The proposal, which would have left some of the most productive and most heavily inhabited areas of Pakistan literally high and dry, brought the two countries to the brink of war in 1948.

The war was averted by the intervention of outside influences and particularly by the proposal of the International Bank for Reconstruction and Development that the diversion should be postponed until alternative arrangements for water supply to those affected in Pakistan could be studied and implemented. After ten years of patient investigation and negotiation, a feasible alternative arrangement was reached and incorporated in an Indus Waters Agreement. The arrangement comprises the construction of a big new storage dam at Mangla on the Jhelum river with a series of huge link canals to carry water from the Jhelum to those areas in Pakistan which have hitherto depended on water from the Ravi and Sutlej rivers. The Mangla dam and the link canals are now under construction. The considerable financing for this undertaking is being provided by an International Consortium organized by the International Bank.

DEVELOPMENT SUPPLEMENTARY TO
THE INDUS WATERS AGREEMENT

The investigation leading to the Indus Waters Agreement coupled with the serious drawbacks of the existing system of irrigation in Pakistan have naturally evoked inquiries as to how the whole water supply system in Pakistan might be improved irrespective of the diversion of the Ravi and Sutlej rivers to India. These inquiries cover two separate aspects—the possibility of further storage and the possibility of using groundwater for irrigation. These aspects must now be described for a full understanding of the technical potential of the Indus Basin region.

The Tarbela Dam.—The combined annual river flow of surface water in the Indus Basin amounts, on the average, to 167 million acre feet of which 70 million still go to the sea, because at the time that this surplus is available the canals are already using full discharge. Survey has, however, revealed a number of other possible storage sites in addition to Mangla, of which the most prominent is on the Indus at Tarbela where the river emerges from the high mountains.[2] The Tarbela site affords yet greater storage potential than that at Mangla, and the water could be diverted into the irrigation system after the flood season by link canals from barrages lower down on the Indus, from the Chasma barrage to the Jhelum river, from the Taunsa barrage to the Chenab river, and thence, to most of the canal system. A feature of these new storage sites at Mangla and Tarbela is that, in addition to providing reservoir water hitherto unavailable, they can also supply large quantities of hydroelectric power.

Utilization of Groundwater.—The hydroelectric power is important for the much greater utilization of a water resource, the significance of which has only come to be appreciated in recent years, largely as the result of trying to find a cure for salinity. The technique for reclaiming land affected by salinity is essentially to provide additional water and wash away the salts by drainage. The process has to be spread over several years as the land cannot immediately absorb the large quantity of water involved. Reclamation of this nature had been practiced by the Irrigation Department for some years, but suffered from a number of drawbacks, such as inadequacy and unreliability of surface water supply, excessively high groundwater impeding drainage, and a subsequent return to low water delta and low cropping intensity which tended to bring back salinity by capillary attraction.

In 1958, a very large-scale experiment was conducted in the Rechna Doab, utilizing for reclamation purposes not the surface water, but the groundwater, wherever this was sufficiently free from salt content. For this purpose 2,000 tube wells were sunk in a rectangle covering a million acres of land.[3] It was intended, by continuous operation of these tube wells, to make a three-pronged attack on these drawbacks: (1) by drawing down the water table to ten feet to eliminate flooding and to permit draining; (2) by supplying continuity of excess water to wash down the salts; and (3) by supplying a new source of water in addition to the surface water to enable not only a full delta instead of a low delta for the crops, but also a much higher intensity of cropping (150 per cent instead of 75 per cent), thereby eliminating the fallow with its consequent encouragement of a return to salinity.

The Rechna Doab experiment has yet to be evaluated, and in some respects the actual reclamation process has been disappointing. However, it has led to a realization that, altogether apart from the reclamation objective, Pakistan has in its groundwater an extensive potential reservoir of additional water supplies. Although some of this groundwater is too saline to use, particularly in the southern part of the Basin, and some must be mixed with surface water before it is usable for irrigation, subsequent survey has revealed that underneath a total of 29 million acres of potential irrigable land, 19 million acres has suitable groundwater. This aquifer contains approximately 300 million acre feet although the intention is only to pump from it the recharge element which comes from irrigation, seepage, and rain.

SUMMARY OF THE TECHNICAL ASPECTS
OF THE INDUS BASIN

It is time to summarize the meaning of these technical points in the general problem of development. Primarily, they signify that in a world which is becoming increasingly short of food and in a critical region where population pressure is heavily increasing, where existing standards of living are low, where rainfall is low, and where, in spite of irrigation, land is rapidly deteriorating on a large scale from salinity, a uniquely hopeful prospect of altering this situation for the better is now in sight.

The provision of additional storage of surface water plus the large-scale utilization of groundwater could, technically speaking, contribute to this prospect in a threefold manner: (1) by lowering the water table and curing the land of salinity; (2) by increasing the yield per acre through the provision of sufficient and sufficiently reliable water; and (3) by enabling, thanks to the same provision, the intensity of cropping to be doubled on the same land within the year.

Sufficient and sufficiently reliable water could also have multiplier effects on production. Although not the only factors (price and market outlet being critical also) they are very important in giving farmers confidence to use inputs critical to yield and income such as better seed, better cultivation practices, fertilizer, and pesticides. The worthwhileness of investing in expensive inputs is enormously enhanced if one can rely on the certainty of water.

The importance of this prospect is not limited to the benefit accrued by the 29 million directly affected acres in Pakistan. By solving the Indus Waters dispute the Agreement also permits irrigation of large new areas in India and makes available hydroelectric power, thereby raising the possibility of surplus food, fiber, and industrial products both for local consumption and for foreign exchange-earning export trade.

In short, the technical aspects in the Indus Basin offer the opportunity to West Pakistan to be a demonstration country for progressive growth towards higher standards of living in Asia, where communist alternatives may become the refuge of despair if inequality, poverty, and population pressure continue unabated.

It is only right to point out, however, that the Indus Basin proposals involve a huge investment cost which is largely expected to be financed by the Western world. The attainment of an economic rate of return, and indeed the attainment of the hopeful prospect suggested by the technical aspects, will depend on the degree to which farmers respond to opportunity, on the length of time they take to respond, on the availability of services (efficient administration of water and power, better seeds, fertilizer, pesticides, credit, transport, marketing), on competent and sufficient advice, on an attractive price/cost ratio, and on political and social stability over the period concerned.

In other words, success is largely dependent on human and institutional factors. The Indus Basin investment is thus a classic example of a current problem in the relations between developing and developed countries where money, ideas, and technology from outside (whether East or West) have to fit in or not fit in with local money, ideas, and technology and above all, with implementation in an environment beyond external control and in the hands of the local people themselves. It is a tremendous challenge not only to our technology and resources, but to human cooperation and psychology. It is at this point that we must look at the human and institutional aspects of the Indus Basin.

HUMAN AND INSTITUTIONAL ASPECTS
OF THE INDUS BASIN

THE HUMAN SCENE IN 1959

I must here divert to a personal note which explains the year 1959 above. In that year the Pakistan Government set up a Food and Agriculture Commission to look into the problems of agriculture throughout both East and West Pakistan, and I was invited to join the Commission as a nominee of the International Bank. The purpose of mentioning this is that it affords an eye-witness' opportunity to describe the human and institutional situation in the Indus Basin at that date, the problems that seemed to arise from that situation, and the recommendations which the Commission made to meet those problems. Later on we shall look at the situation as it appeared in 1965. The period affords quite an interesting case study—the kind of exercise employed at the Harvard Business School—and you can make up your own minds concerning how you would have answered, or would answer today, the questions involved. These are not academic questions. They are the real hard-core puzzles of development.

RAINFALL AREAS IN THE INDUS BASIN

Although this chapter is essentially about the irrigated areas, there is one fact about the rainfall areas in the Basin which cannot be overlooked. They are very overpopulated. The Potwar Uplands, which lie in the north between the foothills and the irrigated area, have already been mentioned. Overcropping and overstocking have led to spectacular erosion there. Although conservation might improve this region, the pertinent point is that future generations must find their sustenance elsewhere. Higher up in the foothills the catchment areas of the rivers present a parallel problem. Overpopulation and overstocking have led to deforestation and erosion, here more critical because of its tendency to turn rivers into torrents and cause extensive flooding in the plain below. Again the implication, exclusive of conservation measures, is that future generations must find their sustenance elsewhere.

Here a distinction has to be made between the Punjab or
northern and the Sind or southern part of the Basin. Irrigation
started in the Punjab, and the "doab" lands were largely settled
in canal colonies in family farms of 25 acres. By 1959, considerable
changes in ownership had taken place, many family farms had been
fragmented, and this region was becoming heavily overpopulated.
In the Sind, development came later and is indeed still going on.
Here much more of the land was in the form of large, privately
owned estates. The rural society arising from those circumstances
was a mixture of owner-occupier, mainly on increasingly small
holdings, and of sharecroppers seeking a living as tenants of those
who held land. A land reform measure had recently been passed
with the intention of reducing the size of the large estates and
making more land available for the landless. However, the ceiling
had been placed fairly high at 500 acres of irrigated land per
individual, aggregation had been permitted in the sense that each
member of a family could be a separate landowner, and areas
planted to orchards were exempt. Thus, only two million acres
became available for distribution, and 60 per cent of this re-
linquished land was naturally of the poorest quality and needed the
greatest degree of development.

The most important deficiency in the land reform, however,
was the omission of any measure to abolish sharecropping, and,
although laws were passed in the Punjab to fix the landlord's
share at 40 per cent only, the actual division increasingly threw
the burden on the tenant as more and more people sought some
place on which to subsist.

The concept of landownership dated back to the original land
settlement of British India under which a landowner was held to
be entitled to receive rent from the actual cultivator in the form of
a share of the crops, but had the duty in turn to pay the land
revenue tax to the government. As the land revenue was only
reviewed every 30 years, a landowner tended to do very well,
and the ambition of all was to become an owner and sit back and
draw the sharecrop rent. Very few landowners were interested in
agriculture. They were often absentees and merely collected their
share through an agent. Their main interest was in the financial
and social prestige which landownership conferred. In fact, a law

of 1950 prohibited eviction of tenants without recourse to court, and although this gave the tenant more security it inhibited the landowner from direct cultivation himself. The tenant was mainly interested in subsistence, in food for himself and fodder for his animals, even if this meant growing sorghum and encouraging weeds in cash crops which he had to share with his landlord. The result of this relationship was that there was little incentive for either party to invest in modernization of farming, and primitive methods and low yields seemed almost ingrained in the system.

There were, and indeed still are, a number of new settlement areas being opened up where new barrages were of fairly recent construction, but the opportunity of settling landless people thereon as owner-cultivators was largely inhibited by a practice of selling the land to the highest bidder, who was often an absentee investor rather than a farmer, or of distributing the land to grantees, mainly in the Army or the Civil Service, who also were frequently absentee investors. Both tended to work their holdings by the sharecropping system.

To complete the human picture, it must be appreciated that at the time of partition some 8 million Hindus, many of whom were among the best farmers in the Punjab, left for India, while some 10 million Moslems came in as refugees from India. Although the ex-Hindu lands were allocated to these refugees many of them came from an urban background and also tended to work their holdings by the sharecropping system. It must also be appreciated that this tremendous exchange of refugees caused profound dislocation, for much of the banking, commercial, and administrative cadres in British India had been in the hands of Hindus.

THE INSTITUTIONAL SCENE IN 1959

The last sector to receive any attention towards overcoming the problems of this dislocation was the rural sector, and in 1959 the main feature of the institutional scene was the general ineffectiveness of the agricultural services. Priority in the new country was given to industry and, apart from continuing investment in the engineering aspects of irrigation, such as construction of barrages and canals, the subject of agriculture had been turned over to the provincial government where it was subsequently starved of funds.

As a result of all this history, the interlocking chain of inputs which have so significantly improved agricultural production in the developed world was practically nonexistent in Pakistan in 1959. In the research stations many of the best personnel had left for India, and those who remained were more engaged in ivory tower papers for their own prestige than in solving the practical problems of the fields around them. The extension service was low in caliber and low in numbers. The field assistant at the bottom had little pay and no transport, but his unit area averaged 100,000 acres or some 15,000 farmers. In point of fact, he seldom left his market town for it was his duty to check the distribution of supposedly better seed and fertilizer. In reality, little better seed emerged from the research stations. There were few foundation farms, no facilities for cleaning and fumigation, and no adequate system of multiplication. Most of the seed supplied was heavily adulterated. There was little demand for fertilizer because of unreliable water supply, too few demonstrations, and a fluctuating policy towards subsidizing its cost. An embryo free pest control service had been inaugurated mainly to deal with major outbreaks. In these three important inputs—seed, fertilizer, and pesticides—private enterprise showed no interest whatever. As in Tennessee when the Tennessee Valley Authority (TVA) was created, when people are poor it is unusual for private enterprise to sense any potential profit in improving their conditions.

Such profit as private enterprise did envisage in Pakistan in agriculture consisted in creaming off margins in marketing and moneylending. With the exception of certain statutory markets in the Punjab, where abuses were restricted, most marketing was subject to swindling on weights, and deductions by the merchant buyer were countered by adulteration by the farmer. In any case, many farmers were forced to sell at low prices on harvest to landlord or moneylenders in order to get credit for consumption. Cooperatives had existed, but were moribund. There was an Agricultural Bank, but this only lent against mortgages and so serviced only the larger landowners. Machinery was hardly used for cultivation except by the rare landlord who was interested and lucky enough to run his estate by direct means. The universal prime mover was bullock power with half the land required for fodder as its fuel. The sowing was usually broadcast by hand. Both practices make elimination of weeds difficult, whereas the shortage of water led farmers to favor a very low stand. Finally, the official attitude to farm prices offered no incentive to increased yield. High export duties were deemed essential to the exchequer and low food prices essential for the urban and industrial population. If shortages occurred, resort was had to cordonning and requisitioning. If yields were good, prices fell.

THE FOOD AND AGRICULTURE COMMISSION 1959/60

The essential fact facing the Commission was thus an immense contrast between the technical possibilities leading to a bright future and the human and institutional limitations leading to increasing disaster. The primary problem seemed to be how to organize matters to bridge this gap, how to energize a stagnant agricultural sector which with its seriously deteriorating land, increasing population, and increasing imports of food was a drag on all prospects of development. Fundamentally, it appeared a problem not of discovery, but of organization and implementation; the great need was not the provision of advice, but to get something done. In other words it seemed essential to plan and to manage. Let me illustrate this by discussing some of the questions which arose.

THE CASE FOR THE PACKAGE DEAL

The high investment cost of providing additional water, the population pressure, and the need to raise rural incomes and foreign exchange all demanded speedy improvement in yield. Technically, there could be no question that the decisive factor in raising yield significantly would be to use a combination of inputs, and raising yield significantly was in its turn critical to a farmer's interest in extra risk and effort. Concentration on one input, say fertilizer, thus seemed of doubtful value. On the contrary, attention to the interlocking nature of all relevant inputs seemed essential. Timely and ample water, properly leveled and prepared land, seed of good quality and tolerant to high fertilizer application, stand in plants per acre relevant to sufficient water and fertilizer, fertilizer itself, and finally pest control—all these must be combined for the full impact to be gained in yield. Nor was this all. Credit, to get out of moneylenders' clutches and get a full price, improved marketing, and a satisfactory price versus cost of inputs ratio, had equally to be part of the interlocking chain if the farmer's incentive was to be aroused and his income raised. In other words, the case seemed to call for a package deal covering all these aspects in a perspective plan. There seemed no prospect that the stimulus might come spontaneously from farmers themselves. Organization by the state seemed an essential prelude.

THE MINIMUM ESSENTIAL NEEDS THEORY

In opposition to the above arguments in favor of a Package Deal strategy, the Commission had to take account of a viewpoint which might be called the Minimum Essential Needs strategy. A great advocate of this viewpoint was Dr. Kenneth Galbraith, then United States Ambassador in India. His view was that, whatever the validity of the arguments in favor of the Package Deal strategy, the plain fact was that in developing countries one could only concentrate on a few essential points. Staff and knowledge were not available for more. In relating this theme to Pakistan it might be that drainage water and fertilizer were the minimum essential needs and that all other features and constraints were of lesser importance and would have to wait.

WHAT AGENCY FOR IMPLEMENTATION?

If a decision on strategy favored the Package Deal concept, the next problem was to decide what agency could best insure that the package of needed inputs was available and could also persuade farmers to use them. Here again there were a variety of alternatives. There was the view of those who felt that state intervention should be kept to a minimum and that private enterprise, particularly in matters of supply, would give the best results. Critics of this view, whatever its ultimate virtue, felt that private enterprise, as already indicated, had so far shown no interest in increasing agricultural production nor in organizing supply to an apparently unprofitable sector. Its only evident interest appeared rather in the nature of a constraint, taking the benefit away from the farmer at the point of marketing and squeezing him on credit. Upon assuming that active government intervention was therefore necessary, the question then arose as to whether the job could be done satisfactorily by routine government departments and with routine government attitudes and regulations or whether some separate organization devoted exclusively to the task of increasing agricultural production ought to be established. If routine government departments were favored, the problem then was how their different contributions could best be amalgamated and their boundaries defined so that different aspects of the package were coordinated. If a separate authority was favored, it must then be decided whether this should take the form of an interdepartmental board of interested government departments or, like the TVA, be something quite outside routine government lines.

In considering a solution by way of reinvigorating routine government departments, a prominent phenomenon in 1959 was that although many different departments of government impinged on the problem of agricultural production from different points, there was very little coordination among them. Above all, there was no one agency to which the farmer could turn who could handle his problems as a whole and effectively. All preferred the traditional advisory role without the burden of seeing that the necessary supply of inputs relevant to this advice was available. Cohesion between these inputs and credit and marketing, so vital from the farmers' viewpoint, simply did not exist.

The lack of any agricultural progress in these circumstances naturally led to the suggestion of a unified command. Members of the Revenue Service (the Civil Service of Pakistan) favored a district team approach with the district magistrate as team leader. They felt that he alone had the power and reputation to control independent departments and to subdue departmental empire-building. They also considered that the newly-created Basic Democracies should be associated with the planning and direction of local development and that, as the nurturing of those new bodies was the special duty of the Revenue Service, the team leader must come from that service. This particular District Team solution was in fact being adopted at that time by the government of India in their Special Districts program, and was adopted in Pakistan in 1959 for a crash program to increase food and cotton production.

Members of the technical departments were less enthusiastic about serving under a generalist from the Revenue Service as team leader, especially for a long-term program which was the purpose of the Food and Agriculture Commission inquiry. Some preferred an interdepartmental board with an independent manager in specific project areas, particularly following up tube-well investment by the state to combat salinity.

RECOMMENDATIONS OF THE FOOD AND
AGRICULTURE COMMISSION 1960

ORGANIZATION

Faced with these divergent alternatives the Commission, after considerable uncertainty, came to the following conclusions in regard to organization.

1. In view of the stagnant condition of agriculture and the prospect of declining yield owing to salinity, it was essential to create some competent instrument of implementation.

2. In this respect the minimum essential needs theory, however tenable for a crash program, was less valid in the long run than the package deal and interlocking links theory.

3. The really critical element to raise yields substantially lay in the application of all inputs to a crop in a timely manner, and the removal as far as possible of all constraints. Just as concentration on the engineering aspects of water supply was ineffective without a follow-up of improved farming, so separation of extension from supply of inputs, separation of supply of inputs from credit, and separation of the whole complex from marketing would be ineffective. A unified command capable of integrating all these aspects was essential.

4. The scope of the unified command must be confined to the prime task of improving agricultural production and farmers' incomes and not dispersed, as in Basic Democracy, over all interests in village betterment.

5. Private enterprise could not at the start be relied upon as a competent instrument for implementation.

6. Left to operate on their own, the individual government departments were not adequately coordinated for the job. The Irrigation Department was engineer-orientated and had no agricultural expertise. The departments of Agriculture and Animal Husbandry, despite the fact that the task might be regarded as their speciality, were weak in personnel and reputation. The Cooperative Department was largely discredited. The Community Development Department, the great hope. at one time in India, was disappointingly ineffective, and its village level workers, jacks-of-all-trades in theory, got no support from other departments.

7. The District Team solution, although theoretically offering a

unified command, had serious disadvantages in practice because the Revenue Service was already heavily overburdened with law and order, taxation, political guidance, and chairmanship of endless existing committees.

8. The government services as a whole were not geared to the task of development. Their decisions were highly centralized in regard to administration, finance, and stores, and lacked the flexibility to permit essential rapid action in the field. Their personnel rules favored promotion on seniority, not merit, and this made it difficult to expel useless men.

9. There already existed a semi-autonomous agency in the Water and Power Development Authority which had itself been created because the routine Irrigation Department could not handle satisfactorily the urgent development needs in water and power. Analogously, it was desirable to set up a semi-autonomous Agricultural Development Corporation which could concentrate on the sole job of agricultural development, could establish a unified command, and could have the advantage of formulating its own regulations in regard to recruiting (from a wider choice of Army, commercial, or even expatriate sources as well as selecting personnel for temporary duty from government departments), promoting, paying, and sacking staff, and in regard to administrative and financial decentralization.

10. The Board of Control of the Agricultural Development Corporation should be a small, independent, full-time board nominated by the President, and not an interdepartmental board, the drawback of the latter being partly the risk of continuing routine government methods and partly the risk that ex officio part-time members would be more interested in their own line departments than in the success of the Corporation.

11. The task of the Agricultural Development Corporation would be to implement the Package Deal concept in specified Project Areas, while the routine government departments would continue in all areas not declared to be Project Areas, where they would endeavor to implement the Minimum Essential Needs concept, particularly in regard to encouraging additional water (surface and tube well) and fertilizer. Within the declared Project Areas the Agricultural Development Corporation would take complete control and all staff relating to agriculture would come under the command of its project manager. The Department of Agri-

culture would, however, continue to be responsible for all research, and the Irrigation Department would continue to control all surface water up to canal turn-outs.

12. Although the Commission set out a very large panorama of potential projects, it visualized that each of these would only be taken up according to a phased program, the government then declaring it to be a Project Area and so under the unified command of the Corporation. The objective was concentration at first on prescribed limited projects to discover satisfactory solution patterns, not diffusion and dilution of staff over wide areas as in a crash program. Typical suggested examples of such project areas were: one district from a region of high production, or one salinity-affected area such as part of the Rechna doab to follow up the tube-well investment theme, or a new colonization area like the G. M. Barrage.

13. An important feature of the program of project areas was that when the Corporation had finally established a satisfactory system or organization in a project area, it was visualized that it would work for a gradual transfer out of its own activities, that cooperatives or farmers' associations would take on its managerial function, private enterprise would compete to provide supplies, and extension would revert to an advisory position. When this happened the new instrument would have served its purpose.

14. It was suggested that the Field Wing of the Corporation should handle the project areas. The Commission further recommended that the Corporation should establish a Supply Wing to take over the duty of supply of improved seed and fertilizer for the whole country, thereby relieving the Department of Agriculture of a burden which had very seriously hampered its primary task of extension and demonstration.

PRICES

Apart from its recommendations on organization, the Commission gave concurrent support to new policies intended to improve farmers' confidence in the prospect of profit from investment in inputs. In 1959, a complete change was made in this respect. A policy of liberalization was introduced to encourage food production. Cordonning and requisitioning were abandoned and collection was left to private enterprise. In order to give both farmer and townsman a fair deal, a system of buffer stock operation was established to keep satisfactory limits to the price of wheat. The system enabled a guaranteed minimum of 13 rupees per maund (82 2/7 pounds) to the farmer, but controlled the maximum at 16 rupees per maund by purchasing or selling the buffer stock. The system was made possible thanks to Public Law 480 supplies. Apart from this food stabilization measure, the export duty on cotton was reduced from 125 to 25 rupees per maund. The Commission further recommended that a subsidy of 50 per cent should be applied to the cost of fertilizer and maintained for at least three years.

LAND TENURE

There were people in 1959 who believed that the greatest single cause of reluctance to adopt modern inputs to improve yields was the high rent which the great army of sharecroppers had to pay in crop percentage to the landowners. It might be thought that the Commission would have advocated some radical change in this aspect of land reform. This thought would be all the more relevant to those who have witnessed the profound effect on the improvement of agriculture in Japan and Taiwan which has been attributed to the "Land to the Tiller" program in those two countries, and which is said to be the basic foundation for their remarkable progress.

It must be remembered, however, that a number of circumstances facilitated that successful land reform. There was, of course, a powerful United States military presence in favor of the reform and, in Japan, a local socialist government in favor of it also. There was heavy pressure from powerful tenants' associations, and there was a real fear of communist alternatives in adjacent China. Apart from these spurs to radical action, the subsequent success of the measures owed a great deal to three other factors: (1) a long tradition of successful cooperatives, (2) a highly literate population, and (3) in the case of Taiwan, a large influx of highly skilled refugees.

By contrast, in Pakistan in 1959 there was no outside influence controlling policy. There was a local conservative government representing largely the landowners themselves and the Army and Civil Service, all with vested interests as current landowners. There were no tenants' associations to exercise pressure. The peasantry was largely illiterate. There was a great shortage of skilled people. Cooperatives had been a conspicuous failure. There was, therefore, neither a desire among those who controlled the country to push through a "land to the tiller" program, nor were there present those other factors so essential to its ultimate success. Under the circumstances it is not surprising that the Commission made no radical recommendation about land reform and merely contented itself with advocating a statutory reduction in the land-lords' share to 40 per cent and a sharing of input costs accordingly. This was a pretty useless recommendation, considering the real situation depended on the pressure of demand for land; but the comparison with Japan does illustrate that a timeliness of relevant factors may well be a *sine qua non* of successful land reform. In Pakistan, undoubtedly, the problem remains and will be referred to again later.

The report of the Food and Agriculture Commission raised a storm of opposition from the Establishment. Government depart-ments saw little need for a special authority, and the International Bank and the American advisers to the Planning Commission were equally inclined to the routine solutions of improved extension services and cooperatives. The military government of Pakistan, however, accepted the recommendations and set up an Agricul-tural Development Corporation.

THE REVELLE REPORT, 1962

The opposition to the Agricultural Development Corporation led to considerable delay in its creation. It also led to a considerable military bias in the staffing of the Agricultural Development Cor-poration and to the allocation of its projects in the difficult new colonization areas of the Sind rather than in the established areas of the Punjab. In the meantime, the salinity problem caused increasing anxiety and, following a visit by President Ayoub of Pakistan to the United States, President Kennedy sent to Pakistan a White House panel of experts, headed by Dr. Revelle, to assist in finding a solution.

The Revelle report, although for the most part a highly technical document dealing with salinity, made much the same criticisms of the lack of cohesion between government departments as had the Food and Agriculture Commission. More particularly, it agreed on the need for a new executive instrument under a unified com-mand to follow up the investment in tube wells and additional surface-water supplies. This instrument was intended not only to secure satisfactory reclamation of saline land, but also to stimulate maximum agricultural production on the lines of the package deal strategy. For operational purposes it recommended that the salinity problem should be tackled over a period of twenty-five years at a unit rate of approximately one million acres per annum by government investment in tube wells. The annual units concerned were called Scarps (Salinity Control and Reclamation Projects). The type of unified command favored by the panel, however, was the interdepartmental board with independent project management, and it recommended that the instrument of implementation in the Scarps program should be a Land and Water Development Board.

The recommendations of the Revelle report were also accepted by the government of Pakistan with the result that there now arose in the country the following situation: (1) An Agricultural Development Corporation with a field wing to conduct a program of project areas (now covering some 10 million acres and four out of the five main barrages on the Indus), and a supply wing for supplying seeds and fertilizer to the whole country; (2) A Land and Water Development Board with a program of Scarps (so far mainly in Scarp 1, the original Rechna doab tube-well project); (3) The routine government departments to stimulate agricultural production in the rest of the region not covered by the above two agencies.

The position in 1965 was that these three somewhat different approaches to the problem of modernizing agriculture were being pursued with little coordination and with no definition of the ultimate boundaries each was intended to attain. In the meantime, the resolution of this somewhat confused picture was becoming increasingly important since the huge investment in storage and groundwater required some estimate of its rate of return as the money was immediately required. To make the picture more confusing, analysis by the Planning Commission of the country's agricultural progress in the period of the second five-year plan, 1960-65, suddenly raised the question of whether any of this emphasis on organization and package deal strategy, or even on state initiative and state investment, was really as important as had been supposed. The problems of policy posed by this latter analysis must now be explained.

THE AGRICULTURAL SITUATION IN 1965 AND
ITS EFFECT ON PROBLEMS OF POLICY

The most striking phenomenon about agriculture in the Indus Basin in 1965 was that it had taken a remarkable turn for the better. During the Second Plan period, 1960-65, gross agricultural production increased about 30 per cent, a rise which substantially exceeded that of industry in value. Foreign exchange earnings from agriculture, largely from cotton and rice, rose by 80 per cent.

To WHAT WAS IT DUE?

It would be nice to claim that this heartening change was due to all the advice about planning and organization and to the new agencies which had been set up. It would be difficult, however, to attribute much to these sources. The Agricultural Development Corporation had been largely preoccupied with infrastructure work in the new colonization zones and had hardly started to apply the package deal strategy in its project areas. Its supply wing was generally criticized as being no better than its predecessor, the Department of Agriculture, in servicing farmers with better seeds and fertilizer. The Land and Water Development Board was only operating in Scarp 1. Certainly the draw-down in the water table there had restored some land to fertile condition, but the reclamation follow-up had been disappointing; many of the government tube wells had developed faulty strainers, and the administrative weaknesses which the Food and Agriculture Commission had feared from an interdepartmental board solution had, in fact, transpired. Of the routine government departments, that of Agriculture, relieved by the creation of the Corporation from the duty of supplying seed and fertilizer, had certainly put in more time on demonstrations. However, there was little improvement in the research and extension services, and although application of pesticides had been increased, the quality of the operation was still the subject of adverse criticism. There had been very little improvement in the provision of credit and none in the system of marketing. The sharecropping system was unchanged.

How then had the remarkable change from complete stagnation to substantial growth in gross agricultural production come about?

The Planning Commission analysis attributed the result physically to two inputs: (1) increased irrigation water, and (2) a complete change in the attitude toward fertilizer. As regards the latter, consumption of fertilizer nutrients rose from 19,000 tons in 1960 to 86,000 tons in 1965, passing from a state of indifference in the farming community to one of black market shortage. As regards the former, irrigation water supply increased in the period by 20 per cent, canal water from rivers by 2 million acre feet, groundwater from government tube wells by 2.5 million acre feet, and groundwater from private tube wells by 4.5 million acre feet. The expansion of canal and government tube-well water was, of course, a planned development, but the contribution from private tube wells, 26,000 of which are estimated to have been installed during 1960-64, was a surprise, largely unplanned and unnoticed until a survey was made in 1964. Most of these wells were put in by private drilling rigs and financed by landowners and speculators without bank credit.

It would be reasonable to link the change in the attitude towards fertilizer to the increase in water, and particularly to the reliability in timeliness afforded by tube wells. However, it seems probable that the spontaneous investment in these dual physical factors was itself induced by a third factor: the marked improvement in the cost/benefit ratio of production. A substantial and maintained fertilizer subsidy, reduction in the cotton export duty, lower internal prices for industrial products particularly textiles, and regular and higher prices for the main agricultural products are believed to have played a considerable part in farmers' response (and tube-well speculators' response) to opportunity.

Additionally, there may have been other imponderable influences such as the effect of land reform on landowners' interest in their estates, the effect of political stability under the military regime, the Basic Democracy compared with the political turbulence which preceded it, and, last but not least, a series of climatically satisfactory years. This last point is one of caution to those who recollect how India appeared at one time in the 1950's to have solved its food problem, only to find that the influence of favorable weather was giving a misleading confidence that other constraints had been overcome or were unimportant.

One other aspect merits mention and also suggests a need for caution in making deductions from the above analysis. That is the difficulty of knowing whether the increase in gross production was the result of extra yield per acre or was mainly due merely to extra area cultivated. It is very difficult to assess this point. Claims have been made in Scarp 1 that there has been a substantial increase in yield per acre, but a recent survey made on a representative number of water channels does not corroborate this claim. Undoubtedly, some of the increase was due to new zones brought into irrigation for the first time, but apart from this, it may well be that the farmer's first reaction to getting additional water was to extend the amount of land (i.e., the intensity) devoted to crops within his farm. The point is important because it does pose the question of whether or not the provision of water is likely to be the end of the easy gains, leaving still to be solved all the constraints connected with poor seed, low stand, bad cultivation, lack of interest in other inputs, lack of credit, poor marketing facilities, and discouraging terms of land tenure. Is the phenomenon just a get-rich-quick gimmick for tube-well investors, or is it the prelude to a breakthrough in spontaneous adoption of all the other inputs beyond the water? The answer affects, of course, the degree of importance which may still need to be attached to organization and planning.

WHAT OF THE FUTURE?

The remarkable growth rate from 1960 to 1965 naturally raises doubt as to whether the emphasis put on the need for a unified command and a special instrument to implement a package deal strategy was all that justified in 1959 and 1962, and certainly whether it is the right policy to continue with it in 1965. It might be that under the apparent stagnation and indifference, human nature was not really so inert and so bound by constraints as had appeared. Once a source of additional water became apparent, and once an attractive cost/benefit ratio made farming profitable, farmers themselves responded spontaneously. Was it not these factors, rather than state agencies, which were the keys opening the door to growth? Should future policy then react more towards a *laissez faire* solution? Need one worry about organizing package deals covering all inputs at once? Given the start by additional water, farmers had already shown great interest in fertilizer. Could it not be assumed that they would quickly follow by demanding better seed and pesticides, and would not private enterprise now respond by organizing availability of these inputs far better than had the state agencies? Should not future strategy be biased towards giving maximum scope to those leader landlords and merchant investors who were prepared to put down their own tube wells, thereby off-loading this problem from the public purse and the delays of public administration?

Undoubtedly, this is the kind of strategy now being advocated by the Harvard Advisory Group to the Planning Commission and with them many others in Pakistan. There is among them a general belief that Pakistan is potentially on the verge of an agricultural breakthrough, provided no untoward discouragement should alter this trend of private enterprise confidence. In support of their view of a spontaneous follow-up to the use of inputs other than water and fertilizer has been the readiness of farmers to purchase high-priced, recently imported, Mexican wheat seed. This seed, because of its higher yielding qualities, is expected to spread like wildfire without the intervention of any government process of multiplication.

The example of Mexico is taken to be a prototype for Pakistan to follow. The immense progress agriculturally which Mexico has made within the short space of ten years is largely attributed to the utilization of priority inputs of water, fertilizer, and improved seed by private enterprise, free of government agencies and controls, and in the absence of any extension service. It follows that no country with scarce resources like Pakistan can afford to ignore the potential which this private initiative indicates. In fact, a strategy for maximum growth rate demands its utilization as much as possible.

An example of the outlook raised by the Mexican analogy is the recent forecast that before 1975 West Pakistan will so have multiplied its wheat production that 6 million acres of wheatland will have to be diverted to other crops.[4] An example of the importance attached to the potential breakthrough is that Pakistan itself would thereby be a prototype example of agricultural development for surrounding countries. The Planning Commission has estimated a 33 per cent expansion of irrigation water for 1965-70. This water program, which includes 12,000 government tube wells in the Scarps, 40,000 private tube wells, and some additional river water, is expected to increase crop production by 23 per cent. Increase in fertilizer use is expected to add another

12 per cent, and improved seed, pesticides, cultivation practices, and new areas to complete a total rise of 50 per cent in gross agricultural production in that period. After a 30 per cent increase during 1960-65, this would certainly demonstrate one of the greatest agricultural advances in history.

However, here the problems of policy become topically critical. Is there a danger that this sudden swing-over to *laissez faire,* so subtly in keeping with Western world, and particularly United States, ideology, may be exaggeratedly optimistic, just as the conclusion, in 1959, that no growth was possible without a great deal of state organization may have been exaggeratedly pessimistic? Are all the other constraints just bogeys which a spurt of private enterprise will blow away, or are they still real obstacles to growth which will not disappear unless an organized effort is made to eradicate them? Suppose the conclusion to be drawn from the production statistics is not so much that the bulk of farmers are suddenly full of initiative to increase yields from their own resources and to use all inputs to make a breakthrough if only government will leave it to private enterprise, but rather that every farmer is ready enough to take more water and increase his area of cropping. Pressure of population alone and numbers to support per family would produce this result. For the bulk, this might not indicate much more than a readiness to take the first and easiest step to improve subsistence. The important uncertainty here is that if this should be true, the additional water input may indeed be the end of the easy gains. To gain more may be much harder and may yet require considerable government stimulus and organization.

Let me finally pose my last question, and this is one which I feel is of the greatest importance because it faces us in so many other developing countries, and it brings us right up against the communist alternative. To what extent in our pressure for maximum growth, and in the conviction that encouragement of private enterprise initiative is the quickest means to this end, are we risking the danger of serious inequality and the social and political tension which might follow from it?

Let us take the analogy of Mexico. It has made spectacular progress, but has this come from the country as a whole? Certainly not. The agricultural growth has been achieved by concentration on a limited number of regions and upon the more enterprising farmers. In fact, 3 per cent of the farmers produce 50 per cent of the crop sales, mainly on large commercial farms. The other side of the picture is that the remainder of the rural population, comprising some 50 per cent of the population as a whole, is altogether outside this progress. In this subsistence sector the holdings are very small, the techniques are primitive, the yields and incomes are very low, and the opportunity of gainful employment is confined to about 150 days in the year. The ensuing poverty and hunger are accentuated by the existence of many who have been unable to get land at all.

Thus, the true picture is that the remarkable success of a program of channeling investment into those sectors which can yield the surest, largest, and quickest economic return has had the adverse side effect of accentuating the demarcation between the relatively few "haves" in the urban and commercial farming communities and the great multitude of "have nots" in the subsistence countryside and in the consequent urban slums. Politically and socially this imbalance is dangerous (remember the country is next door to the United States!). Economically, it reacts adversely on the costs of industrial production, for half the population are not consumers of factory products at all. Without doubt the central problem now facing the government of Mexico is how best to narrow the gap and broaden the base of participation in progress without reducing the growth rate or impairing programs which have proved their economic effectiveness. It will take a great deal of government initiative and organization to solve this problem.

It would be relevant in this connection to remember also the recent history of Syria which, like Mexico, had a spectacular agricultural growth rate after World War II, thanks analogously to private enterprise investment in pumps and machinery. In the case of Syria the actual production was, like that of Pakistan, on a sharecropping system. However, because the owners of equipment and capital seemed to benefit most, leaving the bulk of the actual cultivators poorly off, the situation ended in revolution, and a total estrangement between state and private enterprise.

In regard to Pakistan, those who advocate the importance of private enterprise to the breakthrough make no secret that the spearhead on which they are relying is the more substantial landowner with initiative and resources of his own. There are sound statistical reasons for this view. Figures for the distribution of farm size indicate that 7 per cent of all farms are over 25 acres, 43 per cent are from 5 to 25 acres, whereas 50 per cent are less than 5 acres. In area, however, the 7 per cent of large farms cover 43 per cent of the land, the 43 per cent of medium-size units cover a further 48 per cent of the land, and the 50 per cent of small farms cover only 9 per cent of the land. As a spearhead, the large and medium farms clearly cover the bulk of the area. Nevertheless, anxiety must arise as to whether, under a private enterprise system, the group of smallest size farms are going to have access to tube-well water at all. Yet such farms represent 50 per cent of the farming population. This seems a very valid anxiety, for it is this group which has the least resources to invest and the least access to credit, spares, and repair facilities or to extension advice on tube wells or any other matter. Another major anxiety under the private enterprise system is the cost of tube-well water to those who do get access to it, and the monopoly position in which the owner of the tube well is placed, particularly on critical occasions of shortage in surface supplies. Currently, tube-well owners expect to recover their capital cost within three years, and any system of contractor sale of water could be very expensive and exploitive to the farmers concerned.

The shortage of land among the bulk of the population, the continued high rental sharecropping system, and the possibility of having to pay high for private enterprise groundwater may not be so clearly deterrent to the adoption of modern inputs as had been earlier feared, for current results suggest simply that tenants are forced to work harder in order to support their increasing families. They do raise a specter, however, that a very large segment of the farming community is not likely to get much income value from its work, and as incomes increase among other classes, a sense of inequity among this segment may well impair the whole stability of rural life. As in Mexico, therefore, a very real dilemma is likely to face the government of Pakistan—how best to broaden the base of participation in progress without reducing the growth rate or discouraging that contribution from private enterprise which is proving its economic effectiveness. It will take a great deal of government initiative and organization to solve this problem. An organization is needed which must break into the vested interests of landlords and moneylenders, must provide more land for those without it, must give more help through farmers' associations to get the bulk of the rural people out of poverty and into a stake in progress, and must provide more planned employment in public works to attain these ends. Help in defeating unbalance is surely as important in Western world policy as financial investment itself.

I apologize for the length of this chapter. "Put it all on one sheet of paper. We haven't time for more" is the demand of our age. Is it also a disease of our age? Should we apply the principles of machinery to human society, imagining that every part can be labeled and fed into a computer to get the answers? Or should we apply the principles of biology? Maybe that is another policy problem facing us. However, the real climax of this story, I venture to suggest to you, is that the key problem of our age is how we can both create growth and take care of the "left-outs," and yet attain a civilization that we can all enjoy as individuals. Surely, that is the mutual challenge to both our Western world and the communists and the context of all policy planning in the developing world now hesitant between us. However, need it always be a challenge of extremes? Must state and private enterprise be enemies rather than allies? Or does the future call for capitalism with a socialist conscience and socialism with a capitalist virility? Let me leave that last question with you.

NOTES

1. A fifth river, the Beas, is often mentioned, but since it joins the Sutlej before it reaches Pakistan, it is omitted here.

2. The survey has been made by the United States firm Stone and Webster. The overall consulting ⸱engineers for the Indus Basin are Sir Alexander Gibb and Partners of the United Kingdom. Also associated are the United States firm Harza International, the United Kingdom consultants, Hunting Technical Services, Ltd., and the Dutch consultants, Ilaco.

3. The initiative in this operation was largely undertaken by the United States firm Tipton and Kambatch.   ⸱

4. This striking suggestion is made in the remarkably stimulating reports of Dr. Norman Borlaug of the Rockefeller Foundation, adviser on wheat production to the Government of Mexico and, recently, Pakistan.

11

Problems of Policy in Planning Agricultural Development in Africa South of the Sahara

Arthur Gaitskell

It is difficult sometimes to remember the extent to which geography and history still mold our environment and chart our endeavors. Today technology seems of universal application and Henry Ford's celebrated remark that "history is bunk" reflects the feelings of impatient men of progress. Africa soon corrects this superficial judgment, and any talk about development there has to start with geography and history, for they enormously affect the issue.

THE PHYSICAL BACKGROUND

Generalities often obscure the truth, but with a subject like Africa, a broad canvas is legitimate. The particulars can be etched in later. Examined on the map, the continent itself is huge, a fifth of the world's land surface. Examined from within, a first impression is that man is dwarfed by the immensity of nature. Climate and physical conditions control on a continental scale, and man merely fits in.

The Sahara stretches from the Red Sea to the Atlantic, and its fiery dryness dictates a climatic battle fought in the skies over the

width of Africa below. Southward, the pattern of rainfall gradually and jerkily increases. Grass begins to grow and then trees.
However, it is a continental pattern imposing bands of similarity
from the Ethiopian foothills to Nigeria. Next come the rain forests,
fringing the west coast with a deep belt and straddling the center
of the continent for hundreds of miles. In the east, rises the high
mountain land of Ethiopia with its fantastic scenery of deep
gorges, but east and south of it, a huge band of dry, low-rainfall
country stretches from Somaliland to Uganda. The dry land sweeps
around the highlands of Kenya and extends down through the
interior to the lush area around the great lakes of the Rift Valley
which link up with the forests of the Congo. South of all this
primeval scenery, the continental pattern is repeated. Another
huge band of thinner bush country runs from the coast in southern
Tanzania across Zambia to the coast in Angola. South Africa completes the picture with subtropical Natal on the east, but the
skeleton coast on the west is chilled to desolation by a polar
current.

Of course, there are exceptions to these generalities, but even
the particular in Africa is on a giant scale. The Nile swamps in
the southern Sudan are the size of England. Lake Victoria is the
size of Ireland. Mount Kilimanjaro near the Equator lifts its snowy
cap to 19,000 feet from the dry plain in a mass a hundred miles
wide, and the Mountains of the Moon that bastion the Congo
rival it. The Eastern Rift Valley with its steep walls, its tall extinct
volcanoes, and its wonderland of game makes a cut in the earth's
crust 500 miles long. In the southwest the bushy Kalahari Desert,
where no surface water lies, is 500 miles long and 300 wide, and
the Okovango River disappears into it in a delta swamp the size of
lower Egypt. Even the well-known rivers—the Nile, the Niger, the
Congo, and the Zambezi—follow the pattern. They were never
highways. Protected by cataracts, they were for centuries mysteries emanating from heaven knew where in the unknown.

Africa with its great deserts, its huge forests, its vast horizons
of savannah and miles of bush, its gigantic swamps, its wild animal
life, its strange mountains and mighty rivers, is the untamed
continent par excellence. Hence, its past allure for the explorer and,
one may expect, its future allure for the tourist and the developer.

The Historical Background

The effect of the physical environment on human evolution

The above broad canvas matters because, to an exceptional degree compared with other continents, this physical environment conditioned human history in Africa right up to our own times, both from within and from without.

From within, what could human beings do amid such formidable natural phenomena? On the whole, two main activities could be followed to keep alive. The people could be pastoralists in the large areas of low, irregular rainfall. They could graze camels, sheep, goats, and cattle as the incidence of rain, water, and the killer tsetse fly permitted, a simple life engendering a fighting spirit, but no settled conditions. Alternatively, they could be cultivators, but mostly on high land, where there was a combination of rain, streams, and good soil, or in the forest belts. The immensity of distance, the huge barriers of mountain, swamp, and dry, waterless bush, wild beasts, and dangerous diseases like malaria, yellow fever, and sleeping sickness discouraged conquest of empty land. In general, people remained in isolated tribal communities, fighting each other for the precarious viable portion they had acquired.

In such a society the main activity was for subsistence, and here is the place to bring out an important contemporary result of such conditions: the absence of any diversity of skills or jobs. There was relatively no division of labor—no merchants or bankers, few traders or towns, little commerce, no bourgeois class, and none of that middle element in society which has so furthered the progress of our technology. A job classification survey in the villages and towns of Elizabethan England or Mediaeval Europe, or even in the Roman Empire would reveal much more diversity of occupation than would be the case in most of Africa right up to our times. One has only to read the explorers' stories at the end of the nineteenth century to realize how very lately humanity in Africa has had the chance to emerge from extremely primitive conditions. Perhaps we forget what a beneficent advantage the great flat plains, the good soil, and the reliable climate have been to our own maturity in Europe, and, from that start, to taking advantage of similar conditions where we could find them in North America and elsewhere in the world.

Undoubtedly, another cause of the delayed maturity of Africa, springing from the physical environment, was the extreme difficulty of getting into the continent from outside. Of course, there were also exceptions to this generality. There was trade on the east coast with India and the Persian Gulf, and there was trade on the west coast with Europe. There was the slave trade fingering into the interior. There were the coastal staging posts of the Portuguese around the continent and of the Dutch in South Africa. However, there was no real stimulation or penetration from these contacts until superior firearms gave outsiders advantage over those within and until the invention of the steam engine and the expansion of railways enabled them to conquer distance. Only in the late nineteenth century did this combination coincide. Moreover, when it did coincide, it was at a time in history when Western Europe led the world in material progress and when its nations fought to extend their rival empires. The rapid carve-up of Africa into colonial appendages of Europe followed, with boundary lines drawn on maps to suit European solutions and superimposed on tribal communities and small kingdoms which had hitherto had no cohesion into countries. This so recent predecessor of our times among historical facts also enormously affects the setting of our efforts for development there today.

THE EVOLUTION OF EUROPEAN CONTROL

The effect of the colonial period on the position today can be seen from some of the features which characterized it, particularly in economic and political aspects.

Until World War II, active planned development for the local people was rarely regarded as a priority by colonial governments. The ideology of colonialism was indirect rule through local tribal chiefs. The preservation of tribal peace was certainly a priority, but so also was the retention of customary ways against any upset by modernity. Many colonial administrators regarded themselves rather like game wardens in a Garden of Eden. Such economic development as occurred was left to expatriate private enterprise and watched with some suspicion as liable to swindle the inhabitants of the Garden. European, Levantine, and Asian traders might buy for export local products like palm oil, cotton, cocoa, oil seeds, and groundnuts, and sell in exchange imported manufactured products. Expatriate companies might open mines or estates and employ local people as labor, but the idea that the local people themselves should or could develop their own economy in a rational modern way hardly existed. Such education as they got was mainly provided by Christian missions to supply clerks and underlings for the administration.

Two prominent results of this state of affairs were that most of the infrastructure (and this in itself was very limited) of each individual country was orientated to the external world rather than among countries within Africa itself, and that all the forward links, the manufacturing and so on, tended to take place in and benefit the countries which bought the primary products rather than the countries within Africa.

Some exceptions to the latter result occurred in those parts of Africa which proved attractive for European settlement; this undoubtedly provided more diversity of employment and a great contribution in discovery and experience, but the main benefits where settlement was extensive, as in South Africa and Rhodesia, went to the European settlers who appropriated for themselves a very large portion of the land and a monopoly of political power.

Somewhat suddenly after World War II, the economic policies of the colonial powers swung right around to active government encouragement of local development, a change materially due to the large funds accumulated by marketing boards set up to stimulate supplies for the war and to the higher world prices prevailing for colonial products. However, hardly had this change taken place when colonialism itself came to an end, and its executive officials departed. The reason for this was the galloping race toward political independence, for political policy also swung right around. The war itself was largely responsible for the pace of this change. Large numbers of local people were recruited for overseas service in the allied armies. The B.B.C. broadcast five times a day that the allies were fighting for world freedom, and the allies could hardly exclude their own supporters from the objective. India, after a long period of tutelage, obtained its freedom, and the example was very quickly taken up by the small educated class in African countries who claimed the same right to self-rule. Undoubtedly, the colonial powers, who had long before switched from a concept of Empire to one of trusteeship, would have opted for a longer qualifying period, but this rapidly became impossible without the use of force, and force would have destroyed the cooperation that was essential between the teacher and the pupil.

SUMMARY OF THE PHYSICAL AND HISTORICAL BACKGROUND

Let us summarize now how the position looked as a result of this physical and historical background in those African countries which obtained their independence so recently.

The concept intended by the transfer of power in the minds of both the colonial powers and the local leaders was that of a modern democratic state which could join others as an equal in the United Nations Organization, itself a hoped-for alternative to imperialist wars. It was a concept very much in the Western world image, but it was suddenly grafted onto a background which had hardly evolved biologically in keeping with it. There was a very small educated class, hastily crammed in administrative and democratic procedures in a short period before independence, and which, together with others less educated, was suddenly elevated to positions of prestige and power. The great bulk of the people, however, had hardly changed. They remained largely illiterate, rural subsistence farmers, whether pastoralists or cultivators, some with cash export crops attached but not incorporated rationally in their holdings, which gave low yield and low income. Savings hardly existed, and the low general standards of living meant low national revenues.

There was no large middle class, no burgesses, bankers, artisans, foremen, accountants, salesmen, and none of the intermediary skills on which our societies rely. Education, rapidly demanded by all as a means of getting away from rural poverty, actually alienated the young from rural life and encouraged them to drift into towns in search of jobs which were seldom forthcoming.

There was no historical period for national cohesion such as characterized the formation of our own countries. African countries were simply inherited from the map-drawn boundaries of the colonial powers. These boundaries were preserved, but they frequently papered over marked tribal differences and even marked racial and cultural differences within them, as can be so clearly seen today between northern and southern Sudan, northern and southern Nigeria, northern and southern Kenya, northern and southern Uganda, within Ruanda and Urundi, and within the Congo. An additional feature of the colonial inheritance is that a great many of the countries concerned are small, too small to form satisfactory units for economic development. This condition, of course, is not a feature confined to Africa. Countries in Europe and many parts of the world are finding themselves in the same predicament, but in Africa it does mean that countries which have not really had time to establish internal cohesion are faced at the same moment with a great need to make the most of a rational economic development and to obtain also some regional cohesion in their future planning.

Finally, this development has to be conducted in a tough raw environment, demanding exceptional capital and human resources in a continent of vast distances with little inter-country infrastructure, over large areas of difficult soil, irregular rainfall, and waterless bush, and in the face of debilitating human and animal diseases.

Africa has some advantages against these formidable handicaps. Since it is a latecomer in development, there has as yet been no capturing of the land by big landowners (except by the Europeans in their settlement areas), so that there is no intractable problem of land reform of the type which so stultifies development in Asia and Latin America. Nor has there been any capturing of education or industrial power by a small class, so that the equally intractable problem of gross inequality hardly yet arises. A third point is that presently there is no appalling population pressure in the continent as a whole, although this is rapidly becoming a problem in pockets where the best conditions of subsistence have promoted overcrowding. Finally, given the input of capital and modern technology, the continental resources are not negligible, and the opportunity does offer the chance of planning development so that a reasonable balance between agriculture and industry is pursued, that industrial concentration is avoided, that an intermediate technology suited to the conditions of local society rather than export of Western technology suited to the conditions of our society can be prepared, and that a fair society without undue inequalities can be created.

To this picture must be added the additional complication of international ideological conflict with different ideologies competing to direct the belated continent. African leaders need to tread warily if they are not to lose the advantages of being latecomers, if they are to keep cohesion, if they are to gain economic as well as political control of their own destinies, and if they are to develop their resources and raise their standards of living. The outcome may largely depend on our money, knowledge, markets, sympathy or indifference to their predicament, and their ability to fit in with us.

PROBLEMS IN GETTING AGRICULTURE GOING IN AFRICA

THE IMPORTANCE OF AGRICULTURE TO THE ECONOMY

The biggest problem in spurring agricultural progress in many developing countries is the universal disregard, if not contempt, for it compared with industry and urban life. In newly independent countries in Africa there was at first, and to some degree still is, a much greater interest in industry, although for a variety of reasons at least equal attention to agriculture has come to the fore recently. Industry has been found greedy of capital in a capital-scarce continent, and the use of foreign capital entirely for industrialization is criticized on the grounds that it subordinates the country to foreign ownership of economic assets. In the absence of a middle class, industry has had some difficulty getting started, and its employment ratio has been low. Moreover, with the vast majority of the people living in rural areas on very low incomes, the internal market for industrial products is very restricted, and costs are high. It also needs a great deal of foreign exchange and, apart from countries with large mineral assets, the main contributor to this purpose could be increased agricultural exports. Even in countries with big mineral assets, like Zambia (with its large copper deposits), the marked contrast between such centers and the stationary countryside has caused a great deal of imbalance and social disruption. It has also become apparent that if agriculture really progressed, it would offer more chance of employment opportunities through backward and forward links within the country than any other activity. A prominent mining magnate recently said that behind the farmer stands an array of ancillary trades and professions: road and rail transport, fertilizers, textiles, food processing, stock feed, starch, paper, canning, timber, tobacco, leather, power for irrigation, cement, and all the additional services that are by-products of these activities. The picture of an enhanced agriculture supplying the raw materials for new industries and food for the growing number who no longer grow their own, and industry supplying agriculture, as rural incomes rise, with new inputs to further production and new consumer goods, is no longer so strange an objective. Indeed, it is rapidly becoming a compelling objective as the urban drift of the young raises problems of delinquency and subversion, as statistics make clear that the only openings for the majority of school-graduates will be self-employment on the land, and as rising imports of food, which could be grown within the country, run away with the foreign exchange needed for development. Finally, just at the time when the potential importance of better yields and better rural incomes is coming to be appreciated, many countries are finding that the current state of agriculture is not merely stationary, it is actively going downhill.

TRADITIONAL SYSTEMS OF LAND TENURE AND THEIR EFFECT

Cultivators.—A socially interesting fact about traditional land tenure in many cultivating areas of Africa was that the land was held to belong to the ancestors and to the unborn children in a sense of tribal trust. Within this concept an individual could claim a holding for his subsistence according to his need, that is to say, the number of wives and children he had, but not for aggregation. When the need decreased by death, the holding reverted to the community for reallocation by the chief to others in need. The land was farmed on an extensive bush rotation. A holder would cut down and burn the bush and plant his crops on that spot until the decreasing fertility of the soil forced him to start the process again. His animals merely grazed in the bush and were not integrated with his cultivation. The system suited a society needing only subsistence, when land was plentiful and when the hazards of disease, tribal raids, and the slave trade kept the numbers of people and of stock small.

However, after colonial powers took over, security and health improved, and people and stock gradually multiplied. Stimulated by trading demands, land came to be wanted for money crops as well as for subsistence, but there was no thought-out plan as to how the two could best complement each other. Under this dual pressure, and prevented by the colonial power from invading their neighbors, many tribes have begun to find their portion of viable Africa uncomfortably overcrowded.

It is important to understand just what this system means to the land and to the society. In the first place, the bush rotation can no longer be preserved, and land which ought to be lying fallow to retain fertility has to be allocated to someone to use. The yield naturally falls. As the pressure becomes more extreme, there can be no fallow. The land is then under continuous cultivation, which in sloping country presents a great erosion hazard. The animals have no bush on which to graze, and so they climb the hills, destroying the trees and grass cover and increasing the erosion. In the next stage not only are the yields low, but the family holding itself begins to be fragmented. After a while a typical holding is no longer in one place, but is in a series of small patches scattered over quite a distance; it ceases to be a manageable farm. Finally, some families have no land at all on a continent where land is the only security against starvation. It may well be imagined that sometime before this stage is reached every individual will be desperate to hold his bit of land and may well lose it by litigation and bribery. The original social virtues of traditional tenure are then as lost as the agricultural virtues of the bush rotation.

Deterioration of this kind has begun to occur in many of the most favored and best endowed lands in Africa, particularly in the highlands of Kenya, the mountain outcrops in Tanzania, and in Ruanda and Urundi. However, the danger is widespread and runs through Rhodesia, the Congo, Nigeria, and many French associated territories. It is quite true that there is still extensive land in Africa, undeveloped for lack of water, the presence of the tsetse, or unfavorable rainfall. However, this is a reserve for which it is essential to find a better system, and it is constantly exposed to the risk of haphazard extension of the traditional system.

Pastoralists.—Something of the same deteriorating nature has also been happening in the great pastoral areas of Africa since the advent of colonialism. Under the colonial shield, and with improved veterinary control, herds have increased, and the pressure of humans and animals has begun to have the same devastating effect on land as on the cultivating areas. Indeed, in many parts of Africa the destructive effect of excess herds in the drier pastoral country has been more dangerous, for the disappearance of grass and tree cover has changed perennial streams to intermittent torrents and turned many a pastoral landscape to desiccation. One may rightly remember the once fertile shores of the Mediterranean and their change into the deserts of today. The risk is increased by the conservative nature of the pastoral tribes where, as in the Bible, for centuries a man's prestige was reckoned in numbers, not in quality, of stock. It is also more difficult to combat because the owner of excess stock tends to regard the excess as a bank to draw on in a poor year and to exchange for food and other necessities.

WHAT CAN REPLACE TRADITIONAL LAND TENURE?

The dead-end road just described is obviously the complete antithesis of that main objective of development—to increase yield, incomes, and jobs in the rural areas. The problem is what can best be put in its place. There are examples of different patterns all over the world, and African leaders must be puzzled as to how to know what is going to suit Africa best. Let me try to illustrate some of the problems of policy which confront them. In the cultivating areas, something is obviously needed long before the dead-end road is reached. Instead of the custom of bush rotation, it is necessary to introduce some system of farming which retains a unit in one place where a permanently satisfactory rotation can preserve the fertility of the land. The first thought naturally turns to discouraging the habit of turning animals loose in the bush for grazing and instead to using their manure for fertilizer and planting crops in rotation to feed them. A defined unit of management is essential to get over one great weakness of traditional land tenure: the absence, under that particular communal ownership, of any incentive for preserving the fertility of the land itself. In a stabilized unit the cash crop, instead of being a chance appendage to subsistence with no plan to produce it to best yield and quality, would take its place in a rotation or, if a tree crop, as a fixture which could be well looked after near a homestead. A next stage would be to fence in the unit so that, by separation from neighbors' scruffy herds, improved stock can be carried and protected from disease with a possible addition to income from dairy products.

Upon such a stable base can then be applied measures to control erosion such as contour and tie ridging, with a direct sense of individual benefit. To such a base can also be supplied, as a package, those factors which have so revolutionized Western world farming, namely: machinery to reduce hand drudgery, high quality seed, fertilizer, pest control, credit, and marketing facilities.

An important corollary of such a suggestion is that the user of such a unit (which technically could be individual or communal) would need some kind of title, stronger than mere allocation traditions from a chief, which would give enough sense of security to invest in improvements.

As with the cultivating areas, something is needed, long before desiccation sets in, which can turn the great pastoral areas of Africa, often no worse than those of Queensland or Texas, into modern productive units. Again, a defined unit with managerial responsibility is essential. Onto such a unit can then be applied rotational grazing with reserved pastures for emergencies, planting of selected grasses, control of stock numbers to the carrying capacity of the land, new water points by borehole, dams or excavated reservoirs, marketing facilities and, ultimately, fencing, thereby enabling improved breeding. By such methods the descent to desert could be arrested and the contribution of many areas to national incomes greatly enhanced.

I find it difficult to exaggerate the importance of converting the presently used lands in Africa to the pattern of a basic stable unit of this kind and of controlling settlement in the presently unused areas to a similar solution. This is not purely a theoretical solution. In territories in the British Commonwealth the most advanced example is that of the Swynnerton Plan in Kenya. The purpose of this plan was to change a rapidly deteriorating region (that of the Kikuyu tribe) into individual consolidated holdings with title and to integrate into these stock, subsistence, and cash crops so as to give a considerably enhanced family income in place of universal rural poverty. The cash crops might be tree crops such as coffee and tea or field crops such as pyrethrum and pineapples, or merely livestock, dairy products, grain, or vegetables, or combinations of these according to location. The essential points in the success of this plan lay in registration of title, a sound rotational unit, insistence on high cultural standards through a quadrupled extension service and farmers' training centers, credit loans, and marketing organization. The demand for consolidation and farm planning has, in fact, outstripped the resources in staff and money to satisfy it, and undoubtedly this pattern is one of great significance to other parts of Africa.

Another example, in what used to be a British administered territory, is that of the huge Gezira irrigated area in the Sudan with its standard unit holdings, planned rotation, and package deal services to farmers. This scheme has been the central dynamo of economic development in the Sudan, and this pattern also has features of important application to other regions of Africa.

One of the most advanced examples of planned land usage, converting traditional tenure into stabilized individual units both in cultivation and pastoral areas, was that introduced by the Belgians in the desperately overcrowded mandated territory of Ruanda Urundi. The *paysannats,* started in French colonial countries, and the native land units started in Southern Rhodesia are further examples of the search in colonial times for a new African land use system.

Before concluding, however, from these examples that a solution of continental application is around the corner, a very strong word of caution is essential. The projects referred to above were not just introduced in a theoretical manner. They were the outcome of a great deal of research with respect to satisfactory crops and satisfactory techniques in particular localities and of gradual adaptability to local human reactions. In Kenya, a large part of their success can be attributed to the pioneering work of European settlers, who not only first established the best way to grow the crops concerned, but who also supplied the improved livestock and the marketing organization for subsequent African benefit.

Let me give a few examples of how easy it is to be wrong about the assumed adaptability of solutions and also of how very large the element of risk still is in development. I would like to underline the latter point because those in developing countries are sometimes apt to forget how many people went broke in the growth processes of the developed countries.

The most notorious example in British colonial history of wrongly assuming the adaptability of solutions was the "Groundnut Scheme" in Tanzania, which cost some £25 million before it ended in failure. This project was started after World War II on the assumption that large areas of undeveloped bush could be rapidly made productive by mechanical cultivation and, by growing groundnuts, could contribute at once to alleviate a world-wide shortage of fats. Groundnuts were, in fact, grown on a small scale by Africans in these areas before the scheme was started. There were three main reasons for the subsequent failure. The rainfall records based on a few adjacent rain gauges turned out to be quite unreliable when applied on a much bigger scale, illustrating how very intermittent and local the incidence of rain is in many parts of Africa. The roots of the bush and the abrasive nature of the soil made the costs much greater and the feasibility of using machinery much smaller than had been anticipated. And finally, when groundnuts were grown in large block areas, they developed virus diseases which were not obvious as a hazard in the previous African small-scale plots.

A rather different warning, this time against assuming that one knows what human reactions are going to be, could be taken from two projects in West Africa. In the French territories, a big irrigation scheme was initiated near Sansanding on the Niger River very much with the intention of imitating the Gezira project in the Sudan. The technical conditions were satisfactory, but the region was largely uninhabited, and the assumption that farmers could be recruited from other areas turned out to be wrong. People just did not want to go there. The other example was rather similar. The Nigeria Agricultural Project was initiated in British Nigeria, also largely on the lines of the Gezira Scheme in the Sudan, but without irrigation. This project also was started in a comparatively uninhabited area. Word was sent to neighboring chiefs to encourage immigration to the new project. As a result, all kinds of malcontents and misfits were dispatched and proved very unsuitable as farmers. The project ended in failure.

An illustration of rather a different kind, this time of the risk of assuming the adaptability of techniques, could be taken from the Kilombero sugar scheme in Tanzania. This project, in its initial stage, is an estate rather than a settlement project. The Kilombero Valley was a largely undeveloped area, but experimental plots suggested that it had considerable potential for sugar production. The project was financed by the Commonwealth Development Corporation, the International Finance Corporation, and others, with a stake from the government of Tanzania. Management was entrusted to a Dutch Company with great experience in sugar production in Java. It turned out, however, that the techniques used in Java were not appropriate in Kilombero. Yields and sucrose percentage fell far short of estimates, and capital had to be written off, pending discovery of the appropriate techniques. The project continues, new techniques have been discovered, but a new wilt hazard has again affected the yields.

This story illustrates how important it is to know the appropriate techniques and to establish the prospects of profitability before suggesting to Africans that they can scrap their traditional methods and get a much better income from individual unit farms. Indeed, today the Commonwealth Development Corporation is adopting, in many parts of Africa and elsewhere in the world (in Uganda for tea, in eastern Nigeria for rubber, in Malaysia for palm oil), a policy of putting down first a nucleus plantation and, after that has proved commercially successful, grafting onto it surrounding settlements of small holders who can then grow that crop with confidence and thereby greatly enhance their income. The ultimate purpose is not plantation agriculture, but enhanced incomes on a stable unit for rural farmers. However, the nucleus plantation serves first as a proving ground and later as a nursery, a training school, a processing plant, a continuing contact with new scientific research and better varieties, and an organized marketing outlet. Ultimately, the whole project can be turned over to a farmers' association or cooperative.

An interesting and successful example of this kind of policy can be taken from Swaziland where the Corporation took over 130,000 acres of undeveloped bush, dammed a river and established irrigation, and experimented with rice, citrus, cattle, and sugar. When sugar on a nucleus estate had proved to be a paying crop (with a quota in the Commonwealth Sugar Agreement), Swazi subsistence farmers were invited to take up unit holdings in the remaining undeveloped area. Supervisors and credit facilities were made available to them as aids in developing and using the land very profitably.

In turning for a moment to the pastoralists, the same caution to say "I don't know" has a certain validity before assuming that control of stock, rotational grazing, new water points, fencing, and marketing outlets are automatically successful solutions. One may have more confidence where European farmers have already pioneered profitable ranches in the locality, but very often the true carrying capacity of the pastures, the degree of irregularity of rain, the possibility of growing supplementary crops for stock feed, and even the minimum stock needed by an individual household to maintain it with a decent income, are all unknown factors which only experience will reveal.

It is evident that allowing the continuance of traditional land usage leads to a dead-end and does not contribute to increased yields, incomes, and jobs. It is of great importance to survey and experiment, both technically and socially, before assuming the adaptability of solutions. Now let us go on to consider certain other problems which face African leaders, even if everyone has agreed that a stabilized unit farm is an unavoidable basic step for progress.

One of the first questions which arises is: "Is there time for waiting for ideal solutions?" It is all very fine to talk about the need for caution and research, survey and pilot scheme, but what about the political pressure for a higher standard of living, the urban drift with no jobs and the delinquency and subversion risk this entails, and the urgent need to improve foreign exchange earnings? I put this question deliberately for two reasons. It explains why African governments sometimes have to go ahead with settlement schemes, which are subsequently criticized for partial failure and excessive cost, without all the knowledge it would be nice to have. It also underlines the necessity for aid in money and personnel to solve the unresolved facts if only workable terms, mutually acceptable to outsider and local countries, can be discovered. I would like to amplify later the problems of what sort of aid and the difficulty of fitting-in.

A second question which arises is: "What kind of rational stable unit should replace traditional tenure?" Should it be the state farm, the collective, or the individual farm under private ownership? And, if it is the last, should one encourage large-scale private enterprise with capital and initiative of its own or should one plan for family farms with cooperative services?

I would like to comment shortly on these alternatives, but first let me suggest that there seems to be no reason why they should not all be tried in order to discover which gives the most satisfying results. There is still plenty of land in Africa. From the standpoint of economics, it is important for the land to be used productively; however, this does not necessarily mean that it is the best solution socially. Conversely, what seems socially desirable is not necessarily the most productive solution.

A simple example of successful state-run farms in Africa might be those managed by the settlement ministry in Kenya pending transfer, and usually division, to African ownership. However, these farms had been previously developed, or partially developed, by

European farmers, and the settlement ministry itself had some European personnel with considerable previous knowledge of these very farms. A different example can be taken from Ghana where state farms were pioneered from scratch. It would appear that these farms have been less successful, the main difficulties being the scarcity of competent managers and excessive labor costs owing to a large payroll with poor output. Competent management would appear to be a key factor for overcoming these difficulties as is illustrated by another example, this time of a very successful ranch, run at Kongwa in Tanzania by a state authority, the Tanzania Agricultural Corporation. State farms, however, suffer from a social disadvantage similar to plantations. All the workers on them are employees. Although in time farming may come to be regarded like industry, simply as employment in a land factory, at present this solution seems very remote from the social state of affairs in rural areas where everyone farms as an individual, and the objective is to raise this individual's income and his participation in progress.

A theoretical advantage of state farming is that thereby the land can be laid out in the most satisfactory manner for the effective use of modern inputs. The collective tries to achieve the same result without the drawback of turning the farmer into a mere employee. It might be supposed that since traditionally the land was communally owned by the tribe, and since a great deal of mutual help between neighbors was also a characteristic of traditional farming, and since, further, decisions concerning which land to use for what crop and when were often made by the local chief representing the community, collective farming could be followed rather easily and naturally instead of the traditional pattern. It would merely imply pooling the land, already communally owned, for usage in a modern, instead of an out-of-date, manner. During colonial times many group farming schemes were started on this supposition. Very few of these were successful. It is not easy to be sure of the reason for this. It would appear, judging from collectives outside Africa, that the conditions for voluntary success result either from extreme overcrowding when each individual's holding is so small that pooling land with his neighbors could not offer him a worse living than he is getting at present (as may have been the case in parts of China), or from extreme group patriotism in the face of external enemies (as in the kibbutz in Israel), or from a small, tightly knit family group (as in the Arain tribe in Pakistan).

In Africa, it would seem that far more identity was felt for the individual usufruct aspect of traditional tenure than might have been supposed from the communal ownership aspect. At any rate, as land became attractive for cash as well as subsistence crops, and as it became more overcrowded, the desire for individual rather than communal security was obviously paramount. As yet, there seems to be little evidence that collective farming will have much appeal in Africa, except by compulsion. It is true that, as in Algeria, some European farms in Kenya have been bought and run by groups of Africans, but unlike the state-sponsored collective solution in Algeria, those in Kenya are really joint stock exercises.

Therefore, if the preference in Africa is (with due experiment) likely to be toward individually-owned farms, the question then arises as to whether the enterprising "leader" should be encouraged, or whether the community as a whole can be modernized on the basis of individual family farms with collective services. A decision on this matter is extremely important socially, owing to the long-term risk of excessive inequality if the bias is all toward the enterprising and the acquisitive.

In fact, it is often very difficult to avoid such a bias. Extension service personnel can seldom work with more than a fraction of the enormous number of subsistence farmers, and they naturally start with those most interested and responsive. Many extension methods concentrate at first on developing a cadre of "master farmers" and align their scarce credit facilities only to "adopters" of improved practices. If land is available such farmers are then encouraged to take up bigger holdings and on a larger scale. There is obviously a very great deal to be said in favor of these methods, and the economist will often add that the enterprising individual who can build up his own savings and use his own initiative thereby relieves the state from drawing on its scarce capital and personnel, and is thus an enormous asset in development. In fact, many people in the Western world go further and maintain that this is *the* way to obtain rapid agricultural growth; they quote the example of the dynamic growth achieved recently in Mexico and, to a lesser extent in Pakistan, thanks to a free rein given to private enterprise. Undoubtedly this is true, but equally true is that a high degree of imbalance has been created in the process. In the case of Mexico, 50 per cent of agricultural production comes from 3 per cent large private farms. However, 50 per cent of the rural population has no share in the progress at all. By continuing to live with low yields, very low incomes, and few employment opportunities, their prevailing poverty and indeed, hunger, present a real risk of serious social tension. The example of Syria also offers a warning. After World War II Syria went from comparative stagnation to spectacular agricultural expansion thanks to private entrepreneurs who used their own capital for machinery and pumps and employed the rural population on a sharecropping basis. The unequal distribution of the benefit has resulted in a revolution and thrown the country into the communist fold.

In Africa, it is very pertinent that people should hesitate before scrapping the traditional communal tenure which operated as a constraint both on excessive aggregation of land by any individual, as well as on the acquisition of land for speculation and not for use. Indeed, some Europeans and Asians have already introduced these questionable practices to the continent, and there might well be a fear that once communal tenure was abolished the land could fall into the hands of the rich and the strong without any guarantee that these would also be enterprising.

There are, therefore, strong social reasons, in spite of the need for change, for continuing to retain some control over the terms of tenure and over the transfer of land and, without necessarily discouraging the enterprising and larger operator completely, to place a great deal of emphasis at this stage on encouraging family farms with cooperative services.[1]* The advantage of such a policy is that it does not conflict much with traditional tenure and is based on the fact that the vast majority of the rural population live today on family farms for their subsistence and livelihood. I use the words "at this stage" advisedly because as employment opportunities in industry and services arise, the family is apt to depart, leaving the farm dependent on expensive hired labor at which stage it may be too small to offer a remunerative living. This, in fact, has happened in Europe (in settlement schemes in Italy and Spain), and when it does happen the concept of family farms may need to be revised. It should, therefore, have no ideological rigidity about it, but rather be treated as a pragmatic policy for the existing situation in Africa.

*Notes for this chapter begin on page 238.

If one believes, therefore, that current land usage must be altered and that the best replacement is a pattern of individual consolidated units of family farm size with collective services, the next policy problem concerns the type of tenure. Registration and security of title are essential, when conditions get crowded, to put an end to constant litigation and serious fear of losing one's holding. They are also essential to confidence in investing in improvements. For these reasons, and to facilitate mobility of exchange of land and encourage the enterprising, a freehold type of tenure is often advocated. This has, in fact, been adopted in Kenya. However, to avoid the risk of excessive aggregation and to insure that land is properly developed and used in the national interests, many people think it essential to attach conditions to land tenure and thus, prefer some kind of leasehold. This also presents an opportunity to prohibit fragmentation and to avoid one great constraint on development—an excessive cost of acquiring land. For these reasons Tanzania has abolished freehold. These different solutions to the problem of new tenure in two countries side by side in Africa illustrate the difficulty of choice. Possibly the English words "freehold" and "leasehold" are too stereotyped and all tenure ought to be subject to certain controls (as of course it was in the traditional system) which should not, however, frustrate investment in improvements or create a sense of insecurity. The controls might well vary in different localities and periods. Clearly, settlement schemes in which the state has invested capital need penalties which will weed out unsatisfactory farmers. Clearly also, no country should forget that in two generations half the land in Burma passed into the ownership of Indian moneylenders from absence of any control of mortgage. Nor should Africans ignore the enormous advantage they now have in the absence of latifundia which so frustrate development in Latin America. Please do not think these are side issues. If balance between a fast growth rate and a fair society is to be preserved, wise decisions on the terms of tenure are likely to be of critical importance.

Consideration of the terms of tenure touches on another thorny problem—the degree of discipline necessary in these days for success. A country that needs to increase its agricultural exports in a highly competitive world stands a better chance of doing so if it can get high yields and good quality at low cost and at the right time. This depends to a large extent on using the right technical methods in a timely manner. Colonial administrators often employed a combination of incentive and penalty for this purpose. The discipline was frequently resented, sometimes not understood. The problem is not to abolish it and leave a vacuum, for that would defeat a very necessary purpose, but to replace it by voluntary acceptance and understanding. Again, please do not regard this as a disreputable legacy of colonial paternalism which can now be ignored. Its replacement involves a tremendous task of extension.

IMPLEMENTATION

I come last to the biggest problem of all. One can argue about the choices in the problems just described, but the biggest problem is getting the decisions carried out, getting the job done. With all the handicaps bequeathed by geography and history, Africa stands in need of outside help in many counts of men, money, and markets. Do we want to help? Do Africans want us? Can we fit in with each other?

Let us start with what seem to be the key agricultural needs. Undoubtedly, research heads the list, and here the drawback of being a latecomer continent leaves an enormous deficiency gap and extreme dependence at first on outside help.

Next comes the whole sphere of educating people to apply the results of research—agricultural colleges to train extension workers, farm planners, and demonstrators, training for surveyors and for systems of registration of title, and farmers' training centers to show farmers and their wives that practical application of new ideas and methods can improve their standard of living.

Then there is the wide vista of administrative needs in order for the results of research and education to be made feasible. I refer to such management problems as the production and distribution of better seeds and better varieties of tree crops, of fertilizers, pesticides, tools, carts, machinery, and improved livestock.

Intimately linked to these are the supply of credit and the organization of marketing. Both raise an important question of policy regarding the ownership of processing plants. Should there be a deliberate objective to locate the ownership, ultimately at any rate, in the hands of the producers? Control of deliveries at a processing plant very greatly facilitates control of credit. Indeed, in some countries where farmers' associations are firmly established, such as Japan and Taiwan, control of deliveries enables the placing of bulk orders for fertilizers and other supplies and the raising of credit to pay for them against the farmers' promissory notes. This arrangement has been a key factor in the remarkable increase in agricultural production in those countries, which incidentally may be a better prototype for Africa than most western countries can provide. Ownership of processing by producers should also enable processing and marketing to be conducted at cost with resultant benefit, when operated efficiently, to producers' incomes.

A vista of this kind demands a particular type of help, and one which is very rarely available. I mean men who can teach farmers' associations how to manage efficiently these administrative needs of supply, credit, processing, and marketing. I rate this very much as a key need. It is easy enough in Africa to wish to eliminate the middleman for he has usually been a foreigner, but the real purpose of the exercise, to bring a better income to the producer, is all too easily lost through extravagant costs and inadequate commercial and accounting expertise in the farmers' associations.

In addition to these specific needs for agriculture there is the complementary need for improved infrastructure, main and minor roads, railways, port facilities, forestry and watershed protection, management of river systems for irrigation and power, water distribution to make unit settlement possible, housing, hotels, and health services.

A feature of this formidable list of needs is that few of them are easily applicable to bankers' loan terms. They were largely grant-aided in colonial days. They need more grant-aid, or undated low interest aid, on a much bigger scale today.

Of course, it would be quite wrong to imagine that all the continent can be made productive at any rate for years ahead. Vast areas will continue to suffer uncertain rain, and India has shown just now how sterilizing this is to all plans for improved land use. For this reason I would like to add one panoramic question. Would it not be wise in Africa to think in terms of "regional development poles," to select areas where infrastructure, industry, agriculture, services, and, where applicable, tourism, can be planned in a complementary manner? This is a technique now being used in Spain and Italy to correct the imbalance which has left large parts of those countries undeveloped. Would similar "development poles," where diverse aspects are coordinated and planning dovetailed, be points of spearhead advance, prototypes for the future? Such a concept implies a combined strategy in which government investment in infrastructure, private enterprise, and farmers' associations all play a part in reasonable harmony. Assuredly, advance on a broad front everywhere may dilute resources and defeat effective impact.

I do not want to leave the impression that nothing is happening in Africa to aid development. A tremendous amount is happening. European banks are financing cooperatives. There is an African Development Bank struggling with short resources to encourage regional planning. Mining companies are financing agricultural experiments. Plantation companies are assisting smallholders. Development corporations with joint capital structures of British, German, Dutch, international, and local government capital are investing in industry in partnership with private enterprise. International agencies are financing surveys and infrastructure. The Freedom from Hunger Campaign is playing a part in financing agricultural training. United States AID and other bilateral aid is helping. The Peace Corps and the British Voluntary Service Overseas are there. American and other foundations are prominently contributing. The French have an enormous number of technicians there, uniquely providing continuity of service because they are carried on the home strength, a very important element, for our post-colonial, short-term contracts give no time for fitting-in and break the thread of progress. The Russians are there and the Chinese are there. However, even with all this abundance, few agencies know what the others are doing. Would "development pole" planning bring us closer together, make our efforts more effective, and help to keep Africa out of the ideological battleground?

Let me close by discussing the most difficult legacy of colonialism, the problem of fitting-in—a problem bedevilled by the inconsistency, for which we in the Western world are responsible, of advocating with one hand and with great sincerity the national right to political independence, yet practicing in parts of Africa monopoly of power and privilege by European minorities.

Even if we set aside this inconsistency (and one must remember that one is dealing in the whole continent with only 5 million Europeans compared with 200 million Africans), the problem of fitting-in is a difficult one. On the African side, one of the strongest emotions confronting outsiders is the desire of Africans to be in control of their own destiny economically and culturally as well as politically. This does not mean that they are not perfectly able to appreciate that all nations today are economically interdependent. The cry "neocolonialism," which is apt to puzzle and annoy when political independence has been granted, reflects a very real feeling of resentment at the sense of still being subordinate in much of the profitable production and trade of one's own country. It suggests exploitation in the interests of foreigners rather than nation-building in an African image, and it seems probable that there will be no real contentment psychologically until the degree of local share in the nation's economic life reaches the stage when nobody really minds whether a business is foreign-owned or not.

To fit in with such an emotion means, for us, a tremendous change in traditional attitudes. It means deliberately helping Africans to participate in and control their own economies instead of just picking individual plums for expatriate private enterprise profit as we used to in the past. It means a change in our economic theories to realizing that capitalism is on trial today for what it can put in, not what it can take out. It means a deliberate switch from relying chiefly on European to relying chiefly on African purchasing power and, therefore, deliberately encouraging development of the latter.

It would require a separate chapter to discuss methods of adjusting ourselves mutually to this objective. However, such methods would include joint capital structures with local governments and individuals, Africanization, time limits to foreign ownership, and transfer of investment interests from lines of business, which local people now want to run themselves, to others where they are still glad of our help. Nor is it possible to pursue here that ultimate problem of "trade not mere aid," the theme of the new UNCTAD organization, which affects the whole developing world.

Unfortunately, the challenge to make these adjustments comes to us when the value of aid is under great criticism, when our own balance of payments crises are reducing rather than extending our readiness to increase aid and investment overseas, and when there are significant deterrents in many parts of Africa. There is the immaturity of new governments, the inadequate administration and corruption, the latent psychological antagonism to expatriates, and the difficulty of getting expatriate personnel who can tolerate the changed conditions which no longer offer them prestige and who can fit in with local attitudes. There is the tendency to arbitrary dictation. There is the insecurity of local governments, the risk of conflict through tribal jealousies and of subversion through discontented younger challengers. Finally, there is anyway small profit, and the much pleasanter, less risky, more secure, paying alternative of investment in our own Western world environment. There is also the question of whether or not we really are wanted in Africa by the Africans. Moreover, one cannot escape the feeling that in the end everything depends on African will-power. Our enterprise was built up by ourselves. Can one really build up the enterprise of other people?

In short, it is very easy to succumb to hostility, doubt, and indifference on either side. On such occasions I have always been encouraged by the words of a man who probably did more than most men in history to shape men's minds into a new mold. I mean the scientist, Charles Darwin. He once wrote these words: "I have often experienced what you call the humiliating feeling of getting more and more involved in doubt the more one thinks of the facts and reasoning on doubtful points. But I always comfort myself with thinking of the future and in the full belief that the problems we are just entering on will some day be solved; and if we just break the ground we shall have done some service, even if we reap no harvest."

What a great challenge it is, a challenge expressed for so many of us, beyond the United States, in the words of President Kennedy in his inaugural address on January 20, 1961, when he said: "To those people in the huts and villages of half the globe struggling to break the bonds of mass misery, we pledge our best efforts to help them to help themselves, for whatsoever period is required—not because the communists may be doing it, not because we seek their votes, but because it is right."

NOTES

1. To preserve this balance is not necessarily easy and involves some choice in the size of unit to encourage. Let me illustrate this with two examples. In Kenya, when European estates were being purchased and split

up for use by Africans, the International Bank and the Commonwealth Development Corporation, who were financing this subsequent development, preferred the new settlers to be yeoman farmers whose enterprise was already proved and who had some capital of their own. They were concerned that the subsequent potential income of the farmers would repay the investment. These considerations determined the size of the unit and gave a bias toward the "leader" concept. Naturally, it had equal justification for the economy of Kenya as it was likely to promote the best chance of production, savings, and taxation revenue. There were, however, a large number of landless unemployed thronging the capital, Nairobi, at the time, and if the opportunity for settlement was to be confined to the enterprising who had capital, what was to be done with the landless unemployed? A parallel "high density" scheme of settlement was added which, although based on smaller units and unlikely to provide as much to the economy, at least provided subsistence and alleviated some of the unemployment problem. The long-run hope is that in time, as employment expands in industry and services, many of the high density settlers will find better alternative living, and the farming units can then be enlarged. If the whole European area had been devoted to high density settlement there would be slower or no economic progress. If the whole had been devoted to yeoman farmers there would have been a bigger crisis about the landless unemployed.

Another example can be taken from the Swaziland project already mentioned. Here, at first, the Corporation started the smallholders on 12-acre units. Some of the more successful were then given 60-acre units. The latter brought in an income of over £1,000 per unit. This income was so vastly above the surrounding subsistence level that the Corporation reverted further development to the 12-acre size in order to spread the benefit more widely.

12

Planning Characteristics of
Low-Income Agriculture

J. Price Gittinger

M
ost less-developed countries have undertaken programs of planned agricultural development and have established separate groups concerned with agricultural planning to prepare these programs.[1]* Discussions of planning for agriculture have generally assumed a justification for these separate groups without further examining what might be the nature and the programming implications of some of the structural characteristics which differentiate agriculture from the other sectors of a developing economy.

This chapter explores more explicitly several of those features which set apart the agricultural sector as economic growth proceeds. These characteristics impose limitations on the approach and content of the planning process and on suitable programs for agricultural development. They are, to an extent, the justification for separate planning for agriculture and for what are sometimes rather separate techniques of planning. They help identify more clearly the role of planning in agricultural development (Barter, 1963).

Many of the points touched upon here have a familiar ring for agricultural economists who have been working with problems of more advanced agriculture, for a number are simply the same

*Notes for this chapter begin on page 265.

kinds of considerations that have long been common currency in undergraduate classes. In the low-income context, however, where the emphasis is on overall economic growth and agriculture's role in this process, these considerations take on a new complexion and timeliness.

STRUCTURAL DIFFERENCES OF LOW-INCOME AGRICULTURE

Commonly, a planning activity in a less-developed country will have some sort of overall economic group which undertakes the more aggregative aspects of planning and which bears responsibility for formulating overall fiscal and budgetary measures. There are then separate planning activities for four major sectors, although the details of the distribution of planning responsibility vary from country to country. The four sectors can roughly be identified as: (1) industry, (2) communications and transport, (3) social services including health, education, housing, and other services, and of course, (4) agriculture, including water control. Generally, there is, in addition, some kind of regional planning activity which is often thought of as separate, but which can better be seen as simply a regionalization of the overall economic function and the planning for the four sectors. About the only difference of opinion concerning the need for these separations is whether the responsibility for sectoral planning should belong to the ministries or a central planning agency, or both. An example of this kind of organization in a smaller nation is found in Iran. The Plan Organization at the time of the preparation of the third plan had a Division of Economic Affairs which bore the responsibility for plan formulation. Within this unit was the General Economics Group which was concerned with aggregative aspects of planning and with fiscal and budgetary measures. It also exercised a coordinating function with the sectoral planning groups, and to some extent with operating ministries. Then there were five sectoral planning sections: (1) agriculture, (2) transportation and communication, (3) social affairs and education, (4) industry, and (5) manpower, which concerned itself with population and labor problems (Gittinger, 1965a).

Within this context, some of the more important distinguishing qualities of agriculture and their planning implications may be identified.

COST AND RETURN ORIENTATION

The nature of agricultural production is more cost and return oriented than is the case for many other sectors for which development planning is undertaken.

An elaborate discipline of production economics using advanced programming techniques is devoted to determining optimum production levels and combinations in agriculture. Perhaps more relevant to low-income agriculture is the wide and flexible range of farm management budgeting tools which can approximate optimum production levels and product combinations with much less detailed information about production functions and much less complicated and expensive computational techniques. In program planning, the development of benefit-cost ratios was explicitly directed toward choosing water control systems, mostly dams and associated works, on the basis of their relative return. Such attention to costs and returns in agricultural planning may be contrasted with, for example, the problems associated with planning for schools or health facilities where not only are monetary costs and returns elusive to compute, but where often there is not even general agreement on how important the direct monetary returns arising from these activities are, either in terms of their contribution to national economic growth or in terms of their importance to achieving non-economic objectives.

Even in such a program as rural roads, for instance, where the economic justification is assumed to be much more important than is the case for schools or health facilities, surprisingly little has been done to estimate returns. Only in recent months has any body of experience on estimating rural road returns begun to be reported, and very little of that which has been reported is yet available in normal scholarly channels. In Iran, for example, we were simply forced to give up trying to work out economic criteria for feeder road location despite the fact that all of those involved in the planning group, in the Ministry of Roads, and in the Ministry of Agriculture, were convinced that feeder roads would have a substantial impact on agricultural growth. Recent developments have justified this confidence. Feeder roads have been one of the successes of the current plan, and the change in cropping patterns along these roads has been very obvious. Last season in Tehran, as an example, to the delight of foreigners, but the dismay of farmers, increased supplies of the famous Persian melons became so plentiful as a result of the incentive effects of new access to the Tehran market along feeder roads that the price broke mid-season, and many farmers were unable to pay the costs of harvesting. A similar phenomenon occurred in the supply of spring green onions. Recent research has begun to quantify the effects of rural roads. Bonney (1966) has reported on research in Borneo, and Kasiraksa (1966) has reported on the Friendship Highway in Thailand, to cite two examples.

Of course, this cost and return orientation in agriculture does not distinguish it so sharply from industrial planning as from other sectors.

MANY PRODUCERS, FEW PRODUCTS

Agriculture is nearly unique among sectors for which national economic development planning is undertaken in that it is characterized by a very large number of producers who produce a rather limited number of commercial products. This contrast is even more striking for low-income agriculture than it is for more advanced nations. Not only are crowded peasant societies divided into many more producing units per unit of total national population or area, but they tend often to produce even fewer different commodities, at least commercially, than do farmers in advanced industrial economies. Upon looking at the structure of world trade, only some seventy-five different agricultural products enter importantly into international commerce. This specialization is all the more striking when it is recognized that just three cereals account for some 90 per cent of the value of international grain commerce.

One immediate planning consequence of this juxtaposition of many producers and relatively few products is that agricultural planning almost naturally becomes commodity oriented. Programs tend to be developed for wheat or rice or citrus. In contrast, in other sectors, planning is much more likely to be process oriented, with each grouping producing a number of different products. Thus, we talk of a chemical industry or a textile industry, or health services. Furthermore, in industrial planning it is often feasible to discuss national development programs with only a handful of major producers, such as representatives of the petroleum, metal, or mining industries, or even some kinds of light manufacturing, whereas agricultural planners face one of their continuing challenges just to reach individual producers. In Iran, this point was driven home in an informal conference we were having with the industrial planning section. A point came up about some industrial commodity of concern to both agriculture and industry. Not enough information was available concerning producer attitudes. "Well," someone said, "we'll just have to go out this afternoon and talk to the industry." Indeed, in situations where the number of producers begins to increase and the product range narrows down, there is a tendency for industrial planners to shift responsibility to their agricultural colleagues under such global terms as "rural" or "cottage" industry.

LOW ELASTICITY OF DEMAND AND SUPPLY

Beginning students in economics are sometimes told that one of the assumptions of economic theory is the inexhaustibility of human want. However true this may or may not be in non-Western societies, its main relevance is to manufactured goods and to services, not to food products. Engle's law is clearly valid, even in low-income countries. When this is related to the rather limited number of products which are important in agricultural production, the planning consequence that emerges is that, for agriculture, it makes real sense to begin from the side of estimating aggregate demand. Much attention has been devoted to these estimation procedures, and many suitable techniques have been developed. These are being used increasingly for agricultural planning in low-income societies, and means are being worked out to reduce the obstacles posed by data and administrative limitations. Adjusted for imports and exports, such demand projections for food crops often become the targets for agricultural production. Frequently, they turn out to be well within reach of known techniques and present capital availabilities (though it is, of course, true that food needs in many areas of the world, especially for protein food, remain well beyond immediate prospects for increased production). The agricultural planner's colleague responsible for, say, motor vehicle supply or school planning must genuinely envy the agriculturalist's simpler and neater target-setting approach.

On the supply side, aggregate elasticities are also low. Indeed, it is just this point that is the primary concern of agricultural planning groups. Yet *how* low and means of estimating aggregate supply elasticity in low-income agriculture are as yet almost un-explored. In contrast to the rather satisfactory theoretical position of demand analysis, supply analysis has little to contribute, even in theory, to agricultural planning. Normal projection techniques, which tend to be rather well worked out, cannot be applied to supply projection. It is exactly because they want to *change* the parameters which have historically determined a poor perform-ance in agriculture that many agricultural planners are in business. The USDA has recently sponsored a number of supply projections which are now available in published form. These, however, tend to ignore plans or else they arbitrarily scale them down and then make the projection. An example is the supply estimate published by the National Council for Applied Economic Research (1962) in India. The study took the agricultural targets of the Planning Commission and then discounted the benefits from proposed in-vestments "to make it conform as closely as possible to actual realization on the basis of past trends." It is hard to see how this is any more justifiable than the estimates originally published by the planners except that pessimism can always be defended.

Unhappily, one of the key tasks of agricultural planners is to do just what theory hardly helps us do at all, project supply. Most plans are, to some extent, an estimate of demand and a program of agricultural growth with either the explicit statement that the plan is adequate to bring forth the needed production, or else a clear implication that this is so. But how do the planners know? The plain, unvarnished truth is they do not. There are extremely few "coefficients" which can be used for this purpose. The literature is surprisingly quiet on this topic. Exactly how many tons of rice will an additional extension agent bring forth? Just to ask the question this way tends to make obvious the planners' dilemma. Most supply estimates in agricultural planning are simply nothing other than guesswork. Of course, some "coefficients" or "yard-sticks" are, in practice, used. One is the guess that 5 hectares of additional land will be irrigated for each new masonry well which the Indian Planning Commission uses. Other such yardsticks are used commonly for estimating the impact of fertilizer use on production, and the increased production that new varieties of seed will bring forth. As a result of the informal nature of these "yardsticks," very little exchange of information about them oc-curs. The really important effects on supply remain a mystery. The influences of incentives, of prices, or of institutional development programs on production will also remain a mystery, and until more is known about these relationships, agricultural planning is bound to remain more an art than a science.

It is generally agreed that supply elasticities in agriculture are low, and this distinguishes agriculture from some of the other sectors of the planning activities. In industry, some supply elasticities for light manufactured products, given favorable economic incentive, may be rather high. Textiles provide an example; the increased production of textiles in Hong Kong has provided serious problems in the United States, and Hong Kong, Pakistani, and Indian textiles have proved responsive enough to have had a very serious impact on the British cotton textile industry.

Although low in contrast to industry, agricultural supply elasticities, nonetheless, can be higher than many would otherwise expect. The USDA study on agriculture in twenty-six developing nations comes up with the almost startling fact that the agriculture in twelve of the nations grew at a rate above 4 per cent per year, a rate which surpassed any ever achieved by now economically advanced nations during comparable periods of time (USDA, 1965, V). It is probably this relatively high elasticity of supply in agriculture, and more especially the elasticity of marketable surplus, which has kept the domestic terms of trade from turning more sharply in favor of agriculture with consequent serious implications for industrial development programs.

STRICT ECOLOGICAL CONSTRAINTS

The freedom of movement for agricultural development alternatives is restricted, more so than in planning for any other sector, by the stringent ecological constraints on agricultural production. It is true, of course, that there are some real alternatives such as increasing productivity through more intensive cultivation with the use of techniques already well established, through increasing the quantities of irrigation water, or through the opening of lands for new settlement. However, these choices are always few in number and, except in particular cases, generally are not of very much importance in the overall picture of agricultural development. It is upon the ecological constraints that modern agricultural technology is largely focused. Seen from this point of view, it is even more justified than ever to think of agriculture, at least from the standpoint of agricultural planning, as applied biology. No agricultural plan is without its section devoted to increasing fertilizer use or to improvement of planting stocks. Yet, at best, ecological restraints are pressing, and agricultural plans and the record of implementation are much more directly and extensively influenced by ecological considerations than are plans for industrial growth or expansion of social services. Agriculture can truly be characterized as operating within myriads of microenvironments. Three limits of the environment within which agriculture works can be identified as having important planning and programming implications.

General Environment, Climate.—We are still with Mark Twain when he complained that everyone talks about the weather, but no one does anything about it. Climate is still overwhelmingly dominant in agricultural planning, and almost nothing can be done about it with the major and ancient exception of irrigation. A great deal of the best talent of agricultural planning, therefore, goes into the designing of irrigation developments. Careful research programs are needed to discover more about stream runoff and rainfall records, to study the costs of building irrigation structures versus the benefits from increased production, and to plan for better water utilization. Yet, at best, this is merely nibbling at the edges of the question of climate. Compare what we are able to do in agriculture with the influence of climate on industrialization, for example. Except in the most general sense, industries pay almost no attention to climate. Automobiles may be built with almost the same efficiency in Canada or Texas. Air conditioning makes offices in New York and Singapore identical in climate right down to the cigarette smoke. When static electricity becomes serious for a textile mill, the mill simply humidifies the air.

In other sectors, planning is also less influenced by climatic variation. Schools between the Arctic and the tropics show no particular variation in efficiency which can be traced to climate. Even road building is less affected by climate than is agriculture. For the most part, those who plan in agriculture must simply take the climate as given. About the best they can do is to undertake research programs that increase their real understanding of what the "given" climate is.

Similarly, soil variations are extreme and amenable to little adjustment. Although it is true that there is much which can be done to replace nitrogen loss in soils, there is as yet little we can do to replace eroded soils, to restore lost tilth, or to counter the adverse effects of clearing on tropical lateritic soils. Furthermore, soils vary enormously from place to place, even within single fields. So pronounced is this variation that farmers in European countries often have traditional names attached to particular fields or parts of fields which are used to identify each plot. By this very process, they underline the separate personalities of the different parcels of land lying on a single farm.

Variations in soil and climate, of course, do not pass unnoticed among peasant farmers. The sophistication of their adjustment was first brought home to me when we were studying a Vietnamese village along a river to the south of Saigon. We found some fourteen different, identifiable varieties of rice grown in this one location. When we inquired, we found that an individual farmer with a holding somewhere between one and a half and two hectares might plant five or six different varieties. In each particular type of microenvironment he would plant two varieties. Thus, on lower parts of his holding along the river on an inlet, he would plant an early variety which responds well to lots of water and somewhat brackish conditions in case of poor rainfall during the season, and a later variety which responds in case of flood. Somewhat further, he would plant two varieties which respond to better drained locations, and which would probably produce higher yields, and again one early and one late variety. Yet further, even in such a small holding, he would plant another variety which could resist rather dry conditions. In addition to this, he might plant a bit of glutenous rice to supply the family's need for this type to make the various special Vietnamese confections.

Other climatic limitations need to be mentioned only in passing, but temperature, humidity, and light all impose restraints which are more severe in agriculture than they are for those who plan for industry, communications, or services. Such variation in quality of inputs as those we have been noting would be considered virtually intolerable by the process engineers from MIT, yet somehow we must prepare peasant farmers to cope with them.

Strict Timing Control.—In no other aspect of economic development is timing so important in the production process. A two-week delay in the arrival of a key industrial raw material might cause a plant to lose some 4 per cent of its annual production;

a two-week delay in availability of fertilizer may cost a farmer half his annual crop. One agricultural economist noted recently that agriculture is the only production process where the manager of the fundamental production unit still must wait until he gets up each morning and looks out the window before he can know what his production activity will be that day. Such strict time limitations have serious implications for the way in which management can be organized and in the standards of reliability to which supply and marketing activities must be organized.

Geographical Dispersion.—There is hardly any need to mention, much more than in passing, the impact on agricultural planning of the geographical dispersion imposed on agriculture by a production process which mainly depends on availability of light, a factor over which we have virtually no control. The opportunities for concentrating production which exist in industry and even in communications and education are simply not available to the agricultural planner. Agriculture can only moderately be intensified. An industrial plant can be expanded a hundredfold with essentially no change in its geographical characteristic. A university may be increased from 3,000 to 30,000 students with hardly anything like a concomitant extension in area, and it can change the boundaries of the area it serves rather at will. The opportunities for intensification in agriculture, although at the heart of our strategy of agricultural development, are hardly so striking. Hence, we cannot foresee any dramatic change in the extremely dispersed nature of agriculture, and thus in all that this implies for services, marketing, information, and other matters.

IMPORTANCE OF INCENTIVE STRUCTURES

Agricultural planners, perhaps more than their colleagues in industry, communications, or social services, must make extensive use of incentive devices and more particularly of indirect incentives. This is imposed upon agricultural planning by some of the other features of agriculture which we have already discussed. Of particular importance are the large number of producers and the dispersed nature of agriculture's microenvironment. Under such circumstances, the opportunities for centralized management or coercion are limited, indeed. Barter (1963, 39) notes that whereas industrial management or a labor union cannot hold out long against determined efforts of a strong government, farmers, because of the subsistence nature of agricultural production, can simply retreat into their own farm-household firms and resist agricultural programs not only for weeks or months, but for years. Hence, one whole area of direct control open to those concerned with industry or services is closed to agricultural planners.

Certainly, the use of direct incentives is not limited to agriculture; indeed, the most obvious device to promote industries in low-income countries, that of the protective tariff, is hardly used in agriculture. Nevertheless, direct incentive devices are a major tool in agricultural policy, and almost every agricultural plan, even in low-income nations, makes use of them. Many factors in the structure of agriculture contribute to this. The large number of individual producers makes it difficult to plan directly with them the adoption of new techniques as might be possible with industrial producers or with administrators of health or education programs. Some agricultural development specialists are of the opinion that a new production input must return farmers, at the very least, double their outlay, before it can overcome their subjective uncertainty. Most industrial producers would be more than pleased for half that return, given the availability of capital resources. The fact that the government is so important in the supply of production requisites for modern agriculture, such diverse items as fertilizer, credit, information, and research, or in such expansion programs as irrigation or settlement, makes the use of direct incentives easy to administer, indeed, often too easy. The relatively limited number of important commodities makes establishment of "floor" prices an obvious expansion device and one, though tricky and difficult, that is easier to use than in the industrial sector. One might even include here such institutional changes as reform in land tenure arrangements to increase the impact of economic incentive while at the same time realizing goals of social justice. All of these direct incentive devices quickly overlap into questions of much broader and political content than merely increasing agricultural production to reach specified production targets. The degree to which direct incentive devices will be used depends on many factors. The basic attitude of the government and the farmers about the place of government in encouraging agricultural expansion, the available resources of the agricultural sector and of the government, and the time span envisioned for realization of the output targets are among the most important factors.

A peculiar aspect of the structure of agriculture often forces even low-income nations to subsidize it much more than they otherwise would like to do. World markets for the rather small number of agricultural products are tightly interlinked. As a result, any nation which does not use subsidies puts its farmers into the position of a marginal producer. Unfortunately, it is the low-income countries which wish to expand exports based on a still dominantly agricultural society which cannot afford extensive subsidies, and hence, it is the low-income farmer who finds himself placed in the marginal position. One of the frustrations to the growth of agriculture in low-income countries is the subsidy the advanced industrial nations pay their producers.

EXPENSIVE, DISPERSED INFORMATION SYSTEM

Another problem faced by agricultural planners is the expensive nature of the information systems available to them, and the extremely dispersed nature of these channels. We speak of industrial consultants, but of agricultural extension agents. We organize an industrial census, but, hopefully, a rural sample survey. The means of information dispersal in agriculture are not well understood, even in our own society, and the establishment of new ones in underdeveloped nations has not been notably successful.

One reason why information systems in agriculture have moved slowly may possibly be traced to the influence of Americans in the formulation of the agricultural development programs in a number of nations, and our tendency to misread our own experience in dispersal of agricultural information. Typically, the person who has gone overseas from the United States to help in agricultural development, whether he has been with a government, a foundation, or an agricultural mission, has been drawn from the land-grant college and extension tradition in our own nation. By training and experience, these individuals have become familiar with the agricultural extension service and its importance to agricultural growth in the United States. Thus, they have naturally tended to focus on the extension approach to information when they have been abroad, and American aid programs have been instrumental in helping to establish extension services in dozens of countries. However, the extension service was founded in the United States well after the major expansion of cultivated area, and has never been more than a complementary part of the information flow structure. All during the nineteenth century, information about agriculture in the United States probably came most importantly through word of mouth among neighbors. The next most important sources, and perhaps the most important for technical innovations, were individuals who sold input supplies, and commercial journals aimed at the farm population. Recent concentration on extension information flows led to a tendency to overlook the importance of information flows through these commercial supplier channels. Even today in the United States, more information flows through such channels as salespeople, advertising, and articles in farm magazines and other publications than through the extension service. Given the difficulties of organizing effective extension services, of staff, and of finance, it is likely the planning agencies in developing countries should turn more of their attention to channels other than extension and community development. In particular, imaginative government programs might be aimed at strengthening the information available to dealers of inputs and to helping them improve their sales techniques. The strengthening of information flow through commercial channels imparts the advantage of creating a vested interest in continued and increased commercialization and modernization in agriculture. Experience in a number of developing countries has shown that it is hard to build such an interest into government agencies where the reward of success is to be transferred to the capital rather than to increase one's income within the rural community. Among other channels which need to be exploited more fully are advertising by input supply firms, agricultural radio programs, and commercial magazines which have an important potential for reaching opinion leaders even in communities where literacy is limited.

Given the fact that in many countries millions of producing units must be reached and that the high costs of direct-service information channels, such as extension and community development, are likely to be prohibitive for some time yet to come, there is the need for development of a better concept of cost-effectiveness in the whole area of information flow in low-income agriculture. Some of this is beginning to appear, and there have been a few seminars and a few publications on these topics (Myren, 1964). However, it is surprising how little has been done on communications theory in low-income agriculture, on the effectiveness and cost of mass media as channels of reaching low-income farmers, and on means of strengthening commercial channels of communication.

One obvious communication channel that has attracted too little attention as yet is the use of elementary education to further agricultural development. Special text materials for rural areas, now beginning to be developed in several regions, can make an important contribution to future agricultural development. For one thing, and obviously, schools can teach future farmers about new agricultural technology. Less obviously, the new technology which students learn even in elementary schools may be transmitted through them to their parents, and thus is used long before the students have farming responsibilities of their own. This system is a well-recognized method of the 4-H structure in the United States context. However, the most important impact of elementary education programs on agricultural development is probably neither of these direct influences. Rather, it is likely the much more subtle impact of simply teaching a child that there *are* modern technologies which are applicable to agriculture, not just to airplanes or radios, and that he can command this technology.

Furthermore, elementary educational programs will develop in the child the habit of turning to the printed page for information about new technology, and for many years to come, at least, the printed work must remain the most common source of information about new technology, even in semiliterate societies (Gittinger, 1965b).

HOUSEHOLD-FIRM INTERRELATIONSHIPS

A key distinguishing characteristic of agriculture which separates it from the rest of the society is the close interrelation between the production aspect of the farm family and its consumption aspect. One result of industrialization is the separation of work from residence, which has extensive implications on the whole range of investment and production decisions. Development plans in the industrial, transport, or social development sectors can largely be framed on the basis of pure investment decision considerations. Even in agriculture, those investments for which the government is largely responsible, such as water control measures, can be made on the basis of criteria which are to a great extent pure investment criteria. An example is benefit-cost analysis for irrigation.

However, when the investment process in agriculture depends not on government initiative, but on that of individual farm families who are at the same time consumers, a whole new range of considerations enters into the decision process and must be explicitly taken into account by the agricultural planners. For one thing, farmers are likely to be influenced by the time required for the investment to pay off. In Indonesia, for example, coconut production is falling sharply. One reason ascribed to this development is that farmers know that it will be twenty-five years before the tree reaches full bearing. If the farmer is older and his children are already establishing families of their own, the farmer simply does not see the need to plant new trees. Hence, investment decisions, in this instance increasingly important for Indonesia's copra exports, are markedly influenced by the age of the farm family. When seen from another viewpoint, we can simply say that farmers have widely varying time horizons, whereas a joint stock company, in theory at least, has only the time horizon imposed upon it by current interest rates.

Specialists in African agriculture give us another example of household-firm influence on investment decisions. A serious obstacle to increasing both the variety and quantity of food production in a number of tropical African countries is found in the investment pattern in plantain, or cooking bananas. A young farmer establishing his household will set out a grove of banana plants. Once these plants begin to bear they will produce for some forty years or so, the effective adult life expectancy of most peasant farmers in this area. Hence, once established on his holding, the farmer has very little incentive to extend his investment, and any development plans for agriculture must somehow take this pattern of investment response into consideration.

The importance of household-firm interrelationships in labor allocation has long been significant in discussions of American agriculture, and recently Mellor has advanced the suggestion that it must play a large part in any satisfactory theory of agricultural development which may be worked out (Mellor, 1967).

HIGH SUBJECTIVE UNCERTAINTY

Closely related to the household-firm consideration is the question of subjective uncertainty in low-income agriculture. Indeed, one of the major reasons for the importance of subjective uncertainty is the importance of consumption considerations for investment decisions.

Farmers in low-income agriculture quite rationally attach a large discount premium to any innovation in order to allow for their subjective uncertainty. Of course, all innovations, whether in agriculture or other sectors, display *some* degree of uncertainty. The reasons uncertainty may be singled out for particular importance in agriculture are twofold. One source of subjective uncertainty is exactly the same as that which an industrial manager shares: will a new innovation pay off on my farm or plant? However, whereas in industry or communications a technique developed in the United States can likely be assessed accurately by an industrial manager in a low-income country, in part because of his greater control over environmental factors, the microenvironment imposes a much greater degree of uncertainty in agriculture. In agriculture we must organize an extensive fertilizer trial system, for example, or a variety testing program of a much more local nature. This trial program is not so necessary in industry. The very mention of a polyvinyl chloride plant field test is almost amusing. Of course, Allied Chemical can make its recently announced petrochemical complex in Iran work, and millions will be invested in the next few months without giving the thought any further consideration. However, within sight of this new plant in the Khuzestan, fertilizer field trials are still in the early stages, so farmers continue to shun fertilizer on their vegetables, sugar beets, and wheat. This exceptional doubt is rational, one would suggest, given their economic and physical environment.

A second major consideration that contributes to the high subjective uncertainty in agriculture, and makes it more important in this field than elsewhere, is the very low risk-bearing capacity of the innovating firm. Suppose Allied Chemical *cannot* produce polyvinyl chloride in southern Iran; who goes hungry? However, a farmer must be very careful indeed, because the penalties attached to error in innovation are substantial. The trade-offs between gains and losses are severely skewed. For most peasant farmers, a 50 per cent chance to double yield by adopting an innovation does not outweigh a 50 per cent chance of even a 10 per cent fall in production if the farm family is near a subsistence level where any marked reduction in supply means someone in the family must miss meals. A similar consideration applies to the uncertainty involved in shifting to cash crops. In Iran last year, the farmers who were caught with a green onion crop which they could not sell profitably simply lost their investment. But, cannily, most farmers probably anticipated such might be the case and grew wheat too. The great advantage of a subsistence crop is that it virtually eliminates the market risk; anything you cannot sell profitably can always be eaten by the family.

Subjective uncertainty accounts, too, for differing price responsiveness to money incentives in developing agriculture. Thailand is a case in point. Several years ago the combination of a vastly improved transportation system based on a new American aid road and a strong market underwritten by Japanese importers made kenaf, a hard fiber, an attractive proposition in northeast Thailand. Had kenaf demanded the same kinds of soils and locations as rice, this probably would still be of academic interest. It happens, however, that kenaf can be grown on the upland benches lying above the small areas where rice is grown on alluvial soils found along the watercourses. Hence, it was not necessary to choose between innovation and food, and the Thai farmers responded to the new opportunities with alacrity. Kenaf can be seen throughout the area now, and there can hardly be any question about price responsiveness if the conditions are right. On the other hand, the cousins of these farmers in the main rice delta, who can be presumed to be basically just as price responsive, have been slow to take to fertilizer. One reason is a result of the rather unfavorable ratios between the artificially low rice prices and fertilizer costs. Another reason surely is the interaction of subjective uncertainty with respect to innovation in food crops.

The whole area of subjective uncertainty, incidentally, is one in which there is much too little research being done. It is not an easy area to work in, to be sure, but it is important. It would seem to be an appropriate area for the attention of the vast research resources of an American land grant university such as the University of Florida, and one where an American university might be expected to have a marked comparative advantage over a smaller university of limited resources in a developing country abroad.

PRICE ADMINISTRATION AND TAX COLLECTION

The special characteristics of agriculture in low-income countries impose certain limitations on the ability to levy taxes and may offer particular opportunities to mobilize resources through price administration. A number of low-income countries are trying one means or another of taxing agriculture through price administration. Often this does not fall within the realm of the responsibility of the agricultural planner, but it always influences the programs for which he is responsible.

Clearly, in many low-income countries, agriculture is the major production resource. If agriculture cannot somehow be taxed, then the wealth necessary for industrialization and modernization can hardly be found. In general, experience with taxation of food crops has been poor, but experience with export crops has often been successful. The marketing boards in Ghana, and the operation of the rice premium (really an export tax) in Thailand, show what can be done to mobilize resources from agriculture. True, such devices can have serious implications for incentives and for innovation. One suggestion heard in Thailand, for example, is that producers use little fertilizer on rice because of the depressing effects of the price premium on rice. It is possible to devise taxation techniques which can encourage productivity when there are special circumstances of which imaginative planning can take advantage. An example is the classic colonial case of levying a cash tax which forces farmers to grow a cash crop to sell. A more subtle illustration is found in Taiwan where farmers must exchange rice for fertilizer. The price of the rice can be pegged with little regard for the world price, while the fertilizer availability has a desirable impact on rice production.

Often, however, agriculture escapes taxation, and this poses difficult problems for development. A recent study of India, for example, concludes that agriculture bears less than its proportionate share of the tax burden (Gandhi, 1966), although it would be plausible to argue that it should bear more than its share in order to effect a capital transfer out of agriculture to the urban sector. Such questions of taxation devices and their effect on innovation and growth in productivity take on a special character in agriculture because of the nature of the production, and raise many special planning problems.

OUTSIDE PROVISION OF NEW TECHNOLOGY

A characteristic which separates agriculture from industry and communications planning is the necessity to provide new technology from the outside. Normally, one would expect industries, and to some extent transportation and communication systems, to provide much of the finance for generating new technology. This process might be through research but more often, in newly developing countries, it will take the form of buying modern processes from abroad. This is quite feasible since the individual firm can capture the results of its new technology. In agriculture, however, the nature of the production structure means that no one firm can afford to develop new technology, and if it did, the chances of capturing a large proportion of the total benefit from the new technology are virtually nil. Hence, the universal pattern is for the new technology to be provided by the public sector. The problem of generating new technology is intensified by the microenvironment of agriculture, which means that an enormous amount of adaptive research must be done. In industry, by way of contrast, greater control over the nature of the environment and the production process makes it possible for technology to be transferred from advanced countries more readily. Agricultural planners, more than most others, must not only plan production and investment programs, but must plan research programs also. A rather close correlation is necessary in the estimation of research results in the form of, say, fertilizer recommendations, the rate of innovation adoption, and the impact of innovation on agricultural output. Furthermore, provision must be made for the agricultural scientists who will man the research programs. This necessity further complicates the attempts to plan a development program in agriculture.

HIGH COMPLEMENTARITY OF INPUTS

All of these distinguishing characteristics of agriculture and of agricultural planning have tended to point to a final distinguishing characteristic: the high complementarity of inputs in agricultural production and hence, of agricultural planning.

On the individual farm, the complementarity of production inputs is far greater than that of other production processes in development. There are few production processes in early-stage agriculture that can be subcontracted out. The farmer must provide for himself, and in a timely manner, soil, seed, power, and marketing services. As agriculture proceeds, he is able to pass off to the urban sector many of the functions he provides for himself on a subsistence farm, but his production process remains highly complementary. Better seed will not pay off without proper fertilizer. Fertilizer cannot be successful without water. One farmer producing an early crop may only attract all the rats in the village. Timeliness of operation is of the essence. By contrast, the production process in the urban sector is much less complementary in its nature. A new automobile industry can import all the parts and only assemble them at first; then, gradually, parts can be manufactured. Even then, if it miscalculates, it can always import enough parts to make up for any shortage. In health and education the opportunities for this fragmentation of the process are not so great, to be sure, but the tight coordination between, say, elementary, secondary, and university growth is not so important in education as is coordination among elements of agricultural production. To all this is added the necessity to undertake this tight coordination for agriculture within a varied microclimate and by thousands—perhaps millions—of individual managers who have limited access to new information and limited training.

At the planning level, there is also a complementarity problem. A program for fertilizer imports or manufacture is of little use unless there is a complementary program for seed production, for fertilizer distribution, for market structures to move increased production, and for credit to finance the new input. Indeed, it is probably the extreme difficulty of mounting a coordinated set of programs, each of which is dependent upon another for the final success of the plan, that has been the cause of the poor performance of most agricultural plans. It is simply an enormous task to be undertaken by a small planning group working with limited budget resources and with an underdeveloped administrative structure. Innumerable attempts are being made to mitigate the effects of this complementarity. One approach is the package program in India where the complementary inputs are being provided in only limited areas. Another is to try to engage in regional planning where more homogeniety of environment can be expected and where local cooperation can be more easily mobilized. Yet another is to try to concentrate on a single crop—say an important grain crop—and to try to provide the complementary requirements for that crop alone.

In the final analysis, it is the inherent complementarity of the agricultural development process which provides the biggest stumbling block to effective agricultural development programs, and the most interesting challenge to agricultural planners.

SUMMARY OF CONTRASTING CHARACTERISTICS

A summary of some distinguishing features of agriculture in contrast with other sectors is given in Table 12.1.

SOME IMPLICATIONS FOR TRAINING AGRICULTURAL PLANNERS

Given the fact that agricultural planning has these structural differentiations as contrasted with other aspects of economic development planning, some implications for the preparation of agricultural planners, either in formal coursework or in professional seminars, may be briefly touched upon.

Although it is not always the case, in a large proportion of the situations those persons concerned with agricultural planning will be better prepared in agricultural technology than in economics. For these persons, a general review of economics as a science of maximization and an introduction to the main techniques of macroeconomic planning will be essential, but too much detail in the mechanics of mathematical model formulation, still of limited usefulness in agricultural planning, might not be justified. In the line of statistics, emphasis should be placed on review or teaching of techniques of analysis of large numbers, since planners will be using data about size distribution of holdings, range of credit use, trend of production, time series corrected for seasonal variation, and the like. Included should be such techniques as regression analysis and analysis of variance which give an appreciation of the extreme variation which exists in agriculture in such critically important factors for planning as fluctuations in output per hectare, annual yields, rainfall, or response to given input levels. If they are not already familiar with them, an introduction to farm management budgeting techniques and the usefulness of statistical techniques in the microeconomics of agriculture would be desirable in order to stress the importance of microeconomic research to undergird any agricultural planning and to prepare those per-

TABLE 12.1.—Contrasting Characteristics of Agriculture and Other Sectors

Functional consideration	Agriculture	Industry	Communications and roads	Social: education, health, housing
Estimation of returns	Directly related to the firm; theory of surplus value	Directly related to the firm	Difficult to identify; for roads difficult to capture	Difficult to identify; difficult to capture
Nature of the production unit	Many small, dispersed firms; privately owned	Few, large firms; privately owned	Few firms; government control	Publicly owned; variable size
Management structure	Highly fragmented; very timely; resistant to centralization	Concentrated; subject to pyramiding; few highly trained managers	Concentrated; often government operated	Concentrated; schools, hospitals require local management
Production process	Biological; tangible inputs; tangible outputs; complex and variable	Physical, engineering or chemical; tangible input and output; relatively more uniform	Engineering; tangible inputs; intangible outputs; controlled	Intangible inputs and outputs; controlled process

TABLE 12.1.—(Continued)

Functional consideration	Agriculture	Industry	Communications and roads	Social: education, health, housing
Returns to scale	Limited to about one family	Large returns to scale	Large returns to scale	Moderate returns to scale; problems of teacher/doctor-student/patient relationships
Transferability of technique	Moderately transferable; local testing; often gaps in knowledge	Rather directly transferable	Rather directly transferable	Moderately transferable; severe cultural problems of transfer
Environmental control	Very little; weather critical	High control	Generally high control; weather affects	Unimportant
Household-firm relationships	Highly inter-related; extremely important; subsistence production	None or very little; separation of work from residence	None	None or very little
Structure of market	Many producers; few products	Few producers; many products	Few producers; few products	Few producers; few products, i.e., education, health, housing services

TABLE 12.1.—(Continued)

Functional consideration	Agriculture	Industry	Communications and roads	Social: education, health, housing
Market elasticities	Low market elasticity; tendency for wide seasonal fluctuations	Elastic market demand	Elastic market demand	Elastic market demand
Distribution problems	Severe; must distribute inputs; gather products	Generally concentrated production; distribution a problem	Outlets and roads difficult	Moderate to severe because of population dispersion
Communication; diffusion technical knowledge	Difficult because of so many producers; spread of the production process	Can be rather concentrated	Concentrated	Intermediate, but easier than agriculture
Control	Extremely difficult; generally indirect	Simplified by few obvious firms	Easy	Generally easy because of government ownership and control

TABLE 12.1.—(Continued)

Functional consideration	Agriculture	Industry	Communications and roads	Social: education, health, housing
Tax collection	Difficult; evasion easy	Generally easier because of concentration	Easy	Not applicable; but fees assessed
Adjustment of supply and demand	Difficult; supply inelastic	Easy; supply relatively elastic	Supply of services elastic	Difficult; supply relatively inelastic; resources difficult to transfer
Price administration	Nearly perfect competition	Monopolistic	Monopolistic	Monopolistic
Generation of new technology	Government research difficult to capture returns	Industrial research; patent structure	Industrial research; patent structure	Government research; difficult to capture returns
Tendency to dualism	High	Limited	Limited	Limited, but tend to get traditional or poor schools, etc.; some folk medicine

sons responsible for aggregative planning to appreciate and make good use of microeconomic research.

A training background should include a substantial emphasis on ecology in a broad sense to provide an appreciation of the necessity of fitting a farming system into an environment. For those with an extensive biological science background, this education might best be conducted through the use of social anthropology, which will emphasize the interrelationships between economic and cultural factors on changes in agricultural production. In more common ecological studies, plant and animal ecology can be used to emphasize that response which is almost always a result of two or three complementary measures specifically adapted to a particular environment.

Finally, of course, a training program should introduce the most common program approaches in a broad range of fields: crop production, seed production, fertilizer distribution, credit, land tenure, marketing, and the whole mass of agricultural improvement programs. Necessarily, this training must be done in a summary fashion, and so particular attention needs to be given to the matters of how to use and where to find sources of more detailed information when particular needs arise.

NOTES

1. The author wishes to acknowledge two important sources for many of the ideas developed in this paper. A critical initial impetus came from the lecture on "Special Problems of Agricultural Planning" delivered by Mr. P. G. H. Barter (1963) of the Food and Agricultural Organization (FAO) and subsequent discussions with Mr. Barter. Other insights came from comments made in conversation by Professor Egbert de Vries while he was still Director of the Institute for Social Studies. Of course, any errors of fact and interpretation contained in this paper must be wholly ascribed to the author.

LITERATURE CITED

BARTER, P. G. H. 1963. Special problems of agricultural planning, p. 33-42. *In* FAO, Lectures on agricultural planning delivered at the FAO Near East regional training center on agricultural development planning. Agric. planning studies 3. FAO, Rome.

BONNEY, R. S. P. 1966. Road building and economic development in Sabah. Dev. Digest IV(2): 21-33.

GANDHI, VED P. 1966. Tax burden on Indian agriculture. Harvard Univ. Law School. Cambridge, Mass. 240 p.

GITTINGER, J. PRICE. 1965a. Planning for agricultural development: the Iranian experience. Center for Development Planning, National Planning Assoc. Planning experience series no. 2. Washington, D.C. 121 p.

————. 1965b. Mobilizing knowledge for agricultural planning. Looking Ahead 13(7): 1-4.

KASIRAKSA, WISIT. 1966. Economic effects of the friendship highway. Dev. Digest IV(2): 34-38.

MELLOR, J. W. 1967. Towards a theory of agricultural development, p. 21-60. *In* Herman M. Southworth and Bruce F. Johnston [eds.], Agricultural Development and Economic Growth. Cornell Univ. Press, Ithaca, N.Y.

MYREN, D. T. [ed.] 1964. Communications in agricultural development. Report of the first inter-American research symposium on the role of communications in agricultural development. Mexico City. 3-15 Oct. 163 p.

NATIONAL COUNCIL OF APPLIED ECONOMIC RESEARCH. 1962. Long-term projections of demand for and supply of selected agricultural commodities, 1960-1961 to 1975-76. New Delhi. 262 p.

USDA. 1965. Changes in agriculture in 26 developing nations, 1948 to 1963. ERS, For. Econ. Rep. No. 27. Washington, D.C. 134 p.

13

Organization for Local Development in Low-Income Countries

James W. Green

The terms of reference set for this chapter are to compare and contrast some types of organizations which have been utilized for development in countries of South Asia, Central Africa, and Latin America, a knowledge of which may contribute to agricultural development in low-income countries.[1]* Special attention is given to: (1) the local level, (2) specialist support, and (3) staff training.

As anyone who has had more than casual contact with indigenous societies soon realizes, it is possible to gain an adequate understanding of agricultural matters only within the context of the communal life of the people. Likewise, it is possible to have effective organization for agricultural development only as such organization is consonant with the sociocultural structure of the community and administers to its perceived needs for organized activity. Therefore, some of the approaches to organization, especially the more effective, as we shall presently see, have been multidimensional and oriented to community-defined human needs rather than to a particular technology such as agriculture.

The examples drawn upon here are those with which the author has had the most direct experience. Included are the Pakistan multipurpose worker approach, the paternalistic-compulsive ration-

*Notes for this chapter begin on Page 300.

ale of Southern Rhodesia, the separatist-stereotyped extension approach found in the Dominican Republic, and the coordinated zonal approach for institutional change being initiated in Peru. Like all such brief characterizations, these descriptive titles are oversimplifications, and elements of more than one approach may be found in each of them. Their use here is heuristic and descriptive of what was believed to be a major theme of the specific form of development organization used during particular periods of time in these countries.

Obviously, the variety of organizational patterns which have been given trials is great, and these descriptions by no means exhaust the variety. Perhaps experiences of other patterns might lead to conclusions different from those presented at the end of this chapter.

PAKISTAN'S MULTIPURPOSE VILLAGE WORKER APPROACH

The dire need for increasing agricultural production in Pakistan has led that country to try various approaches to the problem. The Grow-More-Food Campaign encompassing the period 1942-51 preceded the Village Agricultural and Industrial Development (AID) program based on the multipurpose village worker approach. The failure of the former led to the latter.

THE GROW-MORE-FOOD CAMPAIGN

This nationwide campaign, which was initiated and carried forward with great fanfare during World War II in undivided India, was discontinued during the hectic period of partition, but was resumed again in both Pakistan and India in the late 1940's. In India, the failure of this campaign approach to increase production led the government of India to appoint a Grow-More-Food Enquiry Committee. The campaign was very similar in what later became the separate countries of Pakistan and India, and the Report of this Committee is believed to be applicable to both countries. A quotation from this report is appropriate to our purposes (Min. of Food and Agric., Govt. of India, 1952, 50-51) (my italics):

> The economic aspects of village life cannot be detached from the broader social aspects; and agricultural improve-

ment is inextricably linked up with a whole set of social problems. The lesson to be derived from the working of the Grow-More-Food programmes thus confirms the experience of States and private agencies engaged in village development. *It is that all aspects of rural life are interrelated and that no lasting results can be achieved if individual aspects of it are dealt with in isolation.* This does not mean that particular problems should not be given prominence but the plans for them should form parts of, and be integrated with, those for achieving the wider aims. It is only by placing this ideal—of bringing about an appreciable improvement in the standards of rural life and making it fuller and richer—before the country and ensuring that the energies of the entire administrative machinery of the States and the best unofficial leadership are directed to plans for its realization that we can awaken mass enthusiasm and enlist the active interest and support of the millions of families living in the countryside in the immense task of bettering their own conditions . . . .

Out of the report of this Committee was born the first official appreciation of the need for a community-wide, multipurpose approach which resulted in the creation of the Community Projects Administration of India. It should be noted that it was the Ministry of Food and Agriculture which came to this conclusion that the purely agricultural approach is not as productive, even for the advancement of agriculture, as is the felt-needs comprehensive approach of community development.

THE SUFI REPORT

The same dissatisfaction which prompted the government of India to appoint the Grow-More-Food Enquiry Committee resulted, in Pakistan, in the decision to study alternatives, as practiced abroad. In 1951, a group of five agricultural officials, representing the Ministries of Food and Agriculture in the central government and the four major provinces (Sind, Punjab, N.W.F.P., and East Pakistan), were invited by the USDA to visit the United States under the auspices of the Point IV Program. For a period of four months, this group studied intensively the organization, underlying philosophy, and techniques developed by the Cooperative Agricultural Extension Service. In addition to the Federal

Extension Service in Washington, the group studied several state extension services, participated in a State Extension Directors Conference in California, and attended a special summer school at Cornell University. The group was headed by M. H. Sufi, Deputy Secretary, Ministry of Food and Agriculture, Government of Pakistan, and the published results of this study became known as the Sufi Report.

In Chapter III, *Recommendations for Reorganization of Extension Service*, the Sufi Committee makes the following comment concerning the situation in Pakistan in 1951 (Sufi Committee, 1952, 26):

> The main feature of the extension work being done in Pakistan at present is its rigid departmentalization. In each Province, the Department of Agriculture, Animal Husbandry, Forestry, Fisheries, Cooperation, Marketing, Industries Health, Education, etc., are separately constituted and each one of them tries to make a separate approach to the people. Each department maintains a vertical field organization with a Director on top and an hierarchy of officials, in a descending order of responsibility and importance. . . . Before we can do any useful educational work in the field of agriculture and other allied subjects, we have to rehabilitate the Extension Staff in the estimation of the rural population.

The committee then recommends a new approach as follows (Sufi Committee, 1952, 26) (my italics):

> This can be done if all the departments, concerned with the welfare of the rural people, pool their resources and make an integrated approach to the farmers. The various departments may continue to do the teaching, the research and the regulatory work on a divided basis; but they must surrender their right to do the publicity or extension work in their own way. *The educational work, now being done by each department separately, should be entrusted to a single Department of Extension, which will be the common and unified channel for the dissemination of information, emanating from all the nation-building departments.* . . . This arrangement will eliminate the danger of over-

lapping, confusion and duplication of effort, which is inseparable from the present divided approach.

Within six months after publication of this report the government of Pakistan accepted the recommendations of these agriculturists, and in July, 1952 Village Agricultural and Industrial Development (AID) was established as the common extension service of all the nation-building departments from the tehsil or subdivisional levels to the village. It was organized largely in keeping with the recommendations of the Committee as to structure (Sufi Committee, 1952, 27):

> We, therefore, recommend that there should be an Extension Agent in charge of each Tehsil or Taluka in West Pakistan and each Sub-division in East Pakistan. In order, however, to reach the maximum number of people and to maintain a closer personal touch with them, each Extension Agent should have about 10 to 15 trained village workers to assist him. . . . The Director of Extension will keep in close touch with the Heads of all the other departments and will have under his command a group of specialists drawn from different departments.

The committee not only outlined the organizational structure of Village AID, but contributed materially to an understanding of its functions (Sufi Committee, 1952, 30-31):

> Now it may be legitimately asked how this new organization is going to be effective in the fields where other departments, acting separately, have not succeeded so well. The answer lies in making an entirely new approach to the problems of farming and rural life in general. Here a somewhat radical change in our thinking is necessary. The old concept of a benign and paternal Government trying to do everything for the people must be given up and replaced by the vital principle of self help. . . . To achieve practical results it will be necessary to translate these objectives into concrete programmes based on the felt needs of the people. The people will draw up their own programmes which they will carry out themselves under the friendly advice and technical guidance of the Extension staff. . . . The programme will set out the goals for im-

provement, both on farms and in homes and villages, will highlight the problems relating to soil conservation, use of water resources, crop production, crop diseases, breeding of livestock, marketing, cottage industries, rural water supply, public health, adult education, youth work, etc., and will also suggest solutions for these problems.

THE FIRST FIVE-YEAR PLAN

In 1953, with assistance from the Ford Foundation, the Planning Board of the Government of Pakistan entered into a contract with Harvard University, which recruited a staff of development experts. After intensive study of all phases of the economy, including Village AID, by the Planning Board in collaboration with these experts, the *First Five-Year Plan—1955-60* was published in 1957 (Govt. of Pakistan, 1957). The place given to Village AID is best described in the words of this plan (Govt. of Pakistan, 1957, 197-200) (my italics):

> The Central Government and the Provincial Governments have agreed that the Village AID programme should be the principal means for promoting rural development and *the channel through which government technical and financial assistance should reach the villages*. Because of the overriding importance of the rural development programme and the crucial role of Village AID in stimulating it, we have given the highest priority in the Plan to this programme. We believe that in general the programme should be expanded as rapidly as techniques for working with the people can be developed and staff can be trained and that financial considerations should be of secondary importance. In our judgment, this programme is so important that it should receive the continuous and energetic support and active participation of the public officials, political leaders and social workers from the highest to the lowest.

These excerpts raise the question of what type of organizational structure was envisaged for Village AID and for the development departments. The answer was that Village AID was to furnish the development officers, supervisors, and village workers while the development departments were to train and place specialists at the development area level (Govt. of Pakistan, 1957, 198):

5. The staff in the development area will consist of village workers, supervisors, a development officer and subject-matter specialists of the various development departments.
6. There will be one village worker for each group of five to seven villages: about 30 village workers for a development area. Working under the leadership of the development officer, village workers will maintain continuous contacts with the villagers and stimulate and guide self-help organizations in their planning and development activities. They will provide solutions to many of the simpler problems and act as liaison between the villages and the technical specialists in the development area.
7. The village workers will be responsible to the development officer who himself will be responsible to the district officer. The development officer will be assisted by two supervisors. . . .
8. The specialists who will give advice and assistance to the village workers and to the villagers in solving their problems will represent the following technical fields: (a) Farm management (Agriculture); (b) Animal husbandry; (c) Cooperation and marketing; (d) Health and sanitation; (e) Works supervision; (f) Social education (Male); (g) Social education (Female); and (h) Other subjects as needed, such as cottage and small industries, fisheries, forestry and range management.

The following statement is made regarding numbers of specialists (Govt. of Pakistan, 1957, 275):

Two agricultural specialists, two animal husbandry specialists, and one cooperative and marketing specialist will work in each development area, covering about 150 villages; in addition wherever conditions demand, specialists in fisheries, soil conservation, etc., will also be employed. Similarly at the subdivisional or district level, there will be a need for specialists in agricultural engineering, plant protection, and in some cases, forestry, fisheries, horticulture, soil conservation and range management.

The relationship of these specialists to Village AID is spelled out as follows (Govt. of Pakistan, 1957, 198-199):

In the development area the specialists belonging to the various technical departments will work whole-time under

operational control of the Development Officers. The technical departments should be enabled to employ other specialists to work in the parts of the tehsil or subdivision not
covered by the Village AID programme. The specialists under
the Development Officer will continue to belong to their
own departments and be responsible to their respective
departmental officers for technical guidance and control.
For administrative purposes also, such as appointments, transfers, and promotions they will remain under the control of
their own departments. The specialists will form a key link
in the chain between village workers and the development
officer on the one hand, and the rural development departments on the other. They will work for formulating and
implementing the rural development programme. More specifically, in carrying out their functions they will: (a)
Assist in making plans for the development of the area in
their respective fields; (b) Assist in procuring required development materials and services from their respective departments and from available sources; (c) Teach village
workers how to carry out effective demonstrations; and
(d) Go with the village workers to the villages to assist
them personally in their work when their special knowledge
and skills are required.

Thus, it is evident, from the above statements, that the Planning Board, based on its field studies of both Village AID and the
technical departments, came to the conclusion that the Village AID
staff and departmental specialists were to work together as a team.
The Village AID workers were trained in the most important skills
in each technical field applicable to their area. More especially,
they were to be skilled in working with village people in order
to determine their felt needs and to increase their awareness of
other needs, to assist in devising solutions to these needs, and,
finally, to work with them in applying these solutions with a
maximum of reliance on the resources of the village people themselves. The specialist was to give the impetus to this process in
his technical field; he was to assist in planning and in obtaining
the material required, and he was to further train and help the
workers to carry out sound technical assistance to the villagers.

The recommendations of the Planning Board required little
change in the internal form and functioning of Village AID. The
number of institutes devoted to the training of multipurpose work-

ers was increased from eight to eleven with an eventual output of workers exceeding 1,300 annually. Staffs of these institutes were assigned by the various technical departments (health, agriculture, animal husbandry, cottage industry, adult education, et cetera), and the substantive content of training was determined by each department. The institutes selected their students from huge numbers of applicants from the village youths, most of whom were matriculates (secondary school graduates).

Development areas were established as fast as trained workers became available. Each area consisted of 100 to 150 villages, twenty to thirty Village AID workers, two Village AID supervisors, and one Village AID development officer who was in charge of work in the area. The holistic felt-needs approach to the villages was followed. Technicians who would function in the manner envisaged both by the Sufi Committee and the Planning Board were requested of the technical departments. They were not only to give the technical backstopping needed by the Village AID workers, but their own expertise was to be multiplied by the workers who would receive on-the-job training in approved practices and who, in turn, would instruct the villagers in those practices.

MAJOR PROBLEMS

Lack of Technical Department Support.—In a few development areas members of technical departments cooperated sufficiently to show the validity of this form of organization. It also worked extremely well in the East Punjab province of India where the Development Commissioner believed in the integrated approach and had the authority to require full compliance of all government agencies.

However, with the exception of the Cooperative Department in West Pakistan, the various technical departments controlled by the provincial governments chose to circumvent the scheme. They pleaded a scarcity of technicians and the necessity for their assignment to areas not covered by Village AID. Although this manoeuvre was obviously in direct opposition to the Five-Year Plan, it succeeded in depriving Village AID of the technical assistance envisaged. The same rationale was used by the technical departments in the allocation of scarce essential materials, the distribution of which they controlled, including printed informational matter, fertilizers, insecticides, veterinary medicines, et cetera. In the main, those community projects such as small roads, and simple agricultural practices, which required only labor or local materials and technical advice, were successfully completed in thousands of villages. After an initial period of suspicion, the village people responded enthusiastically to the first real sustained assistance they had ever received from their government. However, for those crucial projects which required technical competence and materials beyond that possessed by the villagers, or the assigned Village AID workers, supervisors, and development officers, the story is one of frustration and relatively small accomplishment.

Competing Workers.—It is evident from the above description that the Village AID scheme never was put fully into effect in Pakistan. The absence of key elements prevented its functioning as an integrated movement, uniting the resources of the people with those of government. Rather than provide the missing key elements, the agricultural departments set out surreptitiously in 1957, and more openly by 1958, to build up armies of single-purpose village workers to compete with the multipurpose workers of Village AID.

A number of plausible but spurious reasons were advanced to justify the action. It was stated that the multipurpose workers were not as well trained in a particular technology as those who might specialize in one technical field. Although this might have been true, it was irrelevant. As far as quality of training was concerned, it was given by members of the technical departments detailed to the Village AID training institute, and the quality of this personnel and of the courses of instruction were solely the responsibility of the technical departments. With regard to length and depth of training, it was realized at the start that the institute experiences were only the beginning. The training was to continue throughout the life of the worker by means of short courses, but more importantly by on-the-job training provided by the technicians posted in the development area under the operational control of the development officer.

A second reason asserted that the multipurpose workers could not spend as much time on a particular technology as could a departmental man. Although this is quite true, it is equally invalid. The need for technical assistance on any type of village project is sporadic and intermittent. This condition applies particularly to agriculture. By following the felt needs of the circle of villages assigned to him, the multipurpose worker established far better rapport with the people and insured that he would omit nothing of high value to the villagers. If a greater volume of demands for his services was forthcoming from his circle of villages than he could personally meet, his supervisor was able to assist him or to reduce the number of villages for which he was responsible.

A third argument advanced by the provincial agricultural departments was that Village AID was not expanding with sufficient speed to cover the country. This was sheer nonsense as 4 to 5 million people were added yearly. The demands generated for specialist technical assistance, fertilizers, machinery, and other materials and services were exceeding the real supply of these requisites by the time these departments had advanced their false rationale. The Planning Board had foreseen these shortages and had urged in the First Five-Year Plan that agricultural and other technical colleges be greatly expanded and that new sources and systems of supply of materials be instituted. In accordance with this Plan, the technical departments were to spend their scarce resources on meeting the demands for those vital inputs which they and they alone could provide, rather than fritter away these resources in useless competition with Village AID in duplicating its functions. Furthermore, a bit of simple arithmetic showed conclusively that it would take longer for these departments to build, equip, and man their own institutes for training than to expand the Village AID institutes.

Although the lack of technical department support was the most difficult problem, Village AID had others no less important, but more tractable and soluble. Each of these problems is discussed briefly.

Inadequate Training of Supervisory Personnel.—Although institutes were established to train the multipurpose workers, practically nothing was done until 1958 to prepare the forty development officers and eighty supervisors needed to man the new development areas opened each year. These people were recruited from a variety of sources including technical departments and the ranks of school teachers and ex-army officers. Many of these persons made surprisingly rapid adjustment after only a few days of orientation training. However, there was no doubt that they needed a great deal more training in the philosophy and approach of community development, in non-directive personnel supervision, in techniques of in-service training, in coordination with the technical departments, and in other matters. For these purposes plans were made as early as 1954 to establish an academy in each wing of the country (East and West Pakistan). However, owing to internal administrative difficulties and the difficulty of contracting with an American university able and willing to take on the job of training the staff for these academies, it was not until 1959 that they became operational. The academy at Comilla has recently made some notable innovations in community development in East Pakistan. However, this was much too late to affect materially the fate of Village AID. As an interim measure two staff development centers were established on an *ad hoc* basis in 1958. The excellent training provided to supervisors and development officers by Mezirow and his associates demonstrated the great need that had been largely unmet for the previous five years.

Lack of Independent Evaluation.—Although planners, administrators, and legislators are often willing to initiate community development programs, they are unwilling to continue giving them a high priority without proof of their productivity. This was realized at the beginning of community development by Nehru in India. He established the Projects Evaluation Organization (PEO) as an independent agency concurrently with the Community Projects Administration (CPA), later called the Ministry of Community Development. From the beginning, the PEO made independent evaluations of the CPA development blocks and published the whole story. This washing of dirty linen in public was painful, but it greatly helped to solve many problems and, equally important, to inspire confidence in the validity of the results reported by the PEO. Unfortunately, the Pakistani leadership would not take this revolutionary step. In fact, it was not until 1959 that an internal evaluative unit was established. Consequently, when the Planning Board asked for evaluation reports of the results of the First Five-Year Plan, the Village AID Administration could produce very little objective quantitative data to support its claims, although the reports of several foreign consultants attested to the validity of the approach and the great need to correct its many problems and continue the program. However, with the many dissonant voices of the technical ministries and the barely lukewarm support of the mission director of ICA (which provided much of the support of Village AID through the internal sale of United States wheat and rice), the Planning Board felt that it could no longer give top priority to Village AID in the Second Plan.

Local Government Deficiencies.—Community development movements, such as Village AID, are an admirable device for generating enthusiasm, mobilizing local labor and material resources, and creating a better physical and human community, but it requires local government to maintain and operate the institutions and services created. In place of sporadic inspired voluntary effort, the stage of operation and maintenance requires constancy and devotion to duty which seldom inspires volunteers. Thus, local government must pay its employees, and this requires not occasional money-raising drives on a contributory basis, but a regular, dependable source of revenue, including local taxes and monthly rates for ratable services. The Village AID leadership failed to give sufficient weight to this complementary relationship of community development and local government—to see that they are "two sides of the same coin of local responsibility." As a result, practically no effort was made to replace or to rejuvenate the decadent system of district government existent in Pakistan. The result of this neglect was that considerable infrastructure built through the voluntary efforts of communities was not maintained or properly operated, since the central government did not have the resources for such matters of local concern.

UNDERLYING CAUSES

The reader will no doubt wonder how it was possible for the technical departments to ignore the obvious will of the government. The answer lies in the political sphere. Perhaps the most important cause lay in the breakdown of parliamentary government. From its inception as a nation in 1947 to the military coup of 1958, the members of the parliament were designated by the provincial legislative bodies, and were not directly elected by the people. As a consequence, their sense of responsibility to and identification with the people and with a popular movement such as Village AID was much attenuated. Even more important was the erosion of party discipline as evidenced by considerable crossing the aisles, i.e., switching of party loyalty to gain ministerial status or other personal rewards. Governments came and went and none could depend on its party for support for more than a few weeks or months. Prime ministers spent much of their time politicking within the parliament merely to remain in power. With political control greatly weakened, it is small wonder that the career civil servants within each department proceeded to run their affairs without regard to plans of the government as a whole. The fact that the operational departments were part of the provincial governments, and not of the central government, made it even more difficult for the central government to make its will felt. The breakdown of parliamentary government finally resulted in the military coup of October, 1958. A voluntaristic peoples' movement, especially one beset with the problems described above, was difficult for military men to understand. In 1961, Village AID became a part of so-called Basic Democracies, with promotion of agricultural work falling to newly-created agricultural development corporations.

EXPERIMENTAL EVIDENCE

Observation by the writer over a period of five years, and by a number of outsiders who made shorter studies of Village AID, confirmed the judgment of the Sufi Committee and the Planning Board concerning the technical soundness and administrative feasibility of the multipurpose village worker approach, as exemplified by the Village AID program in Pakistan. These judgments were greatly reinforced, not only by the working of the Community Development program in India, but also by the findings of an experiment conducted between 1952 and 1957 by the Allahabad Agricultural Institute in India. The results of this experiment, called the Extension Pilot Project, were published in 1958 (Allahabad Agric. Institute, 1958). In the description which follows it should be borne in mind that the "felt needs" approach is that followed by the multipurpose worker (Allahabad Agric. Institute, 1958, i):

An experiment in Extension was conducted in 428 villages of the Allahabad district to (1) compare the performance of resident village workers having different educational backgrounds and training viz., graduates, intermediates, matriculates, constructive workers and couple units, and (2) compare the effectiveness of four methods of approach (initial emphasis) viz., occupation (agriculture), literacy, home and family, and felt needs.

The results of the experiment concerning the performance of various educational categories of village workers are most interesting and worthwhile, but we will not go into them here. More germane are the results of the comparisons of the four methods of approach. In order that the summary results may be understood, it is necessary to explain what is meant by the methods of approach (Allahabad Agric. Institute, 1958, 12):

> The method of approach, i.e., the initial emphasis which was to be carried on by the Gaon Sathis (village workers) in each circle was different. . . . Each Gaon Sathi worked at attaining the various targets that were fixed. They had to work on both a high target (the initial emphasis of the circle) and the low targets, (the initial emphases of the other circles). Thus, for example, a Gaon Sathi working in Iradatganj circle had higher targets with respect to agriculture and lower targets with regard to literacy compared to the Jari circle, where literacy was the high target. In addition to these there were some general targets—such as, recreation, youth clubs, anti-malaria programmes, etc., which were of uniform size for all circles. The assignment of initial emphasis to the different circles was done at random. In each circle all the five types of Gaon Sathis were assigned.

Success was measured by the number of practices actually adopted by the villagers. The major findings relevant to the four methods of approach were as follows (Allahabad Agric. Institute, 1958, i-ii):

> 8. The largest number of practice changes was affected where the felt needs approach was followed.
> 9. Of the four approaches (emphases) tested, placing primary emphasis on agriculture resulted in the smallest number of practice changes.
> 10. Emphasis on felt needs got the extension programme off to a good start in the first season and maintained a superior rate of practice changes throughout the experiment,

while emphasis on agriculture resulted in the least significant improvement after a comparatively slow start.

11. The initial emphasis on agriculture did not result in a larger percentage of agricultural changes than those in the home-and-family and felt needs circle. . . .

14. The initial emphasis on felt needs resulted in a higher percentage of agricultural changes than of any other type.

It should be remembered that "felt needs" was the approach of Village AID; its rationale was the same as that used by the felt-needs approach group in the experiment—that of doing democratic program planning with the villagers on the problems and goals considered by them to be most important, such as a school, a connecting road to the highway, or other village improvements. After having enlisted the interest and support of the people in successfully solving the problems as they defined them, confidence was built up in their ability and in that of the Village AID worker who had been given methodological guidance and assistance in problem definition, planning, and solution. This confidence in themselves and in the worker induced the villagers to move on to other less acutely felt problems, or to those which required a longer period of time for solution, such as increasing agricultural production. A purely agricultural extension program, as this experiment showed, cannot hope to win this confidence which is essential to increasing agricultural production, because it does not begin with the felt needs of the villagers. Its only hope is to use the felt-needs approach, in other words, to become a multipurpose community development organization, precisely what Village AID was.

An inference

In spite of the many evidences of technical soundness and administrative feasibility, it would appear that adoption of the multipurpose village worker approach by a developing country is unsound. This statement is based on the improbability that any government will persist in its policies and their enforcement for the approximately eight to ten years required to demonstrate clearly the superiority of the multipurpose worker, and to institutionalize the felt-needs approach. This relatively long period is necessary as it requires from one to two years from adoption of this approach to establish the administrative organization, training institutes and academies, coordinative mechanisms (such as the Development Commissioner with operational control over the technical departments as used in the East Punjab state of India), an evaluation organization, and local government legislation. Pre-service training of personnel, for a year or longer, is necessary before the first development areas can be opened. During the first one or two years of operation of an area it is likely that infra-structure and service type projects will predominate. As local government rates and taxes for maintenance and operations of local institutions rise during the second and third years of oper-ations, the demand for means to increase income to pay these rates and taxes also rises. However, teaching improved production prac-tices, obtaining sufficient credit to purchase the inputs required by these practices, developing reliable supplies of materials, and obtaining production increases themselves requires at least another two years. Thus, it requires four to five years before substantial sustained increased production can be expected in the first develop-ment areas to be opened. To affect production materially necessi-tates the opening of many more areas which likewise must go through these stages of development, although the time element for these can be reduced somewhat below that required by the first areas.

There is little historical evidence from Asia, Africa, and South America that the required type of national enlightened strong leadership will persist for eight to ten years. For every Nehru with the vision, the power to coordinate his ministries, and the persistence of his long tenure, there are scores of governments which are here today and gone tomorrow.[2] Therefore, in spite of the overwhelming logic and demonstrated advantages of the multi-purpose worker approach, it is not possible to recommend it except to those with great faith that their prime minister or president will not only remain in power for a long tenure, but that he will persist in his policies and in the necessary degree of effec-tive control of his ministries to bring about real coordination.

SOUTHERN RHODESIA: PATERNALISTIC—COMPULSIVE APPROACH

The first European settlers in the area that later became South-ern Rhodesia arrived in 1890 from South Africa under the auspices of the British South Africa Company (BSA), chartered by the British government. They came under an agreement made between Cecil Rhodes, head of the BSA Company, and the Matabele king, Lobengula. The latter was under the impression that he was admitting gold prospectors, not permanent land settlers. The Matabele, a tribe from South Africa which had conquered the indigenous inhabitants a few years earlier, rebelled in 1893 and were subjugated by the settlers. European settlement slowly continued under the rule of the BSA Company until 1923 when the country became a self-governing British colony with its own constitution and parliament. A new constitution, providing for the first time for participation of Africans in the parliament, was adopted by the electorate in 1961. Racial violence, which had erupted in 1960, continued after the adoption of the new constitution. The African political party boycotted elections held under this constitution and continued to insist on "one man, one vote," i.e., a complete takeover of the government by Africans who outnumbered the Europeans by about thirteen to one. The British Government, in its attempts to mediate and to liberalize further the 1961 constitution, brought on increasing conflict with the government of Southern Rhodesia which finally declared its independence unilaterally in November, 1965.

These few facts represent, of course, an entirely inadequate account of the political history of Southern Rhodesia. They are presented solely to give the reader a sparse historical framework within which to place the events most directly related to the purposes of this chapter.[3]

AGRICULTURAL ORGANIZATION AND POLICY

Phase of Law and Order.[4]—In 1894, the first native commissioners were appointed to various parts of the colony to keep in close contact with the natives, advise them of the few government laws and regulations which affected them, arbitrate in civil disputes, especially those affecting succession to headships and chieftaincies, protect them from unwarranted interference with their tribal laws and customs by outsiders, collect a native hut tax, and issue passes for natives to enter towns. In the same year the first native reserves were set aside to shield them from encroachment by Europeans.

With the control of intertribal warfare and some of the more virulent diseases the African population grew apace, requiring the reservation of other areas which were provided for in the Constitution of 1923. The constitution, plus the Land Apportionment Act of 1930, divided all land into blocks for future use on a racial basis. Until about 1925, the essence of the government's policy was the protection of Africans from outsiders, thus, permitting them to "develop on their own lines." This meant that as long as no large crimes were committed and they paid the nominal head tax, the people in their reserves could follow their own laws and customs. By 1913, little or no progress had been made in agricultural techniques except for the extended use of ox-drawn plows. The main agricultural concern of the native commissioners was that the Africans should grow sufficient food to feed themselves, and that as many as possible should offer their labor on the nearby European farms, thus reducing the need to import labor from Nyasaland or other African countries.

The Development Phase.—About 1925, it became apparent that the traditional methods of agriculture were causing serious deterioration of the land. Soil was eroding both in the arable and in the overstocked grazing lands. To save those precious inches of topsoil, the Native Department decided to interfere in native agriculture; it appointed European land development officers and African demonstrators, the latter trained in two industrial schools. A Native Education subdepartment was established, and some lands were set aside for purchase by those few Africans who would accept detribalization. By 1939, native agriculture had expanded, and increasing quantities of grain and livestock were entering the money economy. However, this expansion intensified soil erosion and resulted in a shift of government interest to soil conservation through the provision of more evenly distributed water supplies in the reserves, promotion of contour ridge construction in arable land, control of the sale of maize to reduce overproduction, establishment of cattle sales facilities, and centralized purchase of voluntarily offered cattle to reduce overstocking. These voluntary measures were adjudged to be insufficiently effective, and compulsory destocking of cattle was instituted under the Natural Resources Act of 1941. In order to finance the many voluntary and compulsory measures aimed at increasing African agricultural development and marketing and decreasing injury to the land, the

Native Development Fund was established in 1948. Funds were obtained from compulsory levies on African-produced agricultural commodities, government grants, fees for such compulsory services as cattle dipping, and other items.

The Native Land Husbandry Act.[5]—Finally, in 1951, the Native Land Husbandry Act was passed to stabilize the native population engaged in agriculture and to enforce good husbandry practices. The device employed for the latter purpose was the granting of individual usufruct rights to arable land demarcated by the Native Agriculture Department, plus individual stock-grazing rights which permitted the owner to graze a given number of animals on the communal grazing lands. These rights could be bought and sold only among tribesmen. The Act was administered in a highly rationalistic manner beginning with aerial photography and the planning of the layout of access roads, wells, dams, blocks of arable land and blocks of grazing land, and primary conservation works to conform to the technical qualifications of the land. This exercise was followed by engineering surveys, and by bulldozers to give effect to the planning. Meanwhile, a census of persons, the land cultivated by each, and the number of cattle they grazed was taken in each village. On the basis of the census, allocations of arable land and grazing rights were made and registered in a land register. Care was taken to remain within the tribal boundaries, but the necessity for speed, owing to the pressure of mounting costs, made it impossible, or so it appeared to many of the land development officers, to listen to the individual complaints and to sort matters out on a personal or group preference basis. A total of £17 million ($47.6 million), including a large loan from the World Bank, was set aside for the implementation of this Act.

Coincident with the implementation of this Act a boom occurred in European farming, creating a keen demand for land. To meet this demand the government proceeded tardily to enforce the Land Apportionment Act by moving large numbers of Africans from the European crown lands and resettling them in the existing native reservations or special native areas. This movement was, of course, extremely unpopular and added to the pressures on arable and grazing lands in African areas to which the natives were shifted.

Once allocations were concluded, enforcement of the conservation and disease control provisions of the Act were entrusted to the native commissioner, with actual control in the hands of the land development officers and agricultural demonstrators. It was their function to destock cattle if they exceeded the total numbers allocated to a grazing area; to see that each owner constructed and maintained contour water courses in his arable lands; to prevent plowing in the vlei or meadow strips which carried away the rain water from the contours; to see that the areas set aside for grazing would not be used as arable land; and to enforce other provisions of like nature. In addition, these land development officers and demonstrators were to teach improved methods of husbandry and to enlist the cooperation of the people in improving agricultural production and marketing.

PROBLEMS OF LAND HUSBANDRY

While the other colonial territories in Africa promoted native authorities, native treasuries, and native courts, i.e., "indirect rule," Southern Rhodesia concentrated on correct land use. There could be few arguments with the technical excellence of the land use procedures employed or with the technical quality with which they were applied. However, the natives were far from grateful, and the relation between Africans and the government became worse. Let us look at some of the reasons for this state of affairs.

Failure to use the Tribal Community.—In Shona society the tribe is a highly visible entity. Its boundaries are usually distinctively marked by rivers, mountains, or other identifiable features. The tribe is led by a chief whose advice is always sought. Likewise, the small village is highly visible with its separate settlement and attached fields and pastures; it is presided over by a village headman. In between these entities there exists the dunhu or sociological community, which is much less visible. Although it, like the tribal area, has boundaries, these boundaries are not always natural features that can be easily identified, nor is the sadunhu so readily identified as either the chief or village headman. Yet, most of the vital facets of communal life have their setting within the dunhu. The dunhu is the locus of man's major relationships with his fellow men, with his gods, and with the land. His relationships with his fellow men are products, first of kinship, as most of his relatives are found within the dunhu, and second, of the sadunhu's court. In his court all cases are civil cases, and it is here that any foundering of a relationship with one's fellows can be sorted out. In this process, the whole community may actively participate in the proceedings. On the spiritual side, the sadunhu himself is a member of one of the "royal" houses of the dunhu on whom the tribal spirits have eventually settled, and only then is he the sadunhu. It is he who has to undertake propitiation of the spirits for the people in their time of trouble. In terms of man's relationship to the land, it is the sadunhu who gives the right to a man to plow or to keep cattle on the land, for the dunhu is the landholding unit. The land can never be alienated, it is only placed on loan to one of its "sons" for use and returned to the dunhu when no longer needed.

In addition to being the situs of these ancient basic relationships to their fellow men, to their gods, and to their land, the dunhu is the locus of modern communal self-help activities such as building roads, schools, churches, and dams. In spite of its functional plainness, the dunhu was seldom used by the implementers of the Land Husbandry Act because their eyes were on the land, not on the men who inhabited it. Complaints by the tribesmen that the land allocated to them was "no good" were dismissed as plainly false by the land husbandry officer, who could frequently see that the parcel allocated was even better than that which the man had previously tilled. What this officer did not understand was that such a complaint was only a way of expressing frustration at the disruption of the basic social interrelationships of the dunhu, which the tribesman felt were quite unexplainable as such to this European. This attack upon the integrity of the dunhu, as one may imagine, did nothing to endear the government to the sadunhu or to his people. Thus, the support of a critical element of the basic sociopolitical system was frequently sacrificed on the altar of technical efficiency and speed.

Removed Land Flexibility.—The traditional system of land allocation by the sadunhu was marked by great flexibility. When a young man of eighteen or nineteen first decided to plow for himself rather than as a helper to his father, the headman of his village presented the young man to the sadunhu who marked out about two acres for his use and gave him his blessings. When the young man married, his area was extended to, say, four acres. As children arrived and his needs increased, so did his land allocation. As the children reached adulthood and went away to plow for themselves or to the city, their father's land allocation dropped proportionally. Obviously, such a system was able to accommodate not only the needs of each older member of the dunhu, but also a large number of new cultivators each year.

Contrast this with the rigidities imposed by the Land Husbandry Act which gave each person a right equivalent to what he was plowing at any given time, without reference to his increasing or decreasing needs. What was correct on the day of allocation was sure not to be in accord with his needs one, two, or more years in the future. Although some parts of each arable block were not allocated initially under the Act, they were soon used to meet the needs of those who were just beginning to plow on their own. Then, with no more lands to allocate, numbers of young men could find no means of entering the local economy, except for such circumventions of the system as were locally contrived.

Misunderstanding of the Significance of Cattle.—Throughout much of Africa a man's status within the community depends upon the *number* of cattle he possesses and not on their condition of fitness or market worth. Furthermore, the family spirits have usually settled on one or more of the male beasts, and these animals thereby become sacred. Cattle are given by the father of the bridegroom to the father of the bride, not as a brideprice, but as a guarantee of the sanctity of the union. As these few examples illustrate, cattle are inextricably bound up with the social structure, and basic relationships are profoundly affected by what happens to cattle. In spite of a knowledge of some of these facts, the de-stocking of cattle was frequently carried out under the Act directly by government officers, using some criteria of "fairness" derived from European culture. Whatever the procedure used, no one was satisfied and calumny was poured upon the heads of those who dared to do such a thing. In a few cases, knowledgeable native commissioners left the determination of the de-stocking procedure to the chiefs, sadunhus, or headmen and their advisors. Their determinations of who would lose specific numbers of cattle to reduce the total number assigned to the area were often quite different from Western ideas of social justice. However, their decisions were in accord with the norms of the tribal social system and were accepted by the people of the tribe.

Compromise of the Extension Function.—As recounted above, the land development officers and demonstrators were employed to implement the Act, or, as the chiefs, sadunhus, and people often saw it, to usurp the functions of the tribal leaders and violate the norms of their society. In many areas the land development officers and demonstrators became "our enemies." It became impossible for them to have any appreciable effect on the adoption of improved practices, i.e., to function as extension agents. The police and pedagogical functions were antagonistic.

Administration-Tribesmen Alienation.—As we have seen, the native commissioners were originally appointed to act as intermediaries between the African tribes and the European settlers and as such were required to pass stiff examinations in knowledge of the local language, customs, and other matters. Although their administrative duties and paper work had been steadily increasing, they were able to get about amongst the people and to "know their mind" until the advent of the Land Husbandry Act. However, the Act and the compulsory movement of people took away the time they had been able to keep free for this purpose. Furthermore, the number of court cases on which they had to sit in judgment greatly increased, partly as a result of their inability to get about and explain matters to the people and thereby gain compliance with the laws. The gap between the Africans and the native commissioners gradually widened, and the commissioners became a favorite target for the nationalist leaders.

It should be stated at this point that a number of native commissioners and members of the head office staff were quite aware of these problems and their root causes before they developed, but their protests were largely ignored by the government. The physical planners and economists were in the saddle and the land had to be saved—never mind the people, they were only ignorant natives!

Consequences of Land Husbandry
and Other Measures

In speaking of the consequences of the Land Husbandry Act and the other measures related directly to the land and to agriculture, it is necessary, of course, to recognize that many other factors were part of the bundle of causation of the events which transpired. For example, the riots in the townships of Salisbury, which erupted almost weekly from 1961 onwards, would probably have occurred without the large influx of land-deprived, jobless young men. However, their presence acted as fuel on the fire. They were men with a grievance against a government which had made it impossible for them to be accommodated, either within their own tribal structure or in the towns, where little employment could be found.

Although some violence occurred in the rural areas, the response more generally was one of non-cooperation and circumvention of the Act. Reaction to the dearth of land led to illegal plowing in the grazing lands, an adaptation which the administration finally legalized since no means of prevention could be found. The same outcome applied to overstocking as it was believed to be impossible to de-stock the land forcibly. In other areas, implementation of the Act had to be postponed as a consequence of the gathering opposition. As the violence in the townships increased, ever more severe security laws were enacted. These led to higher and higher expenditures for police personnel and equipment to enforce the laws and thereby made less government revenue available for development purposes. Many European businesses were forced to close, or to defer plans for expansion, which in turn caused numbers of Europeans to leave the country. Disinvestment occurred, bringing controls on money, which further discouraged domestic and foreign investment. A downward spiral had set in.

SOME ATTEMPTS AT RECTIFICATION:
THE PHASE OF HUMAN PROBLEMS

As intimated above, there were persons both inside and outside the Native Department who raised their voices in protest at putting the welfare of the land ahead of that of the people, but they were largely ignored until much of the damage had been done. For example, several attempts had been made over the years to institute a system of local government in the African reserves and purchase areas, but such native councils as came into existence had so little support of the people, were so dominated by the native commissioners, and had responsibility for so few functions of vital importance to the people that they were more a façade than a reality (Green, 1962). In 1960, I initiated a comprehensive study of African development in Southern Rhodesia, including local government, administration, education, social welfare, agricultural extension, health education, indigenous tribal social structure and values, voluntary organizations, and other features. The purpose of this study was to gain an understanding of: (1) how governmental and private efforts at assisting African development and local self-government might be better coordinated and integrated, and (2) how the African people might be motivated, organized, and educated to participate to the fullest extent in their own development at the local community and higher levels.

Before this study could get underway the swelling tide of discontent erupted into rioting. This further prompted the government to appoint in succession several commissions of inquiry into the structure and functioning of the Native Department, tribal organization, tribal land tenure system, tribal courts, and African education. As with the comprehensive study mentioned above, these commissions were attempting to see "wholes," to understand issues, policies, and programs within the context of basic social structure. A surprisingly large number of their recommendations were adopted and put into operation, including the elimination of the Department of Native Affairs and the creation of non-racial Ministries of Internal Affairs and District Courts. A Ministry of African Agriculture separate from district administration, a corps of natural resources inspectors with police powers to enforce conservation measures, an extension training program, and other organizations and services were formed.[6]

Finally, in mid-1962, an agreement for technical assistance was entered into with the United States in which the government of Southern Rhodesia accepted the permissive, people-centered principles and practices of community development as the basis for district administration, local government, and all technical development at the local level. The new government, which came into power in late 1962, also affirmed its adherence to this document and set about putting it into effect, including such actions as the establishment of a Staff College of Community Development and Local Government, the training and placement of community development agents, and the drafting of a non-racial local government act.

As admirable as these measures were, they were too late. Non-cooperation and violence by the Africans brought a reaction from the Europeans which culminated in the triumph of the "far-right" in April, 1964, the ending of United States assistance, and the unilateral declaration of independence in 1965.

Dominican Republic: Extension as Stereotyped Organization

After the revolution of early 1965 and the subsequent oas intervention, various evaluations of u.s.-assisted programs of technical and economic aid to the Dominican Republic were made as a basis for planning more effective programs of development. One such evaluation (Green, 1965) attempted to determine the present extent of the assumption by the people of responsibility for their corporate affairs, and to make recommendations for augmentation of local responsibility and for increasing the efficiency of governmental assistance efforts. In this investigation major attention was devoted to local government and community development with some attention to cooperatives. However, one of the primary problems encountered in the study of community development led, as will be explained later, to a study of the agricultural extension service. As interesting as were the findings concerning local government and cooperatives, we shall not deal with them here, but shall focus our attention on the analyses of community development and agricultural extension, both of which are highly relevant to the present purposes.

Office of community development

Organization.—The Office of Community Development (ocd) was established in 1963 as a part of the Office of the President of the Republic. It began operations with a Director and two employees, all three of whom acted initially as "promotores" (village-level workers) in a few villages. After more than two years of operations this program covered about one-fifth of the country with forty-five promotores under the direction of five area managers, and a zone supervisor assisted by three engineers. The promotores were trained for a period of two to three months in an institute established by ocd. At the time of the evaluation another group of workers was about ready to cover another 20 per cent of the country.

Approach.—The major task of the promotor was to determine

the priorities for development of the people in each of several communities to which he was assigned. For those needs of highest priority, contracts were drafted by the promotor showing the contributions to be made by the people, by the Office of Community Development, and by any other agencies involved. Before a contract could be signed it had to be judged to be technically feasible by technically qualified personnel. Except for certain types of engineering projects, for which the technical assistance was supplied by the OCD engineers, OCD relied upon the staffs of the various technical ministries such as agriculture, irrigation, health, and education.

This approach had produced some excellent results, particularly in arousing community support and participation in the building of infrastructure such as roads, bridges, schools, community buildings, housing, and small-scale irrigation.

Problems of OCD.—At the time of the analysis of OCD, the program had grown too large to be administered centrally, and the process of approving projects was unnecessarily complicated. It was recommended that control and approval of projects be decentralized to regions. A second problem concerned the granting to the communities of materials which went into infrastructure. The analysis revealed the probability of widespread acceptance if a large proportion of the cost of materials were offered in the form of loans from a community revolving loan fund, repayable by the community from rates levied for the use of the service or from local taxation. Besides lowering the cost of the program to the central government, such a system would have the advantage of tying these *ad hoc* communal efforts in with local government. A third problem concerned the need for training the professional and administrative staff of OCD and the technical ministries involved, as well as local government officials. To meet this need a staff college of community development-local government was recommended. Finally, the need for a systematic program of "before and after" evaluation was evident, and such a program was proposed.

Although all of the problems so briefly described were important obstacles to the full success of OCD, none of them so impeded progress as the inability of the promotores and area managers to obtain technical assistance in agriculture. As is usual in community development programs, the use of community resources to create infrastructure and to assist in its maintenance and operation resulted in greater demand for increasing incomes which, in the Dominican Republic as elsewhere, usually have to come from agriculture. Since neither the promotores nor the area managers were trained in agricultural technology (there are no multipurpose workers in ocd), they had to depend upon the Extension Service of the Ministry of Agriculture to meet the demands for technical assistance in the scores of agricultural projects presented by the communities. However, when ocd made requests for such technical assistance, it was repeatedly told that the scarce extension personnel were not available as they were employed elsewhere in the regular extension program. As a result, the number of agricultural projects demanded by the communities piled up for want of technical assistance, thus effectively preventing their execution by the communities which desired to implement them and thereby raise incomes.

AGRICULTURAL EXTENSION

Organization.—Agricultural extension was initiated in the Dominican Republic in the same year as the ocd. It opened five field offices in 1963, four the following year, and planned five for 1965. Each field office was staffed by an agricultural agent, usually trained for five years in an agricultural college, a 5-D (youth) club agent, and a woman home betterment agent. All three types of agents organized and worked through standardized organizations. Each of the two field offices visited after two years of operation had formed one farmers' club in one of its communities. Since there were estimated to be from thirty to more than fifty communities in each province, each club represented a coverage at most of 2 to 3 per cent of each province. Five each of the 5-D and the home betterment clubs had been formed in each province, thus representing a 10 to 15 per cent coverage.

Problems.—The personnel of the offices visited appeared to be fully competent and able to carry out their assigned duties. Their problems were the usual ones of lack of sufficient transport equipment to make efficient use of the time of the agents; the low educational and economic level of the people, which limited the effectiveness of certain educational approaches; the lack of materials needed to carry out demonstrations; and the lack of other trained agents to assist them in the communities which were not covered.

An Example of a Farmers' Club.—The club organized by the agricultural agent from one of the field offices was visited. It had been formed in a community interested in obtaining advice and assistance and had been very active. When the agent initiated work in the community he had found it necessary to begin with the people where he found them, i.e., to proceed on the basis of their felt needs. The club's first priorities were a community road, a potable water system, a new enlarged school, and a system of electric power distribution. With the assistance of the agent, the community had secured donations by owners of the land adjacent to the old footpath needed to widen the road. They rebuilt the fences on either side of the right-of-way and, although the highway department was not supposed to work on this type of access road, with the help of the agent the club secured the free use of road-building machinery and culverts from the highway department. Encouraged by their success in constructing the road, the community, through self-help, reticulated potable water to a number of the houses in the area. Then followed a new school, constructed with some help from the ministry of education and large enough to accommodate the great increase in the number of school-age children. By mid-1965, a system for power distribution had been planned, but not yet executed. In addition, the agent had established several small market gardens, arranged corn fertilizer demonstrations, and distributed several improved pigs for breeding stock in the community.

From either a community development or agricultural extension point of view, the work in this one community was a success. However, this success had been bought dearly, as little or no impact had been made by this agent on the remaining 97 to 98 per cent of the communities in his province during a period of two years. The question becomes one of the capacity of the country to afford this type of success.

Analysis.—Obviously, the problem is one of proper use of extremely scarce trained manpower, in this case, agricultural extension agents. Young men with a secondary school education were in plentiful supply to meet the needs of the ocd for promotores, but university graduates in agriculture were extremely few in number, and this fact severely limited the expansibility of the agricultural extension service. Furthermore, the promotores, who had received only three months training in community development methods, were able to assist their communities to inventory their needs and determine their priorities, to set goals and make realistic plans to achieve them, and to mobilize community resources and implement their plans. They had been taught to work with not one, but with several communities simultaneously, responding to specific community needs and forming only such organizations as the people felt were necessary. What they could not do was to give the technical assistance needed in the agricultural projects demanded by the people. They were competent to go through the long process of preparing the people to receive and efficiently use such assistance, but they had to depend on others to give it.

On the other hand, the university-trained agriculturist was able to give the technical assistance in agriculture required by these communities, but he was prevented from doing so by preoccupation with the formation of a particular form of organization and the servicing of community needs largely of a non-agricultural nature. Although he was able to perform these non-agricultural functions, his performance, measured quantitatively, was far below that of the ocp promotores. He worked in only one community, but they were able to perform these functions in several and to do so in a small fraction of the time he required. In other words, the trained agriculturist used to a small extent the extremely scarce capacities he alone possessed while performing inefficiently functions which others could and were doing efficiently.

Quite obviously this juxtaposition of roles leads only to the waste of scarce resources and to the failure to use abundant resources. The solution lies in maximizing the efficient use of the scarce resources (the technical expertise of the agricultural agents) by combining it with the abundant resources (the organizational and social process skills of the ocp promotores). In practical terms, this would mean that each agricultural agent would be assigned to provide the technical requirements of community agricultural projects. This he would do in those communities which, with the help of the ocp promotores, have sorted out their priorities, have carried out other projects to which they attached higher priority such as roads, schools, and water supplies, and in which the people are ready, organized, and receptive to the agricultural agent's technical advice and assistance. Furthermore, the promotores would be available to help the agricultural agent in follow-through activities in their respective circles of communities, and to organize and otherwise prepare the people for the agent's next visits. By using the promotores to do the preparatory, organizational, and other non-technical work always precedent to and associated with technical projects, the technical efficiency of the agricultural agent can be multiplied by many times over the inefficient system of separatist agricultural extension organization.

To sum up, extension conceived structurally as organization is a low producer even in the sphere of agricultural production. Extension conceived functionally as advice, informal education, and training of those already organized and motivated to want it is simply good sense.

SOME PROPOSITIONS

What then can we learn from the experiences of these countries which may provide guidance to other countries in organizing for agricultural development? There are many lessons to be drawn, but we will mention only four here.

First, the felt-needs approach is the most efficient way to obtain, at the local level, both general development and development in specific technical fields. To the specialist, whether he is a professional agriculturist, an educator, a public health officer, or a road engineer, the felt-needs approach appears to be too indirect and a waste of time on "nonessentials" and "luxuries," which he defines, of course, as any kind of development in fields other than his own! Another way of putting this proposition is that physical developments are dependent upon human group development, which in turn is dependent upon the freedom of people to make choices and set priorities among the felt needs of their communities, and to assume primary responsibility for their attainment.

Second, organization for agricultural development at the national and regional levels must be an integral part of organization for general economic and social development of a country. Whether or not this integration takes the form of a Five-Year Plan, it is irrational to organize for agricultural development as if it were a self-contained sector. The example of Pakistan shows the futility of permitting each ministry to act as a "government within a government," free to disregard national policies based on a rational division of functions among ministries and on an interdependency of organization.

Third, any new organization created for integrated development, as was Pakistan's Village AID, will need to be allied with the persisting power structure. For, if it is an effective but separate organization, it will appear to be a threat to established bureaucracies, a hindrance to their expansionist ambitions, and thus a target for elimination. Although it is only through national political leadership that an integrated approach is possible, this leadership is so short-lived in most developing countries that it cannot be depended upon for much more than the gestation period and early infancy. The best chances for survival to full adulthood may lie in becoming the developmental arm of the *persisting* power structure, the district administration service by whatever name it is called. It will be argued that such services often use methods and approaches opposite to the permissive, democratic one which is the *raison d'être* of the new organization. However, the experience of Southern Rhodesia demonstrates the possibility of separating the police and judicial functions from district administration, and of turning the energies of the administrators to the development of local responsibility and all substantive fields for which communities will assume responsibility. This approach requires not only the reorganization of both administrative and development agencies, but the training of the administrative and technical officers in "staff colleges" of community development and local government.

Finally, we must say that technical expertise in all fields, especially in agriculture, is an extremely scarce resource in most developing countries, and maximizing the efficiency of its usage must be an objective of any type of organization for development. It requires many years of arduous and expensive training to produce qualified engineers, educators, public health physicians, and agriculturists, each able to deal with the vast variety of technical problems in his field. Often a majority of this talent is used for research, for university teaching, and for technical administration, so that few are available to meet the technical assistance demands of the thousands of communities. It makes no sense to load these people with non-technical (but specialized) functions such as organizing communities and helping them to determine their priorities of needs. These functions can be performed better by the non-specialists, who are in much greater supply. Nor should any technician be given technical duties in other fields. For example, road-making, school-building, and water-reticulation are the proper work of engineers, not of agronomists. No matter how well technicians perform non-technical functions or the technical duties of other fields, the net result is that they are diverted from utilizing their own technical knowledge and skills to the extent that they are involved outside of their own specialty. Therefore, it makes sense for governments of developing countries to insure that their scarce technically trained personnel are used to perform only those functions which utilize their technical competence, while others are used for the time-consuming non-technical work. Experience in the Dominican Republic and in other countries demonstrates that this can be done by training mature persons with primary or secondary school education to become community development agents. These persons become specialists in the art of helping communities to plan and act together to solve their problems and to reach their goals. They prepare the way for the scarce technicians and provide the follow-through when the technicians have gone elsewhere. Not only does such a system make sense in the efficient use of technical resources, but it is consistent with the interrelated life of indigenous communities which makes it imperative to approach them as social and cultural entities.

This approach, it is submitted, is a means of obtaining for the rural sector some of the major advantages from specialization of function already being enjoyed in the urbanized and industrialized sectors of developing countries. The continuing population explosion and the absolute necessity for increasing food production no longer permit us the luxury of the gross inefficiency inherent in any system in which the technical expertise of the agriculturist is dissipated in other work.

NOTES

1. Agency for International Development, United States Department of State. This Agency is in no way responsible for the reliability of the data presented nor for the opinions expressed as they are the personal responsibility of the author. Publication authorized: LIMA AIDTO A-88, 8-29-66.

2. For an excellent study of the theory and practice of community development as articulated in the Village Agricultural and Industrial

Development program of Pakistan, see Mezirow (1963). See also Green (1958) for a more detailed projection of the point of view given in this chapter.

3. The reader who wishes to expand his historical knowledge of this country is referred to Mason (1958).

4. For the division of the history of native affairs in Southern Rhodesia into the phases of law and order, development and human problems, see Div. of Native Affairs, Govt. of Southern Rhodesia (1961). For an elaboration of the history of this Department, see Div. of Native Affairs, Govt. of Southern Rhodesia (1960).

5. For an explanation of the principal parts of this act and advantages claimed for it, see Pendered *et al.* (1955). For a criticism of this Act and its implementation, see Brown (1959).

6. Each of the reports of these independent commissions of inquiry include historical synopses and evaluations of various government measures of interest to those who care to pursue the topics dwelt upon all too briefly in this chapter (Govt. of Southern Rhodesia, 1961a, 1961b, 1962a, 1962b).

LITERATURE CITED

ALLAHABAD AGRICULTURAL INSTITUTE. 1958. Extension evaluation. The Leader Press. Allahabad, India.

BROWN, KEN. 1959. Land in Southern Rhodesia. The African Bureau, London.

DIVISION OF NATIVE AFFAIRS, GOVT. OF SOUTHERN RHODESIA. 1960. Brief history of native affairs department. Ref. No. 14409 (Mimeo). Salisbury.

———. 1961. The division of native affairs: historical. (Mimeo). Salisbury.

GOVT. OF PAKISTAN. 1957. First five-year plan—1955-60. Karachi.

GOVT. OF SOUTHERN RHODESIA. 1961a. Report of the commission appointed to inquire into and report on administrative and judicial functions in the native affairs and district courts departments. Salisbury.

———. 1961b. Report of the Mangwende reserve commission of inquiry. Salisbury.

———. 1962a. Second report of the commission of inquiry into organization and development of the Southern Rhodesia public services. Salisbury.

———. 1962b. Report of the Southern Rhodesia education commission. Salisbury.

GREEN, JAMES W. 1958. A realistic plan for increasing agricultural production through agricultural extension and Village AID. (Mimeo). U.S. Operations Mission to Pakistan, Karachi.

———. 1962. Part I: Native councils. Report on African development and local government in Southern Rhodesia. Govt. of Southern Rhodesia, Salisbury.

———. 1965. Local responsibility in the Dominican Republic: a report of a short investigation into local government, community development, co-operatives and agricultural extension. (Mimeo.). USAID Mission to the Dominican Republic. Santo Domingo.

MASON, P. 1958. Conquest and settlement of Rhodesia. Oxford Univ. Press, N.Y.

MEZIROW, JACK D. 1963. Dynamics of community development. Scarecrow Press, N.Y.

MIN. OF FOOD AND AGRI., GOVT. OF INDIA. 1952. Report of grow-more-food enquiry committee. New Delhi.

PENDERED, A., DAVIES, R. M., ROBINSON, D. A., TOMLINSON, D. S., and MAKINGS, S. M. 1955. What the native land husbandry act means to the rural African and to Southern Rhodesia. Govt. of Southern Rhodesia Press, Salisbury.

SUFI COMMITTEE. 1952. A report on agricultural extension work in the U.S.A. and reorganization of extension services in Pakistan. Govt. of Pakistan, Karachi.

14

Advising on Development Organization

James W. Green

J ust what advice would you give a person who is going
abroad to advise on local development organization in
low-income countries?" This question provided the topic
for the second half of the University of Florida seminar and is the
central theme of this chapter.[1]*

SYSTEMATIC STUDY

When any person has received an invitation to go abroad for
the first time to advise a government on any aspect of development, he may expect that his biographical data has been subjected to careful study by both the host government and the
sponsoring agency. From this study and the previously formulated
requirements of the position, tentative expectations of the ultimate
performance of the individual will have been projected. However,
the invitation which is extended is not based upon this appraisal of
the advisor's *present* capacity to be useful. It is based upon his
potential capacity to meet the requirements of the position. This
approach is followed for two reasons. First, those responsible for
his invitation know that he has no first-hand knowledge of the
general culture and social organization (including economic aspects) of the country to which he is to be assigned, nor with the

*Notes for this chapter begin on Page 314.

psychic, social, and cultural orientations of its people. Second, they know that he knows little or nothing of the development programs and organizations which presently exist in the country to which he is invited, how and why they function the way they do, their interrelationships, and their problems.

In other words, the prior education, training, and experience of a potential advisor on development organization are sufficient only to get him into the country. No matter how many degrees he may have, or how much knowledge he may possess of development in other countries, he begins at zero in the country to which he is assigned. His usefulness as an advisor will depend upon how systematically and thoroughly he studies, in his country of assignment, the general sociocultural context within which his own field of development organization has meaning, the development programs and organizations which are already there, their rationale for operating as they do, their conception of their problems, etc. Therefore, it is necessary that an advisor realize at the very outset that *on-the-ground systematic and thorough analysis must precede the giving of advice.* The advisor who is ready with answers when he first arrives in a country, or at any time before he has had an opportunity to study thoroughly and systematically the particular situation, will only appear ridiculous in the eyes of those whom he is advising. On the other hand, the advisor who spends days and days in systematic hard study in the field will slowly but surely win the right to advise, and with it the respect of host government officials. They will be impressed, not only with his display of energy and humility, but also with the inherently sound quality of the advice he gives. For his advice will then be set within the relevant context of specific knowledge of the particular country and will draw its major strength and support from the particular facts so painstakingly gathered, categorized, analyzed, and presented. Although the theoretical frame of reference is that of the advisor, it remains barren until filled with the particularities of the country or part of the country to which he is assigned. A rule-of-thumb guide for the advisor is to spend four-fifths of his time systematically learning, and no more than one-fifth advising.

TOOLS OF ANALYSIS

Obviously, study of the type suggested above requires suitable intellectual tools. One of the major qualities necessary for the advisor on development organization is the ability to make analyses of complex organizations, their long-term goals and intermediate objectives, norms, structures, functions, internal relationships and systems of communications, systems of allocating and distributing power, historical development, relationships to other organizations, and their problems. Although his approach is analytical, his purpose is holistic, i.e., he systematically breaks down the components of organization and categorizes them in order to understand the organization as a whole. An understanding of the whole is more important than knowledge of particular parts. However, such understanding is hard to come by; it can be obtained only through detailed analysis of the parts and their interrelatedness in enough organizational units of the same type to enable one to see the central patterns and their major variations.

In what manner, it may be asked, does one get beneath the surface to understand how an organization, particularly one in a foreign country, really works, rather than how the manuals and tables of organization and procedure say it should work? There are several techniques for achieving this end, the most efficient of which, I have found, is position-role analysis. This is a highly personalized approach. Although an organization as such is impersonal, it is, in fact, dependent for its existence upon the conceptions and behavior, with respect to his role, of each individual who occupies a position within the organizational structure. Organization itself, then, may be viewed as a structure of relationships among positions, so that a focal position (any position on which one is focusing at a given moment), to be understood within an organization, must be specified in terms of its relationships to all counter-positions and to the typical situational contexts within which it exists.

For example, if one had set out at any time before 1962 to understand the complex of governmental organizations which substantially affected the development of Africans in Southern Rhodesia, one of the principal organizations he would have chosen to study would have been the Native Department of the Government of Southern Rhodesia. A key position within this department was that of Native Commissioner, one of whom was stationed in each of the country's fifty districts. When this position was under study, it could be understood only in terms of its relationship to the positions both within and outside the Native Department with whose occupants the Native Commissioner interacted. This would include the Assistant Commissioner, clerks and cadets within his office; the agricultural and other specialized officers attached to his office; the heads of the independent departments such as health, education, and the police; the chiefs and headmen of the tribal areas; the mayors and town clerks of the local governments in this district; and those holding other positions.

What then is meant by the role of a position? First, it means the *set of expectations* applied to the incumbent of a particular position by the incumbent himself (what he thinks he ought to do) and by the incumbents of the counter-positions (what they think he ought to do). These expectations (rights and obligations) between positions are the structure of action of an organization. Secondly, role means the actual behavior of the occupant of a position (what, in fact, he does). The role, then, may be understood as the product of an interplay between his and others' expectations of what he ought to do and the actual behavior of others. It is this interplay which accounts, in large measure, for the degree of conformity between his expectations of what he ought to do and his actual behavior.

This chapter is not the place to attempt to teach techniques of role analysis, and enough has been said, it is hoped, to indicate the type of framework which one may employ. The application of this theoretical framework in practice is simpler to describe than are the concepts themselves. It consists essentially of having the occupant of the position being studied describe in his own words and in any order which he desires: (1) the functions he performs, (2) his relationships, expectations, and interactions with such others as are concerned in the performance of his functions, (3) the problems he has in performing his role as he himself would like to perform it, and (4) how he believes these problems may be solved. He is assured of anonymity and encouraged through non-directive probing to give freely *his own views* of his position-role and of that of others with whom he interacts. The sole objective of the interviewer is to understand the position-role of the interviewee as the interviewee himself understands it.

It is obvious that the application of this kind of analysis requires a certain type of behavior on the part of the advisor (interviewer). First, a genuine respect for all persons and for their culture is necessary. No matter how much their appearances, standards, customs, and values may seem to differ from those of the advisor, one must know that if he but understood the complex totality of their situation as they understand it, he would find himself in agreement with many things that in his ignorance he does not understand or like. In other words, he must be convinced of the inherent integrity of any culture. He must know that no action can be understood, and therefore rationally accepted or rejected, except as it is related to a complex of conceptions, beliefs, goals, and norms, each with its multiple expectations within a context of mutual rights and obligations and as projected in the roles being played. This approach, in practice, means that the interviewer does not judge what he sees and hears as either good or bad; his sole intention is to discover how the interviewee understands the matter and why he understands it the way he does. The difficulty of adopting a truly non-judgmental attitude should not be minimized, but neither should the necessity for doing so. The interviewer must be sincere in wanting only to understand, as the interviewee does, because any lack of sincerity in this respect will sooner or later become apparent, rapport will dissolve, and he will have to be content with far less than he seeks.

UNITS OF ANALYSIS

To be effective, any new organization for development must be meshed with the matrix of organizations which presently exist. Rather than creating a new organization, it may be possible to carry out reorganization of existing entities through redefinition of functions, retraining of personnel, and other changes. If this is not possible and new structure is necessary, it may consist either of coordinative bodies of existing organizations or of action entities created for a particular purpose. However, whatever changes are recommended, they have little chance of being adopted, or if adopted, little chance of success, unless they "fit" with existing organizations.

The best way of insuring a fit is to study the matrix of organizations within the smallest geographic subdivision of government which contains all or almost all of the field offices of the central government ministries. For example, in countries like Pakistan, India, Rhodesia, and Kenya, which were under British rule, the smallest geographic administrative subdivision is the district. In Peru and the Dominican Republic, it is the province. Within each district or province one begins with the most powerful unit of government, usually the office of the district administration. The District Commissioner himself should be interviewed first, or if he would rather that you begin with some other member of his staff, this should be done. He is followed in turn by the assistant commissioner, one or more of the cadets, and one or more of each type of specialist officer attached to his office. The same procedure is followed for each of the offices of national government located in the district such as education, health, agriculture, public works, roads, and police, i.e., one or more officers at each level of each of these organizations is interviewed in the same manner as described above.

Next, one may begin with the local governments located within the districts, again interviewing at each level such persons as the mayor, members of the governing council, and the administrator, if there is one. If there are tribes, as in Rhodesia, it will then be necessary to interview chiefs, sadunhu, those who hold spiritual power, and other important personages. At all levels it is useful to observe directly as many of the important activities as possible, such as a chief's court trial and a meeting of a local government council. In the district capitals, there are a number of voluntary organizations which have a bearing on development. Such organizations include cooperatives, women's clubs, and civic clubs, and they usually merit one or more interviews.

Finally, there are the primary communities, the basic units of society. Study of a country's communities is a prerequisite to advising on any type of development organization whose success depends upon decisions of the people to act. These decisions, even those of individuals, are made within the context of community structure and are greatly affected by the expectations of behavior attached to all positions within this structure. The primary community is particularly relevant to development in agriculture, cottage industry, health, education, and other types of substantive community development and local government. But, of course, the internal structure and functioning of such communities have little direct relevance for the success of large industrial development, or the development of a primary road system, or jet airports and seaports.

This is not the place to detail procedures of community analysis, but a few remarks may be appropriate. First, the limits of a community must be determined by the people who live within them. Thus, the community, in our present usage of the term, is a grouping of families occupying a geographic locality which they define as their community. Communal life is carried on through the interaction of a set of institutions within the community, such as families, schools, churches or other religious bodies, economic production and commercial enterprises, and some form of overall community political control structure. Usually a community's boundaries in a rural setting can be determined easily by asking inhabitants to name the last person or geographic feature which falls within the community on each of the roads or paths leading out of it. When two or three have independently agreed upon the cut-off point, the information is usually reliable. However, each point is put to the test further by asking the residents of the next community to indicate the boundary with each of the abutting communities previously delineated. If there is disagreement between the communities, then it is necessary to visit those families who have been included or excluded by both and to determine with which community they identify themselves.

After its boundaries are determined, a brief description is made of the community, including an account (history, structure, functions, problems, relationships) of each of the organizations, economic enterprises, and public services presently found therein, both formal and informal. A brief history of each stage in the development of the community as a whole is useful in setting the stage for the last step, i.e., the community's conception of its current needs: what the community proposes to do about them, what outside resources are essential, and how the institution or service created will be maintained and operated. In the course of this community analysis ample opportunities will be provided to learn unobtrusively, and thereby more objectively, of the operations of the various government and other outside development organizations which have contact with the community, or which affect its development. It would be desirable to study a number of primary communities within each district in the manner described above, but time will probably limit the advisor to only five or six.

Since the advisor is holistically oriented, he is particularly interested in the interrelationships among positions, within and between organizations, and within the context of the community, district, or other unit of analysis. Therefore, in preparing for each interview he will find it expedient to review his notes of previous interviews for information of relationships between those previously interviewed and the person (or organization) next in the schedule. Such information is useful in guiding him in nondirective probing for greater specificity of relationship.

Although one district may represent in microcosm the general organizational structure of the country, there will be not only situational factors which are peculiar to one district, but considerable variation in the expectations regarding and actual behavior of each role analyzed within a district. Ideally, a large number of districts would be analyzed in the same manner as that described above to account for as much variation as possible. However, this ideal may be impracticable since the field work in one district may require three months or more of extremely hard work. Therefore, it may be possible to carry out an analysis as thorough as that described here in no more than two other districts. Each of these units should be as representative as possible of such categories of districts as one may have found useful for his major purpose.

After spending nine or ten months in the study of three districts, the advisor may well find it useful to complete his first year of such interviewing at the state and national levels as seems to be profitable, and in the initial analysis of the field data, the formulation of tentative conclusions, and the planning for further field work. At this stage, the remaining field work may be narrowed to the gathering of data on specific types of organizations which are most germane to the advisor's terms of reference. These interviews should be continued until the patterns to which he has become sensitized emerge, and until he feels that he is familiar with, and understands the major variations from, the main patterns.

If there is a real demand by the host government for advice on organization for development, it is highly likely that an advisor will be required to give his views on certain aspects long before he has completed the field work and analysis of his data. This request is particularly likely to be presented when he has completed his first district, since his periodic reports will reflect the fact that he has already gained an objective understanding exceeding that of any of the host country officials. The advisor must meet these demands as best he can, prefacing any advice with a warning that his knowledge is inadequate. It goes without saying that his field study should be resumed at the earliest opportunity.

ORGANIZATION FOR AGRICULTURAL DEVELOPMENT

The advice given so far in this chapter is believed to have applicability to the work of any advisor on development organization. Of particular interest, however, is the "U. S. Extension Service person," when the terms of reference specify agricultural development. It is hoped that what has been said above has shown: (1) the interrelatedness of all aspects of community and national life, including those of an agricultural production and marketing nature; and (2) the necessity of forming development organizations to serve *human* needs, including, but certainly not restricted to, those of an agricultural nature. Even if these lessons have been learned, it may not be amiss to mention some "notions," which have taken root over the years, with respect to applications of the methodology described above.

WAY OF LIFE

The first of these "notions" will come perhaps as a shock to some professional agriculturists; i.e., in indigenous societies agriculture is *not* a way of life but a means to a way of life. The way of life among indigenous peoples consists of human interactions within an interlocking system of mutual rights and obligations. The way in which expectations of families, relatives, and neighbors are fulfilled is a product of their culture, forms of social organization, and psychic orientations. These features taken together determine the *way* of life in any community.

This view is not meant to minimize agriculture which is, of course, a basic means for sustaining a way of life. However, this fact does not make it the central theme or organizing principle. This is attested to by the many instances one encounters in field research of the neglect of farming operations when the social situation demands other activities, or when the required income can be more easily obtained through other channels.

This matter is important because of the actions which one is led to take by one's conception of what is central in the life of the people. For example, attempts have been made to form purely agricultural organizations at the community level for purposes of increasing production. If agriculture were indeed the "way of life," we could expect to form such organizations and to have them flourish and persist solely on the basis of agricultural activities. However, as the experience of a number of countries, including the Dominican Republic (see Chapter 13), so vividly illustrates, agricultural development is seldom foremost in the minds of the people of a community. Other needs and wants more directly related to communal expectations, such as the road, the school, and the water system in our example of the Dominican community, are predominant. A community-level organization with a good chance for survival is the one which can administer to all types of communal needs, including those of an agricultural nature, when a need arises to increase the *means* to support the community's way of life.

AGRICULTURAL RESEARCH

Undoubtedly, there is a dearth of scientific solutions to agricultural problems of tropical areas. An increase in scientific agronomic and animal husbandry research of the long-term type usually carried out in agricultural experiment stations is one means for providing these solutions. Another type of research, however, would appear to offer sizeable returns in a far shorter period of time. I refer to studies of a farm survey type made of the technical practices and management techniques presently used by the most successful farmers in each agricultural zone. Such carefully performed research may bring to light a number of innovations which are highly related to increases in the efficiency of production. To be sure, these innovations will not have been subjected to the same rigid controls and replications as those which evolve from the experimental stations. However, they do have the virtue of being adapted to the area and to the farming system within which they are found, and, therefore, may be more readily adopted by others than are the findings from experiment stations. If there is a belief that the poorer farmers in tropical areas can raise their levels of production, perhaps some of our organizational resources should be devoted to a clearer understanding of the methods used by better farmers and how they came to be better.

PREREQUISITES TO INCREASED PRODUCTION

In the United States and other advanced countries, we have developed systems of markets, agricultural production credit, and supplies of pure seed, fertilizer, and other inputs, most of which are provided by private business. We tend to take these things for granted and to concentrate on the missing factors, especially technical knowledge of improved practices and the motivation for their adoption by other farmers. However, in most underdeveloped countries these things cannot be taken for granted, since they frequently do not exist. It is worse than useless to build up organizations devoted to technical education in agriculture unless it is possible for the producers to secure the necessary production inputs at an economic price, and on reasonable terms of credit, and to be able to sell their production at a remunerative price. Therefore, it is impossible to set forth any rules as to what forms of organization come first; it is necessary to study thoroughly that which exists and the perceptions of the producers and others as to what is necessary, and then to form judgments as to what is possible.

TECHNICAL PROFICIENCY

It is assumed that agricultural extension has as its *raison d'être* the extending to agriculturists of knowledge and skills concerning agriculture. The capacity of the personnel in these extension services observed by the writer (Green, 1961) to meet the technical assistance needs of the farmers is very limited. The personnel often appear to have been filled to overflowing with a rationale of extension methods and techniques, audio-visual gimmickry, and certain stereotyped information, but practically no capacity to perform or to teach the skills required by the farmers. There are extension horticulturists with masters degrees who have never pruned a tree, poultry husbandrymen who cannot cull a flock of laying hens, and dairy specialists who have never vaccinated a cow. No amount of learned talk, of exhortation and persuasion, of drawings and models, can substitute for the ability to perform and to demonstrate the skills needed by the agriculturists. It follows that any type of agricultural extension organization which may be established must focus on the needs of the people, including, at the proper time and place, their very large desire for *bona fide* knowledge and skills in technical agriculture. Therefore, it must prepare its agents *first* as *bona fide* technicians to meet these needs.

CONCLUSIONS

The impracticability of merely copying organizational forms and functions from any other country should be obvious. Broad-scale organization analysis in depth is the *sine qua non* of the organizational advisor. Capacity to comprehend multiple aspects of existing "wholes," to construct, if necessary, new organizations which are functionally integrated with the whole, or to reconstruct existing forms, is the role of the organizational advisor.

NOTES

1. Agency for International Development, United States Department of State. This agency is in no way responsible for the reliability of the data presented nor for the opinions expressed, as they are the personal responsibility of the author. Publication authorized: LIMA AIDTO A-88, 8-29-66.

LITERATURE CITED

GREEN, JAMES W. 1961. Success and failure in technical assistance: a case study. Human Organization 20(1): 2-10.

15

The Role of United States
Universities Abroad

Arthur J. Coutu

This subject is a very broad and interesting one, particularly if attention is directed to recent changes in the general United States philosophy on the role of science in meeting demanding world problems. The overall objective of this paper is to discuss opportunities for greater university involvement in economic development of the low-income countries and to identify possible areas for implementing programs in response to these opportunities.

To accomplish these goals, the paper is divided into four sections. The first section deals with a brief history, which is relatively new, of the involvement of United States universities abroad. In the second section the discussion centers on reasons for greater involvement. This is followed, in the third section, by a discussion of why United States universities should decide to act positively in identifying their objectives. Finally, in the fourth section, comments are directed at issues of continuity and innovation in the role of United States universities abroad. Particular attention is given to problems of the world food situation.

A BRIEF HISTORY

United States university involvement aimed at expanding our understanding of world issues and at direct participation in economic development abroad has a brief history. In 1940, Asian and

Soviet Union study programs were established at a few United States universities. Later, in 1949, the concept of "Point Four" was introduced and a limited number of the agriculture colleges joined in the effort.

The comparative study programs dealing with Russia and China have expanded in content, and the extent of university interest has spread in the United States. However, the predominant Point Four view, that agricultural development abroad was simply a "transfer of technology problem," may have had negative effects on United States university involvement as well as on actual rates of agricultural development abroad. The extensionistic bias that has prevailed until quite recently minimized the role of United States universities in assisting emerging countries to build the human, research, and communication base for a viable agriculture.

During the 1950's the United States acted to overcome the shortage of professional people necessary to staff internationally oriented curriculum and study programs. The implementation of the Fulbright Program that provided for an exchange of United States professors and for opportunities to study abroad was in recognition of this need. This same program recognized the need for training foreign students at United States universities. Certainly, this program has had an impact on the present situation that involves almost 100,000 foreign students studying in the United States. Foreign languages were given greater emphasis at the secondary education level within the United States during the 1950's. Another noteworthy item was the development of the Committee of Higher Education in the American Republics (CHEAR). This committee has been instrumental in developing the role of United States universities abroad.

Generally, the activities in the 1940's and 1950's were quite limited and were considered to be experimental or innovative. However, by the late 1950's and early 1960's many issues had been clarified, and greater United States university involvement was underway. One such issue was a greater acceptance of the idea that United States university involvement with an emerging educational institution abroad involved a whole package of events. This package included such areas as academic organization, financial or administrative organization, staff development and advanced training, the necessary component of research development at the indigenous university, and finally, the building of or planning for physical plant expansion. This change in attitude recognized a responsibility and opportunity for assisting in indigenous university development as opposed to the simpler idea that international activities were primarily for United States enlightenment.

Another most significant event of the 1960's was the report of the committee on universities and world affairs, commonly called the Morrill Committee Report, that was written under Ford Foundation sponsorship (Committee on University and World Affairs, 1961). This report was the first real effort to focus many minds on the role of United States universities in world affairs. The report urged serious study of the need to train United States students in order to enhance our capacity to assist in problems of economic development in low-income countries. The scientific dimension was added to technical assistance efforts and, among other recommendations, United States universities were urged to work directly with indigenous institutions in order to improve substantially their capacity to acquaint United States citizens with the issues involved in United States responsibilities in world affairs.

As a consequence of the committee report discussed above, two major developments occurred during the early 1960's at United States universities. One was the emerging of committees on university campuses to study the potential scope and role and the organizational questions with respect to their international dimensions. Much greater interinstitutional cooperation was the other major breakthrough.

This oversimplified review of United States universities and their international programs suggests the magnitude of thought and work that remains to be developed. Further developments are very promising with passage of amendments to the International Assistance Act of 1961 and the new International Education Act of 1966. These acts, as well as the Food for Freedom Bill, particularly with the research and institute amendment by Senator Mondale, can give real depth to the role of United States universities abroad.

SOME REASONS FOR GREATER
UNITED STATES UNIVERSITY INVOLVEMENT

The primary stimulus to greater United States university involvement is the severity of problems associated with food deficits, population pressures, and educational needs. These problems have existed for many years, but the promising element is that their severity is being more widely recognized.

Related to the above-mentioned needs is the realization that the simple transfer of advanced technologies and low-cost capital into the less-developed industrial and agricultural sectors of emerging countries is inadequate. The very strong extensionistic bias that has prevailed, particularly in agriculture under United States foreign aid for the last twenty years, is beginning to give way to the realization that science must play a greater role in the transformation of traditional agriculture (Schultz, 1967). Since the days of Point Four, in 1949, the short-run orientation of United States technical assistance to agriculture abroad has been premised on the idea that the problem is primarily one of transferring knowledge. This concept oversimplifies the problem of change in traditional societies. Among the components of change are new knowledge, factor and product market development, acceptance or legitimizing of new knowledge, an adequate transportation system, and adequate individual incentive to change.

The development of new knowledge is not a simple proposition of transferring what is known in the more developed world, but rather is a unique kind of ingredient in this developmental mix. Currently, the extension type technician does not have much to extend since essential knowledge is simply not present in the underdeveloped regions. As Schultz (1965, especially 53-68) has suggested, this lack of knowledge relative to new technologies has resulted largely from our failure to put together an adequate number of research stations and our failure to develop research stations of optimum sizes throughout the underdeveloped countries. In-depth research institutions must contain well-trained staffs in many disciplines, adequately supported and programmed for long periods of time.

Another intriguing dimension of this short-run United States philosophy has been the idea that adaptation of known technologies to the emerging countries is a relatively simple activity. As Millikan (1962) has pointed out, it may well be that effective transfer of known technology may be as creative and innovative a process as if the new knowledge had been developed indigenously. In other words, the adaptation process is not a simple one, and much of our effort to promote the adoption of known Western world technologies has met with little success in underdeveloped countries because we have not been overly successful in solving the adaptation problems.

Certainly, one stimulus for greater United States involvement has been and continues to be the sustained confrontation with communism. However, the realization of political stability within the emerging countries is an essential, but insufficient, condition for economic development. Related to this idea has been the humanitarian interest of the United States people towards food famines and their basic belief in further self-help as the real solution to this problem. The self-help program that is most convincing is one that supports the development of indigenous institutions involving human and physical resource development designed to transform traditional societies.

Still another stimulus is made evident by the change in attitude that has occurred with regard to the role of United States agricultural trade with emerging countries. It is encouraging to note that some countries formerly receiving agricultural products under foreign aid programs have emerged from severe agricultural deficits and now are large importers of United States agricultural products (Bachman, 1965). Five years ago, agricultural economists saw very limited possibilities for increased international trade in agricultural products as a solution to the surplus problem in the United States. Recent evidence is convincing that it has been one of the prime forces within the expanding agricultural sector of the United States. Further evidence that such trends may continue are supported by results of studies that indicate that per capita agricultural imports from the United States have increased about 11 per cent for each 10 per cent increase in per capita income (Mackie, 1965). These are important reasons for greater United States university involvement. Particularly significant is the fact that basic issues in economic development are closely related to the service and human resource development capacities of United States educational institutions.

WHAT DO UNIVERSITIES WANT AS
AN INTERNATIONAL DIMENSION?

In the area of international technical assistance, many United States universities have reacted to servicing programs planned, in large part, outside the university system. Generally, such programs have had a short-run as well as an excessively applied orientation. The failure to plan on a long-term basis has resulted in an attitude of temporary United States university-AID (or foundation) relationships. It is essential that United States universities ask themselves what international dimension they seek and then interact with AID and other granting institutions.

Three basic tenets of any United States university involvement abroad have been presented by F. F. Hill (1962): (1) United States universities must provide the knowledge of other countries for government, business, and educational development within the United States. The United States university has a responsibility to assist in enlightening United States citizens with regard to the dimensions of the world's problems and an explanation of the reasons for United States involvement in global activities. (2) The United States universities must provide a greater international dimension for training United States students. It is not adequate to say that we can further divide the present resources and those that may emerge to satisfy the international scientific dimension of United States universities. Rather, it is essential that we consciously train people in the sciences to work abroad. With respect to agriculture, such a training effort involves the development of more physiologists, entomologists, economists, pathologists, and others trained in their disciplines; it also involves those trained in other disciplines such as history, politics, and sociology as well as the languages of emerging countries. (3) United States universities must improve the efforts of less-developed countries to assist themselves in the fields of research and education. This is commonly called the technical assistance dimension of institutional development. The academic aspects involve teaching, research, and adult educational activities. If a United States university embarks on one or more of these three primary areas, it is important that each be developed in adequate depth.

If these three elements are what United States universities want to include in their programs, it is most important that their international dimension be a long-term commitment. As such, the international dimension could become an integral part of the United States university system.

If United States universities must select among these three areas of international involvement, because of limited resources, the third item on the role with indigenous university development may be the most demanding. Further, in the area of increasing food needs, greater United States university program specialization involving interdisciplinary effort may be necessary.

CONTINUITY, GROWTH, AND INNOVATION OF
UNITED STATES AND INDIGENOUS UNIVERSITIES

Of the three broad program components outlined by Dr. Hill, I contend that the prime dimension of the universities in international affairs should be associated with interinstitutional building or development. The realization of the fact that there must emerge stronger indigenous staffs and programs supported by United States universities suggests that the ideal arrangement may be that of a permanent international dimension at United States universities where staff members are looked upon not as taking time out to serve abroad, but as an integral and continuous phase of United States university involvement.

A critical element of this technical assistance or interuniversity involvement is that of continuity. Continuity is defined as a system that allows a United States as well as a foreign participant in any program of institutional building to look upon it as a permanent professional relationship where scientists develop and extend knowledge with respect to particular phases of critical food, educational, health, or related topics. The concept of continuity can be operative with one- or five-year appointments abroad, if it develops the idea that there is a continuous kind of relationship between professional staff members.

The programming of such long-term and in-depth research-oriented programs should replace the conventional United States technical assistance role as advisors and consultants. An ideal in-depth program is a commitment between a United States university department and a similar department within an indigenous institution. Such a programmed effort would shift the emphasis from a United States "expert" who goes abroad to assist an emerging country to a long-term program developed between departments—a long-term program with stated production, staff development, and growth objectives (Hill, 1964, 1091). With effective programming, the initiative of individual scientists need not be reduced.

A key element to effective program development is a commodity orientation that has multiple disciplinary characteristics. For example, a potato program cannot be conceived of within a disciplinary department at the United States institution or at the foreign institution. It must be a long-run interdisciplinary research program. A functional as well as a commodity orientation is possible, but it would be disastrous unless such an orientation is interdisciplinary. At the same time, a commodity and interdisciplinary program can operate with two types of United States professional workers. One type is the conventional long-term foreign assignment at an indigenous institution. Another type is the continuation of former long-term appointees as "campus cooperators" upon their return to the United States campus. In North Carolina, we are attempting to arrange for faculty members who have returned from abroad to commit one-fourth or one-third of their time to continuation of their work on foreign problems. For example, there are North Carolina staff members who have spent five years working in Peru on fertility and pathological and economic aspects of potatoes. Before these people return to the North Carolina State University campus, they structure specific subprojects with Peruvian colleagues that will continue their international involvement.

To develop a program, such as the one outlined above, it is important that a master project for a particular commodity program be well-conceived between the United States university and the indigenous institution. Our experience suggests that it is possible to program the research and the extension phases in terms of long-term technical assistance commitments abroad, whereas additional components or subprojects are carried out on a continuation short-term basis by technicians after returning to the United States. It is without question that the loss of momentum in a man leaving to accept a foreign assignment, and that associated with integrating him back into our domestic environment upon his return, can be minimized if the concept of a master project with a series of long-term as well as short-term subprojects can be structured. The Peru-North Carolina program is undergoing revision, and we are finding that the United States departments, as well as the departments in institutions abroad, are anxious to develop long-term commitments as well as a more professional type of relationship.

Another idea associated with that of continuity is the concept of growth in an international dimension. It is important that the concept of an international dimension not be considered as a substitute for domestic activities. Quite the contrary, it is a concept of development and growth within the United States institution. This suggests that the problem of overstaffing, and the problem of tenure related to this overstaffing at the department level, must be resolved. Perhaps the most realistic suggestion is to conceive of these programs as a long-term continuous type of relationship and that tenure positions be built into the system associated with an expansion of departmental effort. We in North Carolina are considering this a permanent addition to the departmental structure, where we are attempting to build a permanent international dimension as a key component to selected departments.

In the concept of growth and overstaffing, it is an oversimplification to assume that a program will continue indefinitely and that the United States institution can overstaff. However, it is also possible to conceive of floating tenure appointments among departments within the United States university system in order to provide the necessary flexibility.

A concept of innovation in an international dimension, as well as continuity and growth, is essential. It is extremely important that the United States university view the program abroad as one deserving of experimentation. It is particularly significant that we experiment in a purposeful way with alternative approaches to United States university involvement. One of the foremost issues related to innovation is the idea that in most United States institutions the research programs are more basic than those that are preferred abroad. At the same time, most United States institutions are unwilling to regress to take on the more service- or problem-oriented economic development issues faced by foreign institutions.

This problem is a very challenging one and demands the study of alternatives until the United States university involvement is more consistent with both domestic and international goals. A most promising alternative is the development of research institutes that will provide for multiple types of research—applied and basic—for both the U.S. and foreign professional worker and, at the same time, will possess elements associated with servicing critical short-run problems. The institute idea might include extension specialists or persons skilled to deal with applied short-run problems that are research oriented. Such an approach is quite consistent with what the outstanding United States extension specialist is now doing.

Further experimentation involving teams of United States researchers working jointly within foreign institutions deserves additional effort. Innovations with respect to the form that interinstitutional cooperation may take is most appropriate because the educational and research systems used most frequently in the United States may not be most appropriate for much of the emerging world.

CONCLUSION

In conclusion, I shall close with the view that the United States university has a clear responsibility for greater international involvement. The history of this involvement has not been outstanding. However, there are challenging opportunities for innovation and for service by the United States universities as well as those in the emerging nations.

LITERATURE CITED

BACHMAN, K. L. 1965. Agricultural economics and technical aid in foreign development. J. Farm Econ. 47(5): 1079-1090.

COMMITTEE ON THE UNIVERSITY AND WORLD AFFAIRS. 1961. The university and world affairs. Ford Foundation, N.Y.

HILL, F. F. 1962. The land-grant colleges in international affairs. Ford Foundation, Vice President, Paper delivered at a Land-Grant Centennial Convocation at Cornell Univ., June 14, 1962. Ithaca, N.Y.

————. 1964. Institutional development at home and abroad. J. Farm Econ. 46(5): 1087-1094.

MACKIE, A. B. 1965. Foreign economic growth and market potentials for U.S. agricultural products, USDA, For Agr. Econ. Rep. 24. Washington, D.C.

MILLIKAN, MAX F. 1962. Education for innovation, p. 131-147. In Study of world tensions and development. Council on World Tensions, Inc. Dodd, Mead and Co., N.Y.

SCHULTZ, T. W. 1967. Education and research in rural development, p. 391-402. In Kenneth L. Turk and Loy V. Crowder [eds.], Rural development in tropical Latin America. Cornell Univ. Press, Ithaca, N.Y.

————. 1965. Economic crises in world agriculture. Univ. Mich. Press, Ann Arbor.

Index